T0310414

ELINOR OSTROM AND THE BLOOMINGTON SCHOOL

ELINOR OSTROM AND THE BLOOMINGTON SCHOOL

Building a New Approach to Policy and the Social Sciences

**EDITED BY
JAYME LEMKE AND VLAD TARKO**

McGill-Queen's University Press
Montreal & Kingston • Chicago

We dedicate this book to every student of human civilization who embraces the opportunity to learn from and engage with different disciplines, methods, and perspectives.

© Editorial matter, introduction and selection 2021 Jayme Lemke and Vlad Tarko. Individual chapters: the contributors.

Published in 2021 by McGill-Queen's University Press

Published simultaneously outside North America by Agenda Publishing

ISBN 978-0-2280-0414-1 (cloth)
ISBN 978-0-2280-0415-8 (paper)
ISBN 978-0-2280-0479-0 (ePDF)
ISBN 978-0-2280-0480-6 (ePUB)

Legal deposit second quarter 2021
Bibliothèque nationale du Québec

Library and Archives Canada Cataloguing in Publication

Title: Elinor Ostrom and the Bloomington School : building a new approach to policy and the social sciences / edited by Jayme Lemke and Vlad Tarko.
Names: Lemke, Jayme S., editor. | Tarko, Vlad, editor.
Description: Includes bibliographical references and index.
Identifiers: Canadiana (print) 20210133503 | Canadiana (ebook) 20210134011 | ISBN 9780228004141
   (hardcover) | ISBN 9780228004158 (softcover) | ISBN 9780228004790 (PDF) | ISBN 9780228004806
   (EPUB)
Subjects: LCSH: Ostrom, Elinor. | LCSH: Institutional economics. | LCSH: Social institutions. | LCSH: Public institutions.
Classification: LCC HB99.5 .E45 2021 | DDC 306.3—dc23

Typeset by JS Typesetting Ltd, Porthcawl, Mid Glamorgan
Printed and bound in the UK by TJ Books

CONTENTS

ACKNOWLEDGEMENTS

The greatest debt this book owes is to the contributors, who lent their time, patience, and expertise to this deceptively complicated undertaking. Thank you all. We are also deeply grateful to Elinor Ostrom and Vincent Ostrom, without whom the Bloomington school's exciting and interdisciplinary approach to the study of human civilization could never have been possible. Their scholarship and the example they have set with their personal and professional lives is a source of great inspiration.

In their keenly felt absence, we have relied heavily on the knowledge of many of their former students, both those formally enrolled at Indiana University Bloomington and those who engaged with the Workshop in Political Theory and Policy Analysis in other ways. Although there are too many such collaborators to name, we would be remiss if we did not call special attention to Paul Dragos Aligica, Peter J. Boettke, Roberta Q. Herzberg, and Michael D. McGinnis. Their contributions to the intellectual community at both IU Bloomington and George Mason University built an important bridge that has sustained this project and the broader intellectual inquiry it represents.

One of the many lessons that emerges from the work of Elinor Ostrom and her Bloomington school colleagues is the important role that community plays. The impact of community takes both direct and indirect forms, and we have no hope of being able to list the many teachers, peers, students, and scholars who have provided encouragement, intellectual challenge, and professional support. Our most heartfelt thanks to all of them. Thank you also to the Mercatus Center at George Mason University for their support over the years, and to Logan Hansen for valuable contributions during the copy-editing process.

To paraphrase Elinor Ostrom's dedication to Vincent from *Governing the Commons*, thank you all for the affection and contestation.

Jayme Lemke
Vlad Tarko

CONTRIBUTORS

Paul Dragos Aligica is a Senior Research Fellow at the F. A. Hayek Program for Advanced Study in Philosophy, Politics, and Economics at the Mercatus Center at George Mason University, and KPMG Professor of Governance at the University of Bucharest. Among his most recent publications are *Public Governance and the Classical Liberal Perspective: The Political Economy Foundations* (with Peter Boettke and Vlad Tarko) (2019) and *Public Entrepreneurship, Citizenship, and Self-Governance* (2018).

Peter J. Boettke is a University Professor of Economics and Philosophy at George Mason University, and Director of the F. A. Hayek Program for Advanced Study in Philosophy, Politics, and Economics at the Mercatus Center at George Mason University. He is the author of *Challenging the Institutional Analysis of Development* (with Paul Aligica) (2009), and *Public Governance and the Classical Liberal Perspective* (with Paul Aligica and Vlad Tarko) (2019), which both deal with the contributions of the Ostroms and the Bloomington school.

Rosolino A. Candela is an Associate Director of Academic and Student Programs and a Senior Fellow with the F. A. Hayek Program for Advanced Study in Philosophy, Politics, and Economics at the Mercatus Center at George Mason University. Prior to George Mason University, he taught in the Department of Economics at Brown University, where he was also a postdoctoral research associate in the Political Theory Project. He was also a visiting professor of economics at Universidad Francisco Marroquin, and a visiting fellow in the Department of Political and Social Sciences at the European University Institute.

Alice Calder is a writer and economist who seeks to understand the impact of cultural and social influences on our economic actions. Originally from the UK, she received her MA in applied economics from George Mason University and is an alumna of the Mercatus Center MA fellowship. Prior to this she received her BA Hons in philosophy and political economy from the University of Exeter. Her interests lie in the intersection of economics and culture, economic sociology, and the future of work. She also writes on international trade, helping to explain the importance and relevance of this issue to both our economic and cultural lives.

Adelin Dumitru is Assistant Professor at the Polytechnic University of Bucharest. He also teaches classes in political philosophy, rational choice theory, and the history of political and social thought at the National University of Political Studies and Public Administration in Bucharest. His research interests are distributive justice, ethics of immigration, relational egalitarianism and the interplay between empirical and normative theorization in general. He has published in journals such as *Philosophia, Studies in Philosophy and Education, Philosophical Forum, Educational Philosophy and Theory*, and *South African Journal of Philosophy*. He is one of the founding members of the Bucharest Center for Political Theory.

Emil Duhnea is a lawyer with experience in real estate, banking and finance, intellectual property, technology and competition. His research interests include law and economics, the evolution of legal institutions, Austrian economics and public choice, with a focus on monopoly, competition and the original intent and early development of antitrust law. He is passionate about US history and occasionally publishes fiction.

Jayme Lemke has a PhD in economics from George Mason University and is a Senior Research Fellow at the Mercatus Center at George Mason University and a Senior Fellow in the F. A. Hayek Program for Advanced Study in Philosophy, Politics, and Economics. Her specialization is in public choice economics, constitutional political economy, and the political economy of women's rights.

Jordan K. Lofthouse is a Senior Fellow with the F. A. Hayek Program for Advanced Study in Philosophy, Politics, and Economics at the Mercatus Center at George Mason University. He is also an Associate Director of Academic and Student Programs with the Mercatus Center. He graduated from George Mason University with a PhD in economics, where he also received the William P. Snavely Award for Outstanding Achievement in Graduate Studies in Economics. His research applies the Austrian, Virginia, and Bloomington schools of political economy to environmental issues and economic development.

Adam Martin is Political Economy Research Fellow at the Free Market Institute and an Associate Professor of Agricultural and Applied Economics in the College of Agricultural Sciences and Natural Resources at Texas Tech University. His research interests focus on the intersection of philosophy, politics and economics and include Austrian economics, economic methodology, economic development and public choice.

Michael D. McGinnis is Professor Emeritus of Political Science and Senior Research Fellow (and a former Director) of the Ostrom Workshop at Indiana University, Bloomington. He has edited or co-edited seven volumes of papers by Ostrom Workshop scholars, and has published articles on institutional analysis, game theory, arms control, humanitarian aid, faith-based organizations, and US health policy.

Adrian Miroiu is Professor of Political Science at the National University of Political Studies and Public Administration, Bucharest. With a background in philosophy, he has published papers on modal logic, philosophy of language and philosophy of social sciences. More recently, he has worked on social choice, focusing on the role of voting rules in both committee and mass elections. Using public choice models as well as scientometric methods he has published theoretical and applied analyzes on topics like higher education funding, quality assurance in higher education and academic research evaluations.

Virgil Henry Storr is an Associate Professor of Economics in the Department of Economics, George Mason University and the Don C. Lavoie Senior Fellow in the F. A. Hayek Program in Philosophy, Politics, and Economics at the Mercatus Center at George Mason University.

Vlad Tarko is the Head of the Department of Political Economy and Moral Science at University of Arizona. He is the author of *Elinor Ostrom: An Intellectual Biography* (2016), co-author with Paul Dragos Aligica of *Capitalist Alternatives* (2015), and co-author with Paul Dragos Aligica and Peter Boettke of *Public Administration and the Classical Liberal Perspective* (2019).

1

INTRODUCTION: THE BLOOMINGTON SCHOOL IN CONTEXT

Jayme Lemke and Vlad Tarko

When Elinor Ostrom became the first woman to win the Nobel Prize in economics in 2009, she drew unprecedented attention to the Bloomington school of institutional analysis, a wide-ranging research program in institutional economics and political economy. The well-deserved award was the culmination of over 50 years of inquiry, institution building, and hard work (Tarko 2017). Elinor Ostrom and Vincent Ostrom, the founders and most impactful contributors to the Bloomington school research program, saw themselves as artisans. They both studied diverse forms of institutional design and practiced what they preached by building up research teams and their self-directed Workshop in Political Theory and Policy Analysis at Indiana University in Bloomington. In a 2006 interview, Elinor described their study: "Learning science at a university was very much like learning a craft ... We teach our students the best of what we know. Essentially it's a form of artisanship" (Zagorski 2006).

This ongoing and complex research program has developed advanced analytical tools for the study of the production of public goods in metropolitan areas, such as studies of police services and the role of police within communities; problems of federalism, such as how the balance of powers between the multiple overlapping governments that exist around the world can possibly be negotiated; and tragedy of commons challenges in communities of different sizes, from small-scale fishing villages to global-scale climate change. Alongside fellow Nobelists Ronald Coase, Douglass North and Oliver Williamson, Elinor Ostrom's contributions helped form what is now called "new institutional economics". Further, this research program has long been considered one of the main three schools of public choice economics, alongside the Rochester School, associated with the work of William Riker and Anthony Downs, and the Virginia School, as developed by James M. Buchanan and Gordon Tullock. Throughout the volume, the contributors discuss many other disciplines that have been influenced by the Bloomington school.

JAYME LEMKE AND VLAD TARKO

The openness and creative potential of the Bloomington approach is on full display in these chapters. Elinor Ostrom and Vincent Ostrom consistently rejected the idea of there being strict divisions within the interdependent, interconnected world of humans and their projects. This idea carried through into their approach to scholarship as well, where they rejected methodological divides, disciplinary divides, and the idea that phenomena in the world could be easily broken down into binary concepts like market vs state or private vs public. This open-endedness lends the concepts developed by the Bloomington school to a wide variety of applications.

In this volume, we have brought together contributors with diverse expertise to highlight the creative potential of the approach developed by Elinor Ostrom, Vincent Ostrom, and their colleagues in the Bloomington school. The Bloomington school approach is special for so many reasons. We'll start here with just three. First, an essential part of the success of the Bloomington school has been its ability to learn from a variety of different perspectives across the social sciences. Depending on their specific analytic purposes, Elinor Ostrom and colleagues adapted conceptual tools from a wide variety of sources. In addition to their formative influence on new institutional economics, they were critical participants in the development of public choice and constitutional political economy. Vincent Ostrom's inquiries into bureaucracy and hierarchy have been particularly influential in the field of public administration, and much of Elinor Ostrom's applied work dealt directly with environmental and natural resource management issues. In this volume, we attempt to build on this admirable tradition of building disciplinary bridges by highlighting some of the most important of these connections.

Second, the Bloomington school approach embraced multiple methods. The scholarly approach of Elinor Ostrom and her collaborators was to embrace insight wherever it could be found, be that through political theory, history, field work, case studies, game theoretic modelling, laboratory experiments, or big data analysis. They rode in police cars in order to study community–police interaction in the provision of public safety, conducted in-depth historical case studies in order to understand the functioning of centuries-old governance institutions from irrigation systems to national constitutions, and used advanced technology like satellite imagery in order to understand the effectiveness of forest management policies. In the book *Working Together*, Elinor Ostrom, Amy R. Poteete, and Marco A. Janssen (2010) championed the idea of working directly with people with diverse expertise because of the great difficulty associated with mastering all the methods that might be useful for a project on one's own.

This argument in favor of collaboration leads directly into a third reason the Bloomington school research program is so special. Unlike many academics who are more comfortable in the ivory tower, Elinor Ostrom and Vincent Ostrom believed in engaging the world. Their model of scholarly and civic engagement not only brought them together as a working group, but enabled them to integrate themselves meaningfully within their community. In no small part due to their crafting-in-the-workshop model of scholarship, they were inspired to also take these skills into the world around them, and became actively involved in the process of governance and problem solving, at the university, community, and government level. Vincent Ostrom even took his expertise on constitutions to the Alaskan Constitutional Convention. Elinor Ostrom and her colleagues studying environmental common-pool resources were actively involved in the development of a whole new approach to resolving problems of environmental and natural resource management. And of course, few legacies could be more enduring than the team of researchers and the body of work they built up, which can be seen not only at Indiana University, but in universities and research centers around the world.

The contributors use their respective chapters to show how the Bloomington school relates to other approaches to understanding social organization. In Chapter 2, Emil Duhnea and Adam Martin outline the connections between the work of Elinor Ostrom and Vincent Ostrom in political science and public administration and the work of James M. Buchanan and other public choice theorists working from within economics. The Bloomington school has long been an active part of the public choice tradition, taking what Elinor Ostrom called "a behavioral approach" to the study of how institutions shape the choices and strategies of individuals as they work to live better together. In this chapter, Duhnea and Martin note that a unifying theme of the two approaches to the study of public choice is their emphasis on self-governance, or, the study of constitution-building, local problem solving, and other attempts by communities to craft more productive sets of rules to live by. This chapter further illuminates the Bloomington–Virginia public choice connection by discussing the similarities and differences in their approach to constitutional and institutional design, the nature of polycentric institutional arrangements, modelling the complexity of economic and political actors, and understanding institutional robustness.

In Chapter 3, Michael D. McGinnis brings the Bloomington school into conversation with the core ideas and contributions of the new institutional economics, as typified by the research of Ronald Coase, Douglass North, and Oliver Williamson. Similarities between these two approaches are many and well-recognized, as suggested by the fact that Oliver Williamson and Elinor Ostrom shared the 2009 Nobel Prize. McGinnis highlights the fact that both approaches adopt a bounded notion of rationality, within which decision-makers are presumed to do their best given the limits of human cognition rather than to be efficient optimizers, as a particularly important similarity. The chapter also discusses transactions costs and the organizations that people create to minimize those costs as something of a shared project. The two approaches emphasize the importance of these considerations, but wind up approaching practical questions of how to analyze and interpret organizational activity in very different ways. The chapter concludes with recommendations for how to build out the overlap between transaction costs economics and Bloomington research agendas, including through more robustly incorporating the idea of path dependency into understanding institutional change.

In Chapter 4, Vlad Tarko explores Elinor Ostrom's critique of the use of the rational choice model for understanding collective action. Unlike many other critics of rational choice, her aim is not to reject rational choice, but to improve the model. On one hand, she points out that rational choice is vital as a tool for understanding human behavior and for making sense of deliberate attempts to reform institutions. On the other hand, she points out that we cannot fully explain the ways in which communities overcome collective action problems, and the ways in which they manage to create, monitor and enforce rules, without accepting that people's motivations go beyond pure selfishness. Matters such as generosity, fairness and group identity need to be incorporated into the rational choice model. Furthermore, the complexity of institutional reality makes it difficult to have purely rational (consequentialist) evaluations of institutions. The role of history and tradition cannot be evaded. On a policy level, Ostrom argues that ignoring these departures from the standard rational choice model biases institutional analysis in a paternalistic and technocratic direction because it implies that communities are generally helpless in escaping tragedies of the commons. By contrast, a fuller concept of rational choice enables us to better understand the process of self-governance.

In Chapter 5, Alice Calder and Virgil Henry Storr bring the Bloomington tradition into conversation with economic sociology. Their particular focus is on the new economic sociology of Mark Granovetter and Richard Swedberg, which emphasizes the sociality of economic behavior and the ways in which our economic decisions are socially constructed and embedded within systems of relationships. Like the Bloomington school, the new economic sociology is critical of approaches to economics that abstract too far from the imperfections, idiosyncrasies, and creative capacities of real human societies. In this chapter, Calder and Storr discuss a number of common themes between these two traditions, with an extended discussion of how Tocqueville's pioneering observation of early American civil society inspired both groups of scholars. The discussion of how the relationship between the Ostromian concept of the polycentric system relates to the study of social networks in the new economic sociology is of particular interest, as is the discussion of the way both branches of scholarship have managed to successfully incorporate multiple methods into their research.

In Chapter 6, Adrian Miroiu and Adelin Dumitru discuss a less recognized but critically important set of ideas coming out of the Bloomington school about the nature of knowledge, science, and the social world. The Ostroms and their collaborators thought deeply about what it means to be human and what exactly happens when we try to study ourselves and others. Miroiu and Dumitru explore their contributions on this issue with special attention to John Searle's ideas on the relationship between language, shared understandings, and the institutions in place within a society.

In Chapter 7, Jayme Lemke and Jordon K. Lofthouse articulate the relevance of the Ostroms' research program for environmental policy. Both Vincent Ostrom and Elinor Ostrom began seriously studying environmental concerns during their time at UCLA, inspired in part by the water crises that continue to plague California. Since that time, Elinor Ostrom in particular expanded these studies to all manner of common-pool resource situations, winning the Nobel Prize for her contributions. Common-pool resources – like aquifers, forests, and fish populations – are resources that are accessible to many and as such susceptible to overuse and degradation. Ostrom's work showed that communities are capable of coming up with functional, self-enforcing systems of rules to effectively manage these resources without resort to either top-down government control or atomistic privatization. This chapter shows how these lessons can be applied to contemporary environmental policy issues by those working in the field.

In Chapter 8, Peter Boettke takes a Bloomington perspective to issues of central planning and economic calculation. The economic calculation debate – most associated with the twentieth-century experiments in large-scale socialist organization – illuminated the important coordinative capacities of the prices discovered through market exchange. Less settled is the issue of whether or not there are political institutions that may serve an analogous function in non-priced contexts, enabling groups and individuals to coordinate for collective benefit without the need for central command and control. The ultimate question raised is: can a political system be designed that could gather, interpret, and filter information about the changing needs of a diverse citizenry well enough to provide public services that will ultimately do more good than harm? Boettke utilizes Vincent Ostrom's work on public administration within polycentric systems in his exploration of this question. He discusses reasons for both optimism and caution, situating the Bloomington school's contributions to institutional analysis in the context of the tradition of classical political economy along the way.

In Chapter 9, Paul Dragos Aligica continues the inquiry into the relevance of the Bloomington school approach for the field of public administration. Aligica highlights Vincent Ostrom's contributions to the field of public administration by importing a political economy approach into a field otherwise inclined towards centralization and hierarchy. He draws together several important contributions explored in previous chapters, connecting the Ostromian insights on public administration to the metropolitan reform debate, the study of the commons, and the theory of polycentric organization in general. Aligica prompts us to consider how the dominant conceptions of the past have shaped the development of public institutions.

In the final chapter, Rosolino Candela takes an in-depth look at the Bloomington school's approach to institutional analysis and its relevance for understanding the polycentric, federal systems that exist throughout the political world. The crux of the chapter is a case study of Italian unification in the nineteenth century. There has been significant debate in history over whether southern Italy during this period of time suffered from too much or too little centralization of government functions, and Candela shows here how the theoretical apparatus developed by the Ostroms can be used to interpret such complicated institutional questions. The chapter also contains a discussion of the relationship between emergence and design in the Bloomington research program that will be of great interest to many scholars of institutional analysis.

Overall, the combined contributions of the chapters in this volume are a testament to both the scholarship and the lives of Elinor Ostrom and Vincent Ostrom. In the conclusion to her Nobel Prize lecture, Elinor Ostrom summarized the lessons learned from her life's work: "extensive empirical research leads me to argue that instead, a core goal of public policy should be to facilitate the development of institutions that bring out the best in humans" (E. Ostrom 2010a: 665). Our hope is that this volume is a step in that direction.

2

PUBLIC CHOICE THEORY: REUNITING VIRGINIA AND BLOOMINGTON

Emil Duhnea and Adam Martin

The economic theory of markets could be called "private choice" since it analyzes the way property rights generate incentives for individual action. Public choice, by contrast, uses that same theoretical framework to explain political behavior. There are distinct streams of thought within the broader field of public choice (Mitchell 1988). The Rochester school places a heavy emphasis on the use of mathematical and statistical techniques to formally model collective choice problems of elections and voting behavior. The Virginia school of public choice adopts an approach that foregrounds institutions, and treats politics not as primarily conflictual, but cooperative, with an emphasis on exchange. This contractarian and normative tradition is echoed in the Bloomington research agenda, but enriched through an interdisciplinary and empirical approach of its own.

This chapter explores the deep connections between the Virginia and Bloomington schools of political economy, focusing on three main figures: James Buchanan, Vincent Ostrom, and Elinor Ostrom. Buchanan and the Ostroms have led separate, but related, research programs with key areas of overlap and a distinct theoretical approach. Although diverging in important ways, they stem from shared core principles, developed by Buchanan and Tullock in *The Calculus of Consent* (1962), which later inspired the Ostroms' approach to political economy.

The Ostroms' work prepared the way for starting the Workshop in Political Theory and Policy Analysis at Indiana University Bloomington in 1973. The further studies developed through the workshop helped flesh out the Bloomington school's own distinct and rich framework of public choice. Although developed along distinct lines from the Virginia public choice tradition, the Ostroms recognized a debt of gratitude to Buchanan and Tullock's *Calculus of Consent*, and remarked that their own important works *Governing the Commons, The*

Intellectual Crisis in American Public Administration and *The Political Theory of a Compound Republic* "resulted from the stimulus created by the organization of the Public Choice Society" (Aligica & Boettke 2009: 143). But, more generally, as Elinor Ostrom points out (E. Ostrom 2011b: 372), James Buchanan's influence permeated all of the Bloomington workshop's research program and was a driving influence in its development:

> I am deeply indebted for the inspiration that the work of Jim Buchanan has generated for me, for Vincent Ostrom, for all colleagues at the Workshop in Political Theory and Policy Analysis at Indiana University, and our many colleagues in other universities in the United States and overseas. His work is foundational for the study of the sustainability of a democratic system over time. I am deeply appreciative that I first began to read Buchanan's work as a graduate student, and have been reading it ever since. It has served as the foundation for a rich and productive research program over the years.

Our chapter proceeds as follows. The next section summarizes the main arguments in *Calculus* and its role in establishing the public choice research agenda. The following section connects these contributions to the works of Vincent and Elinor Ostrom, underlining the influences that carry through. The final section explores specific common themes of the two schools with a view to compare and contrast their intertwined development.

The Calculus of Consent

The Calculus of Consent is widely credited as a foundational text in public choice economics. In the preface to the collected works edition, James Buchanan credits the success of *Calculus* as a key input into the creation of the Public Choice Society and the journal *Public Choice*. It is widely regarded as a modern classic whose "central views form part of the common sense" of public choice theory (Kliemt 1994) and whose "revolutionary insights irrevocably changed the scholarly conversations" of economics and political philosophy (Haight, Marroquin & Wenzel 2011). Going beyond "strictly scientific contributions", it has established itself as a work of great relevance for liberalism (Berggren 2014).

Calculus has a number of important moving pieces. We focus on three here. First, like all public choice scholars, Buchanan and Tullock analyze politics through the lens of microeconomic theory. *Calculus* challenged the prevailing orthodoxies of both political theory and standard welfare economics. When it was published in 1962, collective action was primarily seen as a tool for enacting welfare-increasing policies in line with the "public interest". Much political theory assumed that political agents pursue the common good, often conceptualized in terms of a social welfare function. The function of this organic state was to use law and policy to steer society toward the most socially preferred state among possible alternatives (Buchanan & Tullock 1962: ch. 1, 275–6).[1]

Challenging this organic view of the state, Buchanan and Tullock stress that public action is a direct result of individual choice and that, contrary to prevailing theories, individuals act just as rationally in politics as they do in economics (ch. 2). The *Calculus* rejects the concept of a social welfare function. The basic unit in their analysis is the individual actor who chooses among alternatives based on their own values. While those values can vary, individuals still choose to gain more of what they value rather than less (17–18, 33–4). By embracing methodological individualism, *Calculus* extends the economic model of utility maximization to political choice.

Second, *Calculus* places primary analytical emphasis on exchange. Since Buchanan and Tullock reject the concept of a social welfare function, how do they evaluate political outcomes? In a market exchange, both parties expect to benefit simply because they have agreed to the exchange. Such exchanges are Pareto improvements as long as fraud or violence are not involved, and no third parties are harmed. Inspired by Swedish economist Knut Wicksell, Buchanan and Tullock argue that, under conditions of unanimity, collective choices take on this character as well. By establishing a condition of unanimity rather than a lower majority, this Wicksellian criterion blocks public expenditures whose costs would outweigh the benefits for each individual participant. If an entire community votes to levy taxes on its members to finance a public good, economics can say that this decision is positive sum for the same reason that bilateral exchange benefits all. So while Buchanan and Tullock invoke the Pareto criterion, they do so in a consistently contractarian fashion: *agreement* is the only criterion for whether an individual is better or worse off.

Rather than conceiving of voting rights as polls about the desirability of a policy, Buchanan and Tullock treat them as decision rights that can be traded just as property rights are traded. I vote for your favored policy, you vote for mine. Choice over a single issue may present uncertainties and even deadlock of conflicting interests under unanimity rule; choice over a series of issues presents individuals having conflicting interests with the opportunity to trade (38, 120–24).

Under unanimity, exchanging votes or logrolling over multiple issues remains Pareto efficient. Agreement among all contracting parties implies an action that will bring gain to at least one party, and not cause anyone else any losses. But the

---

1. Unless otherwise noted, references in this section are to the *Calculus of Consent*.

advantages of this extreme protection of individual welfare are counterbalanced by correspondingly high costs of reaching agreement. Negotiating costs increase as groups become larger and more heterogeneous. Relaxing the rule of unanimity toward a less inclusive threshold can certainly reduce decision-making costs (73, ch. 8). But such departures from unanimity also imply less protection against a majority imposing costs on a minority and can lead to exploitation. We move away from Pareto optimality into a decision process that can make some people better off at the expense of others. Collective action becomes a double-edged sword that can provide public goods but also leave individuals subject to domination by others.

Addressing these difficulties in a third key component of *Calculus*, Buchanan and Tullock's analysis shifts between two levels: *constitutional choice* over the rules of the game and *collective choice* within the rules of the game. Breaking down decision-making into these two stages reconciles the unanimity rule and less inclusive rules such as various levels of majority (ch. 6). Whereas most political economy models throw agents into a predetermined institutional framework, *Calculus* asks how free and rational individuals might constitute such groups in the first place (Buchanan 1987). Such individuals would recognize both the benefits of expedient collective action as well as the dangers.

This constitutional calculus of individual consent is the titular centerpiece of the book. Unanimity becomes more realistic when considering choices over the rules than in day-to-day play within the rules. With a constitution unanimously agreed upon, the second stage of collective choice can employ a variety of less stringent rules for day-to-day operational decisions. As Buchanan and Tullock explain, in choosing what action to collectivize and under what rules to do it, the decision-making costs described above are weighed against the expected external costs imposed by the result on those in the "losing minority" (ch. 5). Rules minimizing the total sum of decision-making costs and external costs are considered optimal (70–73). Although such optimal rules could be envisioned, they are necessarily non-uniform both across a range of possible action as well as across time because distinct courses of action imply unique dimensions of the two types of costs. There is no single, one-size-fits-all decision rule and this is precisely why it will be rational for individuals to have a constitution, that is a set of decision-making rules to govern collective action: "If a single rule is to be chosen for all collective decisions, no constitution in the normal sense will exist" (81).

The constitutional stage sets forth the range of political choice, what particular activities should be undertaken collectively, as well as the rules for deciding them. These decisions will take into account the interests of others to the extent that individuals fall behind a "veil of uncertainty," meaning that they do not know their future interests with confidence. Since they cannot anticipate what side of future policy debates they will fall on, they will be inclined to collectivize those activities that present strong prospects for mutually beneficial political exchange and subject them to appropriately "fair" decision-making rules (78–9). In order to obtain the benefits of collective action, they will choose rules and institutions that would offer balanced protections against exploitation.

Bloomington and the *Calculus*

Calculus exerts a profound influence on the Bloomington school. Elinor and Vincent Ostrom praise the *Calculus* for helping "to clarify the logical foundations of constitutional democracy" (E. & V. Ostrom 2004). In *The Political Theory of a Compound Republic*, Vincent Ostrom points out that Buchanan and Tullock offer a helpful "language and logical framework for understanding the distinctive problems of constitutional choice" (238), and he uses this approach to reframe the deliberative and constitutional process at the founding of the American federal republic.

In particular, Vincent Ostrom appeals to the *Calculus*'s contributions in both the importance of the unanimity rule in the ratifying process of the constitution, as well as in the expediency of cost-minimizing rules for operational decision (52, 67). In reformulating *The Federalist*'s safeguards against majority tyranny, Vincent Ostrom presents the constitution as a set of decision-making rules and specifies that a compound republic is not merely an assembly of autonomous governmental units but, just as importantly, a "compound of decision structures within each unit of government" comprising the federal state (120). It is for these reasons that Vincent Ostrom's analysis of these constitutional arrangements has fittingly been described as a "flying buttress to the *Calculus of Consent*" (Wagner 2016: 18).

Vincent and Elinor Ostrom (1971) defend the relevance of public choice as a framework for understanding public administration "with more radical implications" for policy than the prevailing theory epitomized by Woodrow Wilson. Criticizing Wilson's hierarchical and managerial theory of public administration, the Ostroms highlight the need for an alternative approach. They apply public choice's methodological individualism and Buchananite constitutional cost calculus to show that decentralized and competitive provision of public services may be more appropriate and efficient in meeting diverse collectivities' needs.

The Ostroms also credit the *Calculus* with giving them the "basic tools for acquiring some analytical leverage in addressing particular problems that people are required to address about public affairs" (E. & V. Ostrom 2004). Buchanan and Tullock's work was at the center of the Ostroms' early working group discussions on how to conceptualize local governance and how to efficiently address its specific problems. In line with the *Calculus*'s lesson that no single decision-making rule is fit to properly handle the wide range of collective action situations that arise in society, the Ostroms recognized that collective action problems could be solved more efficiently in a polycentric system of governance more closely fit to the differing scales of each issue. Since public goods and services are neither produced nor consumed in an equal measure, multiple governmental units with overlapping jurisdiction and varying scope and scale of action would allow "the calculus of consent [to be] developed and worked out more fully than in one overarching monocratic system" (E. Ostrom 2011b: 378). It is for this reason that Elinor quotes "a fundamental lesson that we all learned from Buchanan and Tullock" which she wished "to be hung on a wall of every university I visit as well as integrated into the textbooks on public policy and urban governance" (*ibid.*: 377): "both decentralization and size factors suggest that when possible, collective action should be organized in small rather than large political units. Organizations in large units may be justified only by the overwhelming importance of the externalities that remain after localized and decentralized collectivization" (Buchanan & Tullock 1962: 114).

The basic insights of *Calculus* carry through to Elinor Ostrom's work on common-pool resource problems, beginning with her doctoral dissertation and culminating in the development of the institutional analysis and development framework. In her study of Californian water management, Elinor Ostrom drew on the *Calculus* to interpret the equity jurisprudence process used in the Californian West Basin for adjudicating water rights, formulating rules, and monitoring performance in the management of the common-pool resources. Conceptual unanimity and individual rational choice for fair rules were important parts of this process, as it was "to the advantage of each member to support the right of the minority to delay decisions until all interests are fully taken into account" (E. Ostrom 1965: 266–77; E. & V. Ostrom 2004: 106).

Later, in *Governing the Commons*, Elinor Ostrom analyzes the calculus involved in the process of changing status quo rules for institutional choices (both constitutional and collective choices). Her approach is fittingly individualistic, because "individuals who make institutional choices also make operational choices" and in accordance with the standard of rational action "one predicts that individuals will select strategies whose expected benefits will exceed expected costs". The rule-changing process involves individuals evaluating the benefits of the status quo and of the prospective change against the necessary present transformation and future expected costs. As with *Calculus*, the more inclusive the rule, the higher the decision-making costs, but also "the lower the losses will be suffered by those protected by status quo rules" (E. Ostrom 1990: 192–3, 198–201).

Commons concerns

Having established the foundational role that *The Calculus of Consent* plays in the Bloomington approach and explored its key arguments, we now turn our attention to broader themes that Virginia and Bloomington share in common. We focus on the work of James Buchanan as the most distinctive representative of Virginia political economy, although we invoke other scholars where their contributions are salient. We do not dwell here on topics that Bloomington and Virginia share in common with all approaches to public choice. Some version of the rational actor model, for example, is constitutive of all approaches to the field. Instead, we focus on common themes that are either relatively neglected by other public choice scholars or are understood in a distinctive way by Bloomington and Virginia school scholars.

Self-governance

If we had to pick one concept to describe the central concern of both Bloomington and Virginia, it would be self-governance. Self-governance is the key normative commitment and the central social-scientific object of inquiry that underwrites both traditions. Vincent Ostrom makes this abundantly clear in his *Political Theory of a Compound Republic*. He opens with the same question with which Alexander Hamilton begins *Federalist 1*: "whether societies of men are really capable or not of establishing good government from reflection and choice, or whether they are forever destined to depend for their political constitutions on accident and force" (V. Ostrom 1973: 14). This commitment to understanding self-governance animates the questions asked in Bloomington and Virginia, questions that lead to the development of unique and complementary toolkits.

Buchanan's focus on unanimity derives from his reading of Wicksell (1896). Wicksell observed that majority rule disfavors minority taxpayers who suffer net losses in enacting public policy. Instead, he argued for a shift toward unanimity, where each citizen's agreement would imply net benefits. In Buchanan's application to "politics as exchange", if collective action and government is based on a rule of unanimity, then politics has the same positive sum properties as market exchange. From this position, Buchanan mounts an offensive against welfare economics as a form of social engineering. This approach involves imposing values on others and a social function by which economists would measure the welfare of a group of people. Buchanan argues that the normative role of economists is to propose changes in political institutions that the economist expects will receive wide (near unanimous) assent. Whereas day-to-day policy determination will always involve disagreement, individuals may agree that the rules of the political game – or, more modestly, changes to those rules – are on-net beneficial. In gauging efficiency or effect of collective action, Buchanan rejects the notion of a social welfare function and argues that individual consent in a choosing group is thus "the only test which can insure that a change is beneficial" (Buchanan 1959). Under other decision-making rules, a shift from private to collective action does not guarantee the elimination of externalities. Buchanan laments economists' failure to account for this in comparing government corrective action to private market failures (Buchanan 1962). He urges economists to not focus on theories of managerial resource allocation, but on theories of voluntary and cooperative association of individuals (Buchanan 1964). In essence, Buchanan argues that economists should be citizens rather than technocrats.

In many ways, the work of Bloomington school scholars exemplifies Buchanan's citizen economics. Through both the metropolitan reform debate and their extensive study of common-pool resource problems, the Ostroms and their collaborators always sought to understand existing governance practices rather than simply imposing some pre-existing vision of the good society. This is not to say that concepts like efficiency play no role in Bloomington or Virginia. Rather, efficiency is used as a hypothetical benchmark from which to identify potential gains from trade in politics. Those gains remain merely potential, however, until they are validated by an inclusive democratic process. In the Bloomington school, this approach ultimately leads to a call for a new science of citizenship. Vincent Ostrom (1997) argues that, in order to sustain self-governing systems, citizens need to learn both theoretical tools and practical experience to develop their capacities for solving collective action problems. In a self-governing society, the purpose of laws is limited to ordering social relationships among equals, not instituting mechanisms of domination. The design of a "good government from reflection and choice" in such a society relies on using power to check power and on conflict resolution processes to continually uphold, as well as reshape, patterns of order (V. Ostrom 1997: 9–12).

This reshaping was reflected in Elinor Ostrom's empirical work on self-governing communities employing localized knowledge in structuring and enforcing rules for successful management of common-pool resources. Elinor's work examines concrete instances of self-governance and highlights some of its advantages. She situates self-governance as a middle-ground between two solutions to the tragedy of the commons: privatization and government regulation. Self-governance entails that individuals are not prisoners in tragedies of the commons, needing external top-down homogeneous regulation, but are instead capable of creating diverse arrangements for solving social dilemmas (E. Ostrom 2010a). One of the chief advantages of self-governance that Ostrom identifies is that those closest to a collective action situation have the strongest incentive to get the rules right. For this reason, Ostrom recognizes educating citizens on the importance of participating in the "constitution and reconstitution of rule-governed politics" and the "art and science of association" as one of the central themes of the Bloomington research agenda (Aligica & Boettke 2009: 159).

Institutional choice

The problem with a theory of self-governance is that, in collective action situations, individuals are rarely decisive. Except under unanimity rules, some collective decisions will run counter to each individual's desires. Buchanan and Tullock solve this problem by distinguishing between decisions at the constitutional level and decisions at the policy level. This theme carries forward in Buchanan's work. In *Politics by Principle, Not Interest*, Buchanan and Congleton (1998) argue that rational individuals could choose restrictions on the domain of government decisions. If government can only pass policies that conform to a generality norm, then policy ceases to be a means of discriminatory exploitation and becomes a search for mutually agreeable exchange. They propose the generality rule as a substitute for super-majoritarian requirements in areas where deliberation costs make super-majorities unattractive. This rule would prohibit "discriminatory" policies that shower benefits or impose costs on only some groups, and thus – to the extent that it is respected – steer policy choice towards generalized benefits.

Vincent Ostrom's *Political Theory of a Compound Republic* likewise expands on *Calculus*, examining the role of federal structures such as the separation of powers. For Ostrom, a constitution is an operative instrument of governmental *design* wherein general rules are enacted and enforced by government, and constitutional rules are enacted by the people and enforced against government (V. Ostrom 1973: 49–50). The merits of a federalist constitutional structure lie not merely in curbing abuse of power, but more importantly in allowing citizens to participate in various types of political associations pursuing "common measures to deal with common problems" (V. Ostrom 1973: 93). This design entails structuring a multitude of different decision-making rules and balancing institutions of authority in such a way that "constitutional law can specify both capabilities and limits that apply to citizens and governmental officials alike" as subjects of law (V. Ostrom 1991a: 94–5). Achieving this balance is the foundation of a limited government that at once cannot define its own authority at the constitutional level but is also charged with the authority to conduct operational collective decision-making, where the people themselves must in turn submit to its results. The cost calculus of consent is apparent at this point, and Ostrom emphasizes the deliberation period before constitutional choice that took place between the recommendatory process of the Philadelphia Convention and the ratification process in establishing a government "from reflection and choice" (V. Ostrom 1973: 50–57).

In later Bloomington work, the two levels of choice are explicitly integrated into the institutional analysis and development framework. Elinor Ostrom (1990: 50–55) decries that most studies of collective action problems are dedicated to just one level of rules, which she identifies as operational, while the other two relevant levels of collective choice rules and constitutional rules were taken as unchanging. This limited approach treated collective action problems within fixed operational rules leading to the prediction of a tragedy of the commons in common-pool resource management. Ostrom proposes an alternative multi-level approach, distinguishing between (1) operational rules that govern day-to-day resource use; (2) collective choice rules that determine the creation and management of the former; and (3) constitutional rules that stipulate the "arenas" subject to collective choice. Buchanan's calculus regarding what actions to collectivize and under what rules is again at play here, with the costs becoming higher when addressing changes in "deeper" rules. Shifting analysis from action constrained by fixed operational rules to action within different types of rules nested at multiple levels, Elinor identified a framework in which self-governing people could switch among all of the relevant levels in addressing common-pool resource governance and other collective action situations (Gibson *et al.* 2005).

Calculus's distinction between constitutional choice of political rules and collective choices within the rules is the most distinctive *analytic* move that separates Bloomington and Virginia from other schools of thought. Most political economy models treat the rules of the political game as given. The median voter theorem, for example, models collective choice along a one-dimensional axis of quantifiable degrees and ignores the constitutional structure of decision-making rules of a compound republic, where different *types* of decisions are reached through different processes. In assuming a single dimension for political decisions, it also loses sight of vote trading, by which minorities may counterbalance majority rule or expedient political decisions may be taken over a wide-ranging and separate set of issues. Of course, Bloomington and Virginia school scholars make use of these static models as well, but always keep in mind the possibility of moving to the constitutional level.

Polycentricity

Both Bloomington and Virginia converge on a key idea early on: governance is not one singular, well-defined problem. Governance problems are many and varied, just as the ways in which individuals and groups can help or harm one another are varied. Varied problems imply the need for a variety of solutions. One-size-fits-all, top-down governance is unlikely to work very well. Bloomington and Virginia are alike in expressing skepticism about the efficacy of top-down planning. As noted above, an essential idea of the *Calculus* is that there is no suitable decision rule applicable to all collective actions or to all groups. A constitution is a collection of many different rules for many different situations, with optimal rules minimizing the expected costs for individuals. This initial subjective cost-based argument against top-down governance ties into the fundamental lesson that the Ostroms attributed to the *Calculus*: collective activity should presumptively be organized in smaller political units, and decentralization and federalism allow individuals to minimize their costs under government. Elinor Ostrom laments that self-organizing individuals "are invisible" to those who see central direction as essential in governance, and proposes instead policies supporting multiple-level governance structures (E. Ostrom 2005a: 240). Both schools of thought thus commend and study systems of polycentric governance.

Vincent Ostrom articulates the concept of polycentricity in the context of the metropolitan reform debate. Drawing on work developed as early as 1961, Vincent Ostrom summarizes polycentric political systems as composed of (1) many autonomous units formally independent of one another; (2) choosing to act in ways that take account of others; and (3) through processes of cooperation, competition, conflict, and (central or non-central mechanisms of) conflict resolution (V. Ostrom 1991b: 225). Ostrom, Tiebout, and Warren (1961) introduced the concept in addressing the problem of "too many governments and not enough government" with overlapping jurisdictions and duplication of functions in growing local communities. Countering the prevailing solution of centralization of government under one unit, they instead showed that different problems are more efficiently addressed by units of varying size and scope. Tiebout (1956) had already advanced the idea of separate jurisdictions competing for citizens who can "vote with their feet", but under the polycentric model, the competitive processes happen between geographically distinct jurisdictions as much as *within* jurisdictions overlapping the same area. Exit options for individuals are no longer tied to just "voting with their feet", as polycentricity entails the concurrent existence of competing governments where "overlapping jurisdictions and fragmentation of authority yield emergent patterns of order that are at least as consistent with standards of liberty, justice, and general welfare" as unitary states (V. Ostrom 1991a: 136). Polycentric governance enables the functioning of a rewarding discovery process similar to markets. Federalism as a form of polycentric organization allows for the generation and dispersal of information on the performance of existing alternative solutions to public service needs, which in turn facilitates corrections and improvements in competitive "patterns of order" similar to markets (V. Ostrom 1991a: 231–2).

Buchanan likewise writes extensively on federalism in the context of public finance. His earliest works on federalism reflect the influence of Knut Wicksell and a preoccupation for the individual, later developed in *Calculus*. In analyzing the equity of fiscal burden and redistribution within a federal system, Buchanan rejects "as difficult to comprehend" the idea of equality and ethics between states, and instead shifts the discussion to a standard of equality before the law appealing to Pigou's formulation of "equal treatment of equals" (Buchanan 1950: 586–7). Later, applying the public choice framework, Brennan and Buchanan (1980) present government as a revenue-maximizing monopolistic Leviathan and base an argument for federalism on the individual's constitutional deliberation that it would be beneficial to restrain taxing power by decentralizing authority in multiple units. This opens up the possibility of competitive fiscal behavior of decentralized units, and more importantly, the option for individuals and capital to escape predatory jurisdictions and move to more conservative or efficient states. Governmental intrusion is inversely related to the extent of fiscal decentralization and exploitative capacity is similarly related to the number of competing units. As with market cartels, as the number of members increases, the costs of colluding towards exploitation also increase (Brennan & Buchanan 2000: 203–12). It is on the basis of offering a practical exit option among competing jurisdictions that federalism can be viewed as an analogue to voluntary market activity, and government's potential to exploit the citizenry be minimized, making it an "ideal political order" (Buchanan 1995).

Federalism is just one example of a polycentric system, and the concept of polycentricity is much wider in its applicability. Elinor Ostrom argues in her later work that natural resource governance requires a polycentric approach. She counts polycentricity in her set of design principles for enduring common-pool resources, finding positive outcomes when the management and governance of such resources is "organized in multiple layers of nested enterprises" of local, regional and national jurisdictions (E. Ostrom 1990: 101–102). However, she warns that these principles are not "blueprints" and emphasizes that it's not some unique structure that promotes positive outcomes. Instead, it is the ability of citizens to organize and rearrange the structure in multiple governing authorities that communicate, cooperate, and resolve resulting conflicts specific to a variety of local conditions. These authorities, either public or private associations, varying both in scale and in scope, are interdependent and may complement each other in fulfilling public services. More importantly, being separable, they can afford policy experimentation of different types because "when small systems fail, there are larger systems to call upon – and vice versa" and thus they "drastically reduce the probability of immense failure for an entire region" (E. Ostrom 2005a: 283–4).

It is no exaggeration to see polycentricity as central to the concepts of self-governance and democracy for the Ostroms. In this sense, Elinor Ostrom (2010a) casts polycentric governance in stark contrast with Thomas Hobbes' theory of sovereignty. Governance under Hobbes' theory of sovereignty is achieved through a monopoly of power, where rulers with absolute prerogatives are the source of the law. The state is necessarily unitary, and even in democracies, citizens participate in unitary assemblies adopting universally binding decisions. In contrast, polycentric governance allows citizens to share in the prerogatives of governing their own affairs in overlapping and coexisting decision structures ordered according to rules of law. Citizens use power to check power through these arrangements, but also participate in active learning and communication to find ways of solving possible conflicts arising from this cohabitation.

Complex agents

Using rational choice models to understand politics is a *sine qua non* of public choice. But neither Bloomington nor Virginia apply these models in a mechanical or uncritical fashion. Buchanan and Brennan do argue that *homo economicus* is an invaluable benchmark for institutional analysis. However, this exercise is meant to serve as a robustness check on institutional design. If individuals are sometimes selfish, we should look – both descriptively and normatively – for rules that check that selfish behavior. Hume's political maxim that every man must be supposed a knave is wise counsel even if we recognize that humans are more complex. But some puzzles require asking not only how individuals choose between an array of given alternatives, but also how certain options come to be the relevant alternatives in the first place.

Except for his denunciation of utilitarianism (1959), Buchanan's early work is rarely explicit about his economic anthropology. He later develops in more detail a fairly radical form of subjectivism. He argues that preference functions are, at best, a useful mental tool for making predictions about free choices (1979a). It's the choices that are real, not the preferences, which is why Buchanan is so suspicious of social engineering aimed at preference satisfaction (1969: 87–8). He distinguishes between "reactive choice" as modeled by *homo economicus* and "creative choice" as discussed by thinkers like Israel Kirzner and G. L. S. Shackle (Buchanan 1982: 35–6). Creative choice is characteristic of entrepreneurship and represents a richer model of human behavior. Assumptions about preferences and mathematical modelling are necessary for making falsifiable *predictions* about behavior, but a general understanding of social processes is enriched by adopting a more complex model of individuals. This epistemic dimension of decision-making makes its way into Buchanan's thoughts on public finance, where he worries that deficit financing might create a "fiscal illusion" about the scale and scope of government activity (Buchanan & Wagner 1977). It also underwrites one of his most radical arguments for individual liberty: since individuals can imagine new possibilities, we do not know what sort of people we will be in the future. This means we should want liberty for the sake of the future, unknown, "artifactual" selves that we will create with our choices: "Man wants liberty to become the man he wants to become" (Buchanan 1979a).

Vincent Ostrom likewise embraces the epistemic dimension of human action. He argues that the most promising avenues for public choice research would follow the "thrusts at the periphery" that deal with issues related to knowledge, such as Gordon Tullock's (1965) work on the limits of information transmission in bureaucracy and Buchanan's above-mentioned argument about artifactual man (V. Ostrom 1993). Ostrom places language at the center of his account of how groups order their relationships. Language not only allows for communication but "for constituting knowledge, organizing thought, arraying alternatives, ordering choice, and taking actions in arranging present means in appropriate ways to realize future apparent goods" (1993: 166). Like Buchanan, Ostrom argues that the approach of Austrian economics, which emphasizes limited individual cognition and the epistemic function of prices, is a valuable complement to the standard public choice tradition (Buchanan 1979b; V. Ostrom 1993: 169). While recognizing the value of stripped-down analytical models, Ostrom warns that "excessive use of Occam's razor runs the risk of transforming economic reasoning into perverse forms of theology which afflict those who eat fruit from the tree of knowledge without appreciating the limits of human fallibility" (V. Ostrom 1993: 175).

In her doctoral dissertation, Elinor Ostrom draws on Buchanan's mentor Frank Knight to develop a concept of public entrepreneurship. Public entrepreneurs work within the political framework and their assigned limited authority to pursue specific legally established community goods and services (E. Ostrom 1965: 2–8). Her later work deviates from pure rational choice in several important ways. First, she argues that human beings are conditional cooperators and altruistic punishers. Based on repeated experiments on collective action, Ostrom explains individuals' participation as "norm-using" players in addition to rational egoists. As conditional cooperators, individuals initiate and contribute to collective action as long as others reciprocate, while as willing punishers, they rebuke and punish free riders. Together, these two roles "create a more robust opening for collective action and a mechanism for helping it grow" (E. Ostrom 2000a). Second, she uses Herbert Simon's work on bounded rationality. Moving away from models of fully rational and informed individuals, Elinor Ostrom shows that individuals who face knowledge limitations, but repeatedly interact over time, gain new understanding of the constraints they face and overcome collective action problems by changing the framework of rules they operate under. Finally, she likewise emphasizes the importance of language in the constitution of order. She showed that the introduction of "cheap talk" or low-cost non-binding communication in repeated common-pool resource games offered the opportunity for cooperation and efficiency gains (Ostrom & Walker 1991). Elsewhere, she develops a syntax for analyzing distinguishing among different types of institutional statements that describe a "constraint or opportunity that prescribes, permits, or advises actions or outcomes for actors" (Crawford & Ostrom 1995).

The fragility of order

If order rests on so frail a foundation as language, it should not be taken for granted. Because Bloomington and Virginia school scholars pay heed to the distinction between constitutional and operational choice, they are attuned to the possibility that play within the rules can undermine the rules themselves. This can generate a fundamentally pessimistic outlook about maintaining self-governance.

Buchanan's concept of "relatively absolute absolutes" (1989) illustrates this concept. He argues that moral absolutism and moral relativism are both dangerous positions. Moral absolutism denies the possibility of improving upon our core values by insisting that they are time invariant, while moral relativism leaves us with no room to make moral judgements on actions that are potentially disruptive of social order. The highest principles, for Buchanan, are absolute, but only relatively so. Key moral precepts must be accepted *as if* they were absolutely true in day-to-day life, but they are subject to revision through learning and experience. The parallel here with Buchanan's thoughts on constitutions is evident. The problem, for Buchanan, is that there is no guarantee that the absoluteness of the relatively absolute absolutes will be respected. Communities can turn away from the basic principles of self-governance because they dislike constraints (1975) or because they are "afraid to be free" (2005).

This concern about fragility is most evident in the project on anarchy taken up at Virginia Tech in the early 1970s. A variety of Virginia school scholars contemplated the economics of a state of nature in which order was only the result of self-interest (Tullock 1972). Most of these projects did not paint a rosy picture. Buchanan's *Limits of Liberty* is a case in point. Buchanan argues that markets represent a sort of "ordered anarchy" where individuals can pursue their interests within the constraint of property rights secured by the productive state. With the advent of the "redistributive" state, however, it is possible for society to slip back into a world of unordered anarchy as groups struggle for control of state power. This pessimistic tome grew in part out of Buchanan's worries about the breakdown of social order beginning in the late 1960s, most notably (to him) in the academy (Buchanan & Devletoglou 1970).

Vincent Ostrom's *The Meaning of Democracy and the Vulnerability of Democracies* is similarly pessimistic in tone. Subtitled *A Response to Tocqueville's Challenge*, it considers the threats to orderly and mutually beneficial life in a democratic society. Echoing Buchanan's operational level, he recognizes that all forms of governance are a double-edged sword: "Organization in human societies, then, depends on a Faustian bargain – a bargain with evil – where imposing deprivations on others via instruments of evil, that is, sanctions, including those of organized force, necessarily leaves some worse off rather than better off" (139). These sanctions can make life in society worse rather than better. However, he argues that democratic societies, which alone offer the possibility of self-governance, "are especially vulnerable to majority tyranny and to the machinations of boss rule" (215). Among the threats to democracy, not coincidentally, are "newspeak" and "doublethink" (V. Ostrom 1997: ch. 3). Newspeak refers to redefining terms from their everyday usage for political purposes, and doublethink to the way in which such linguistic changes separate political mental models from those used in markets, science, and other arenas. Since language plays a crucial role in self-governance, this wedge between politics and the rest of social life can transform citizens from participants in democratic processes into mere spectators.

Elinor Ostrom echoes some of these concerns, recognizing that tragedies of the commons do occur. But the Ostroms' overall project was a hopeful one. Their goal was to develop a "science of citizenship" (V. Ostrom 1997: ch. 11) in a literal sense. They imagined that individuals could be taught to analyze how rules govern patterns of interaction, to recognize the dangers of power, and to receive some elementary practice in devising rules that are beneficial to all. Elinor Ostrom sums up this hopeful project thusly: "Self-governing, democratic systems are always fragile enterprises. Future citizens need to understand that they participate in the constitution and reconstitution of rule-governed polities. And they need to learn the 'art and science of association'. If we fail in this, all our investigations and theoretical efforts are useless" (Ostrom in Aligica & Boettke 2009: 159; cf. 56–7).

Conclusion

This chapter has surveyed some of the deep connections between the thought of three giants of public choice, James Buchanan on the one hand and Vincent and Elinor Ostrom on the other. From the foundational analysis of the *Calculus of Consent*, all of these thinkers built extensive and highly influential research agendas probing the limits and promise of self-governance. They address some of the most critical questions that perennially afflict democratic, liberal societies struggling against various forms of internally generated tyranny and the threat of institutional erosion.

By focusing on these three central figures, we have necessarily neglected both parallel and subsequent developments in both the Virginia and Bloomington schools. Recent scholarship has only brought these two schools of thought closer together. Richard Wagner (2016) blends the insights of Buchanan, the Ostroms, and others to investigate the complex dynamics of constitutional order. Boettke (2012) places Virginia and Bloomington both in the broader social-scientific tradition of "mainline economics," which includes the Scottish Enlightenment and the Austrian school of economics. Political economy as an academic field still has much to gain from cross-breeding the intellectual fruits of these schools of thought.

3

NEW INSTITUTIONAL ECONOMICS: BUILDING FROM SHARED FOUNDATIONS

Michael D. McGinnis

This chapter explores similarities, contrasts, and connections between the Bloomington school of institutional analysis established by Vincent and Elinor Ostrom and new institutional economics (NIE).[1] Although NIE was not included among the three "schools" or research traditions Mitchell (1988) identified as closely related but distinct approaches to the study of political economy active at that time, new institutional economics can also claim a common origin in the mid-twentieth century public choice movement, in which scholars from various disciplines brought concepts and methods from economics to bear on explicitly political subjects (Mitchell 1999; Aligica & Boettke 2009). As shown in this chapter, these two traditions of research have since gone in quite different directions.

In a nutshell, NIE and the Bloomington school offer complementary perspectives on the origins and sustainability of institutions, political economy, and social order. NIE sees the institutional order as primarily constituted in a network of organizations, and focuses on the principal–agent problem within formal organizations as the key difficulty in building a stable social order. By contrast, the Bloomington school sees the institutional order as a network of action arenas in which political, economic, and social actors work together to realize shared interests while acknowledging that each will nonetheless continue to also pursue self-interested goals. For those working in the Bloomington tradition, the key problem becomes reducing the frequency of free-riding or other behaviors that undermine trust within and across social groups.

---

1. I wish to express my deep appreciation to Vlad Tarko, whose extensive editorial suggestions for revisions and rearrangement helped clarify the argument I was trying to make, and to my colleagues Lee Alston, Dan Cole, and Bill Blomquist for their very useful comments. Of course, any errors of fact or interpretation that remain are my responsibility alone.

This chapter examines a series of similarities and differences between NIE and the Bloomington school in their understanding of basic concepts and their tendency to rely on different, but related, methods of analysis. After this introductory section, I highlight their shared foundations in the basic tenets of methodological individualism and bounded rationality. The following section details how scholars working in these traditions interpret core concepts of institutions, organizations, and property rights in subtly different ways. I then show how these differences underlie more dramatic contrasts in their approach to broader issues of social order. The final section concludes by suggesting ways scholars from these two research traditions might combine their respective strengths to improve our collective understanding of important aspects of political, economic, and social order.

A shared foundation: methodological individualism and bounded rationality

Oliver Williamson (1975: 1) first coined the term "new institutional economics" (NIE), which eventually broadened to incorporate a wide range of related areas of research on political economy (Eggertsson 1990; Furubotn & Richter 2005; Ménard & Shirley 2008; Galiani & Sened 2014). The advanced NIE text by Furubotn and Richter (2005: 35–40) identifies the core topics of NIE as transaction costs, property rights, and the economic theory of contracts. In this chapter, I use the term NIE to also encompass two research areas that Furubotn and Richter (2005) designate as new institutional economic history and historical and comparative institutional analysis. Researchers working in the first of these areas use simple economic models to understand the institutional structure of a political-economic system as a whole, and those in the second area focus on how different configurations of small-scale institutional arrangements can support the persistence of diverse macro-level patterns of strategic interactions between powerful political and economic actors. In short, NIE covers an impressive range of core topics in political economy, ranging all the way from the contractual basis of individual firms to the historical development of fundamentally different structures of social order.

Douglass North and Oliver Williamson are the two scholars most closely associated with new institutional economics. Each has received a Nobel Prize in economics, North in 1993 (North 1994) and Williamson in 2009 (Williamson 2010). Williamson's award was shared with Elinor Ostrom (2010a), but the Nobel committee did not identify Williamson and Ostrom as belonging to a single school of research, beyond recognizing their contributions to the study of economic governance, specifically the commons (Ostrom) and the structure of the firm (Williamson). Critically important contributions from two other Nobelists, Ronald Coase and Herbert Simon, are also discussed below.

Scholars in both new institutional economics and the Bloomington school stand united in opposition to the general presumption in neoclassical economic theory that rational actors can accurately and dispassionately weigh the potential benefits and costs of each option available to them in real-life decision situations. Proponents of both research traditions give prominence to a core contribution from Herbert Simon, the first political science PhD awarded a Nobel Prize in economics (Simon 1979). Throughout his long career, Simon forcefully argued that human choice is subject to constraints inherent in the nature of human cognition, the organizational structures within which we act, and the effects of emotion and normative values on decision-making.

Simon (1955) postulated that the sequence by which options are considered can be critical. He argued that individuals rarely hold out for finding the optimal solution, but instead follow a decision process he called "satisficing," that is, set an aspirational level, start examining options, and then pick the first option likely to reap net benefits exceeding that threshold. If that process is as ubiquitous as Simon postulated, then to understand the decisions made by individual leaders, analysts need to become familiar with the institutional procedures that determine the sequence of consideration, the source of each agent's aspiration level, and the intensity of time pressure felt by that actor.

Simon's model of human cognition implied that humans are boundedly rational information processors capable of only relatively simple decisional tasks, but if those same actors are placed within appropriate institutional settings, in which agents are presented with the information they need to make decisions regarding their particular range of responsibilities, then as agents of corporate actors they can cope remarkably well with situations of great complexity (Simon 1969, 1979, 1991, 1997). Simon's insights help justify the foundational premise in both traditions that institutions matter, both by shaping contexts for decisions and by influencing how individuals understand their material interests and normative values.

NIE and the Bloomington school also share the presumption that boundedly rational actors consistently pursue their own self-interest, even when acting to serve the interests of their organization or to fulfill the terms of a commitment to cooperate with others. There is always a chance that someone may break an agreement or shirk on previous commitments, or manipulate conditions in an opportunistic manner. Anyone seeking to design effective organizations needs to take account of this ubiquitous tension, by building in institutional mechanisms to monitor behavior and enforce sanctions for violations of agreements or social norms.

Researchers in both traditions also share a deep commitment to methodological individualism. Institutional processes assign individuals to play prescribed roles within established organizations, but when push comes to shove, analysts need to understand how individual humans actually make decisions, not just what they should do in that role. Even committed methodological individualists cannot deny the existence of collective entities that, in at least some circumstances, operate as if their agents are pursuing a common purpose.

Coase (1937) decried the lack of explicit attention paid to firms by economic theorists, even in an age when national economies had become dominated by large corporations. The discipline of economics was slow to respond to Coase's clarion call, but eventually the importance of his article was recognized when Coase was awarded the 1991 Nobel Prize in economics. This classic article also inspired scholars who developed the then nascent field of new institutional economics.

Coase attributed the origin of firms (and by extension, other corporate actors) to widespread incentives to lower the costs necessarily entailed in any kind of transaction, including simple market exchange. Parties need to find each other, evaluate the quality of the items under consideration, assess the trustworthiness of the other party, and determine what terms of trade are acceptable. For NIE scholars, the take-away point was that political economists have every reason to expect that leaders of corporate actors will strive to adopt an organizational form that minimizes the transaction costs of production, exchange, and whatever other types of transaction in which they are engaged.

For example, firms may significantly increase profit margins by lobbying legislators and regulators to craft laws and regulations that give their firm (or their market sector) significant competitive advantages, thus allowing them to benefit from artificial rents generated and distributed by public officials. Within NIE, transaction cost minimization and rent-seeking are recognized as foundational to the dynamics of political economic systems.

In an overview of the conceptual origins of the interdisciplinary synthesis of institutional analysis now known as the Bloomington school, Elinor Ostrom (2007a) identifies Coase (1937) as the foundational statement of new institutional economics, one critical component of that synthesis.

> The 'new' institutional economics field has been a major challenge to both economists and political scientists ... Ronald Coase started the first foray in 1937 with his article on 'The Nature of the Firm'. By asking 'Why do firms exist?', he asked an embarrassing question for economists. Why should one find firms existing in the midst of highly competitive markets for strictly private goods? He challenged the presumed dichotomy of the world into markets for production, allocation, and distribution of private goods and hierarchies for the production,

allocation, and distribution of collective goods. Coase answered his own question by pointing to the costs that are associated with all forms of organization that had not been included in economic models of the market. These transaction costs could be substantial and would lead entrepreneurs to try out alternative forms of organization even when they were dealing with private goods.   (E. Ostrom 2007a: 242–3)

Elinor Ostrom (2007a: 243) goes on to highlight how Coase's work influenced later NIE researchers. "North (1981, 1990a, 1990b) initiated a series of studies of institutional change that challenged the static focus of both political science and economics. He examined the growth of the transaction sector in the American economy over century-long periods and demonstrated that transaction costs were a more important factor than production costs in a modern economy." Milgrom, North, and Weingast (1990) demonstrated how "the evolution of property rights in the Middle Ages … was affected by the need to reduce uncertainty in relationships and the costs of transactions" and that "a variety of self-organized institutions had guaranteed the property rights of merchants long before the creation of a state." Finally, Ostrom notes that "Oliver Williamson (1975, 1985) also took up Coase's challenge to examine a diversity of internal mechanisms within firms to keep agents accountable and to reduce transaction costs".

Although Ostrom (2007a) acknowledges NIE research on transaction costs as an important contribution to the Bloomington school, most of her conceptual overview focuses on developments related to other sources, especially public choice and polycentric governance, natural resource management and commons research, and experimental research in behavioral game theory. The Ostrom research tradition overlaps with NIE in many ways, but that overlap is by no means complete.

NIE scholars tend to conceptualize politics as exchanges between public officials and private actors (individual citizens, corporate agents, or representatives of interest groups), but Bloomington school scholars counter that politics encompasses a far broader range of experience than mere exchange. Consider education or health: the active involvement of students or patients is essential if they are going to be able to realize a quality education or good health (E. Ostrom 1996). The same can be said for public safety and many other local public goods (McGinnis 1999b; E. Ostrom 2006). To Bloomington school scholars, "co-production" denotes situations in which the active personal involvement of the consumer (or the beneficiary of an assistance program) is a requisite input for the production of a high-quality good or service.

A basic tenet of the Bloomington school is that governance should be understood as co-production, a form of collective action in which the governed see themselves as an integral part of the governing process. This emphasis on active citizen participation inclines scholars from the Bloomington school to be more willing to incorporate normative considerations into their analyses than other social scientists. In her Nobel address, Elinor Ostrom concludes that the "most important lesson for public policy analysis" from institutional political economy is the realization that "humans have a more complex motivational structure and more capability to solve social dilemmas than posited in earlier rational choice theory" (E. Ostrom 2010a: 664; Boettke *et al.* 2016: 237). She goes on to articulate a radically optimistic vision:

> Designing institutions to force (or nudge) entirely self-interested individuals to achieve better outcomes has been the major goal posited by policy analysis for governments to accomplish for much of the past half century. Extensive empirical research leads me to argue that instead, a core goal of public policy should be to facilitate the development of institutions that bring out the best in humans.
>
> (E. Ostrom 2010a: 664–5; Boettke *et al.* 2016: 237–8)

This explicitly normative claim stands in stark contrast to the standard NIE injunction to policy-makers to "get the institutions right", that is, to select laws and regulations that give policy actors incentives to choose actions that facilitate efficient operation of markets, with scant consideration of non-economic consequences. The following section argues that this stark divergence of world views has its origin in seemingly minor differences in the interpretation of a few concepts that play prominent roles in both research traditions.

Subtle shades of meaning: institutions, organizations, and property rights

Douglass North and Elinor Ostrom have provided influential definitions of the core concept of "institution" that succinctly summarize key precepts of NIE and the Bloomington school, respectively. At first glance they seem similar, but they turn out to have quite different consequences for institutional research and policy analysis.

"Institutions are the rules of the game in a society or, more formally, are the humanly devised constraints that shape human interaction. In consequence they structure incentives in human exchange whether political, social, or economic" (North 1990a: 3). Elinor Ostrom writes, "Broadly defined, institutions are the prescriptions that humans use to organize all forms of repetitive and structured interactions including those within families, neighborhoods, markets, firms, sports leagues, churches, private associations, and governments at all levels" (E. Ostrom 2005a: 3).

North treats institutions primarily as constraints on behavior, but for Ostrom institutions are critically important resources that groups can use to support efforts to resolve common problems or to achieve shared aspirations. Both use the term "institution" to include written laws, rules, and regulations, as well as organizations whose agents have the responsibility to act on behalf of a larger group. Both North and Ostrom acknowledge the importance of informal arrangements such as conventions, codes of behavior, common values, norms, and shared modes of understanding, but they differ in their interpretation of these kinds of informal institutions. In a recent effort to systematize NIE in the institutional and organizational analysis (IOA) framework, Alston *et al.* (2018) draw a sharp distinction between formal organizations and informal norms, but for Ostrom (2005b), the boundary between formal and informal remains intrinsically fuzzy, their subtle interweavings impossible to untangle completely.

Despite considerable overlap in their definitions of institutions, North and Ostrom encouraged quite different analytical approaches to the study of formal organizations:

> Institutions are the rules of the game – both formal rules, informal norms and their enforcement characteristics. Together they define the way the game is played. Organizations are the players. They are made up of groups of individuals held together by some common objectives … The immediate objective of organizations may be profit maximizing (for firms) or improving reelection prospects (for political parties); but the ultimate objective is survival because all organizations live in a world of scarcity and hence competition.   (North 2008: 22)

> An organization is composed of one or more (usually more) action situations linked together by prescriptions specifying how outcomes from one situation become inputs into others. Organizations may be thought of as a tree or a lattice with situations at each node. A particular set of rules structures the situation at each node. A general set of rules partially structures all internal situations and specifies the paths that may be chosen from one situation to the next.
>   (E. Ostrom 2005a: 57)

North clearly designates organizations as actors in a game, but Ostrom's vision of organizational behavior requires further elaboration. "Action situation" is a technical term from the institutional analysis and development (IAD) or social-ecological systems (SES) frameworks used so frequently by scholars from the Bloomington school (see E. Ostrom 2005a, 2011a; McGinnis 2011a; McGinnis & Ostrom 2014; Schlager & Cox 2017; Cole *et al.* 2019). In essence, an action situation is an abstract representation of a site of strategic interaction occurring within social, physical, and institutional constraints. It is closely related to the more commonly used concept of a game, in the sense that both action situations and game models connote settings in which individuals or corporate actors make choices that jointly determine some outcome or outcomes. To define the rules of a game or the working components of an action situation (E. Ostrom 1986, 2005), analysts must specify the players and the positions they hold, the choice options available to them, how those choices combine to generate alternative outcomes, all actors' preferences over those outcomes, and the information and other resources available to each actor, including resources they can use to influence each other.

Action situations differ from standard game models in that participants in the former are presumed to be capable of reconsidering the desirability of the rules under which they interact and to work together to change those rules through some process of collective action. Such efforts can, of course, be costly to undertake and uncertain in effect, but players in game models are rarely assumed to have even that minimal level of self-control over the games they are playing (for an exception, see E. Ostrom *et al.* 1994).

In the quote given above, Ostrom uses the concept of an action situation as a basic building block to construct a formal organization as a complex network of multiple interlinked sites of collaboration or contestation among executives, workers, and other stakeholders. Some component action situations may generate outcomes that shape the decision procedures employed by actors in situations of operational or collective choice, and the very same individuals may (or may not) be involved in both kinds of action situations. In effect, players in an action situation must first come to a shared understanding concerning the nature of the particular game they are playing at any one time. In addition, the overall performance of an organization conceptualized as a network of adjacent action situations (McGinnis 2011b) could be profoundly affected by dynamics within and between informal social networks, which rarely comport with formal connections designated in organizational charts. Frankly, this definition of a formal organization as a complex amalgam of action situations and other institutional arrangements, strategic interactions, normative prescriptions, and social networks is neither clear nor easy to apply in practical applications (McGinnis 2019).

Formal organizations are much more clearly defined within the NIE tradition. In his Nobel address, Williamson (2010) paid homage to the 1991 Nobelist, Ronald Coase (1992), for his insightful recognition of the central importance of transaction costs and property rights to the ways in which corporations are established, and the effects those organizational structures can have on the performance of real economies. Coase provided the theoretical foundation for a robust research program pioneered by Williamson, built on three empirical measures of transaction costs: asset specificity, uncertainty, and frequency (Williamson 1975, 1985, 1996; Williamson & Winter 1993). Each dimension refers to aspects of a potentially repeatable exchange that can generate potential problems between the parties. Take asset specificity as an example. If a product is being produced specifically for the use of one party, and if few other suppliers were available, then the producer could take advantage of this situation by insisting on a higher price than originally agreed, once the buyer has become dependent on continued access to that product. Similarly, if measures of a product's quality are intrinsically uncertain or more fully known by one of the parties, this can considerably complicate negotiations over terms of exchange. Finally, parties who expect to interact frequently should have confidence that they will have later opportunities to renegotiate the details of their contracts, if one or both parties deem that changed circumstances warrant reconsideration. Depending on the mix of a potential transaction's characteristics on these three dimensions, the parties may prefer to structure their interactions in the form of a one-off market exchange, or a long-term contract with provisions for renegotiation or arbitration when needed, or by consolidating themselves into a single organization, or one of many hybridized versions combining aspects of these basic elements.

Williamson highlighted the importance of transaction costs on shaping the organizational forms contracts, partnerships, firms, or other arrangements between economic actors are likely to take in different circumstances. One of Williamson's primary concerns was to deal with the danger that one or more parties might act in an opportunistic manner to exploit future situations. His solution was to find a way for parties to make credible commitments to a good faith effort to live up to the terms of the contract or other form of coordination. This theme of credible commitment lies at the core of NIE research.

A particularly important type of contractual relationship for NIE scholars concerns interactions between principals and their agents. A principal is an actor seeking to accomplish some goal that requires the assistance of an agent with specialized knowledge, skill, or assets. Agents usually have an incentive to shirk on their responsibilities or to hide information or otherwise misrepresent the quality of the services they provide. In response to this ubiquitous dilemma, principals strive to design contractual relationships that specify the agent's rewards for good performance and the information that the principal can require from that agent, in a way that closely aligns the self-interest of the agent to the primary interests of the principal.

Seen through the analytical lens of agent–principal relationships, policy systems can prove very difficult to untangle. Consider, for example, how frequently the executive, legislature, judicial, and administrative branches of a liberal democratic government work at cross-purposes, even though all are acting as agents of the public at large. The public selects representatives to act on their behalf, and bureaucrats serve as agents of elected officials, but bureaucrats, who have more direct control over policy levers, face incentives to shirk by slanting policy implementation to favor their own policy preferences. Rigorous investigations of the logical inter-relationships among these interconnected principals and agents have demonstrated that different configurations of the policy preferences of median voters in legislative bodies and the realized preferences of administrators or judges authorized to resolve policy disputes can result in substantially different patterns of policy outcomes, many of which seem unconnected to public opinion on those same issues, or even to the preferences of elected officials (Shepsle 2010; Alston *et al.* 2018).

For NIE scholars, the security of property rights in different kinds of political economic systems has been a particular point of concern. Most famously, Douglass North has investigated many ways in which property owners can come to feel that their rights to that property are secure (North & Thomas 1973; North 1982, 1990a,b, 2005; North *et al.* 2009). This is such an important problem because sustained economic growth requires investor confidence in the security of their assets. In the absence of secure property rights, owners are unlikely to willingly invest in improvements of those assets, since they have no assurance that they will be able to reap any benefits from those investments. Herein lies the short answer to the big question of why wealth, prosperity, and quality of life vary so widely across countries of the world: countries with insecure property rights fall behind countries whose leaders have solved that problem by establishing political, economic, and social institutions that credibly protect property rights (North 1990a; Alston *et al.* 2018).

In contrast to this emphasis on state protection of property rights, Bloomington school scholars see property as an institution that imparts a highly variable bundle of rights and obligations to a potentially wide range of affected parties. For the purposes of empirical comparisons, Schlager and Ostrom (1992) unpack the concept of property into a small number of configurations of rights: access, withdrawal, management, exclusion, and alienation. Different configurations of rights and obligations can be, and often are, created and monitored in a bottom-up fashion by a community trying to solve some problem of collective action (E. Ostrom 1990, 2010a). Real-world property systems can be incredibly complex, and Cole and Ostrom (2012) move beyond simplistic categories of private, public, and common property to highlight the wide variety of mixed, context-specific, and contingent property arrangements in operation throughout the world.

Complexity of property rights has not escaped the notice of NIE scholarship. For example, Barzel (1997, 2002) weaves an economic model of diverse property forms into his interpretation of the historical origins of the state. In his Nobel address, NIE pioneer Ronald Coase noted that "what are traded on the market are not, as is often supposed by economists, physical entities, but the rights to perform certain actions, and the rights which individuals possess are established by the legal system" (Coase 1992: 717; Boettke *et al.* 2016: 37). Hadfield (2008) explores the complex array of legal institutions needed to protect contracts through the evolution of common law, and several chapters in Furubotn and Richter (2005) investigate alternative forms of property and contractual obligations.

Property over land and its associated resources has been an especially fertile topic for different modes of research in this tradition. Alston *et al.* (1999) investigate changing methods of formal land titling on the frontier of Amazon region in Brazil, while Galini and Schargrodsky (2014) examine a natural experiment in more informal land titling processes in areas near Buenos Aries. Finally, property lies at the heart of the IOA framework, in which the primary purpose of political authority is to secure private rights over property, including the right to make policy decisions, both of which are critical foundations for the vitality of the overall economy (Alston *et al.* 2018).

Allowing for endogenous changes in rules and configurations of rights and obligations compounds the difficulties of analyzing property regimes within the Bloomington school tradition, but in so doing it brings a broader perspective that can have profound implications for policy. In a very influential article, Hardin (1968) argued that commonly owned resources will nearly always degenerate into a "tragedy of the commons" unless external actors intervene by assigning the responsibility of managing that shared resource to some central authority, or by splitting up the commons into separate tracts of private property. Ostrom (1990) demolished any pretentions to universal validity of Hardin's claim by demonstrating that in many places throughout the world community groups dependent on shared resources have insured continued access to those resources by working together to formulate and enforce rules on themselves, provided those rules satisfy a series of "design principles" (discussed in the next section).

However, endogenous rule-making at this level of frequency and effectiveness is possible only if the relevant actors can step back from day-to-day decisions to engage in extended deliberations on what kinds of rules would be appropriate and who should be responsible for enforcing those rules. Not all communities enjoy that level of autonomy or capacity for effective collective action. The next section shifts attention to questions of political, economic and social order at the macro-level.

A question of emphasis: rent-seeking, credible commitments, public entrepreneurs, and polycentric governance

For NIE scholars, the persistence of significant variation in the economic performance of different political economic systems poses a profound puzzle (North 1990a; Alston *et al.* 2018). One essential piece of that puzzle's solution is that path dependence is a common property of historical processes (North 1990a). Past choices limit later opportunities for choice, by opening up new opportunities while discouraging or even closing off other potential directions of change. Furthermore, not all interests are created equal. Actors who have benefited the most from existing institutions have at their disposal more resources relevant to helping them prevail in future contestations over policy change, and their determined opposition may scuttle any reform meant to empower other actors. In effect, power imparts a persistent bias in the distribution of transaction costs, and power holders will act to perpetuate (and to widen) existing inequities.

NIE scholars tend to see politics as a form of exchange, typically between economic principals and political agents. Political executives, legislators or bureaucratic officials can significantly alter the overall performance of the economy, since they are empowered to write laws and enforce regulations that determine the rules under which markets operate. More abstractly, the "state" acts as agent of society, tasked with the purpose of providing national security and other public goods, notably the protection of property rights and other legal guarantees needed to support the efficiency of markets. But, as noted above, agents often have incentives to act contrary to the interests of their principals.

NIE researchers are particularly concerned about rent-seeking. Inherent in the logic of public authority is the ability to use laws and regulations to create artificial scarcities from which holders of those scarce resources can extract rents, that is, benefits beyond what might be expected from free market exchange. Private actors face strong incentives to influence public officials to implement laws and regulations that serve their own special interests, at the expense of the public as a whole. Given obvious rewards to play favorites by distributing benefits to supporters, it cannot be assumed that political leaders will design (or even respect) institutional arrangements that help generate a well-performing economy.

In sum, NIE shares with public choice a vision of the state as a provider of rents to its supporters, and only incidentally as a provider of public goods (e.g., protecting property rights). This dilemma has been highlighted in a compellingly succinct way by Weingast (1995: 1): "A government strong enough to protect property rights and enforce contracts is also strong enough to confiscate the wealth of its citizens. Thriving markets require not only the appropriate system of property rights and a law of contracts, but a secure political foundation that limits the ability of the state to confiscate wealth".

The problem here is one of credible commitment: how can state officials commit to not taking advantage of their coercive capacity? State officials will need to reward their supporters in some way, and all institutional arrangements can have uneven distributional consequences (Knight 1992). Without credible limits on state extraction, rent-seeking may become so pervasive as to destroy the economy, as competing interests strive to make deals with state officials to protect their own interests at the expense of competitors and of society at large.

To consider possible resolutions of this dilemma, NIE scholars draw upon the tools of game theory to understand how institutions define the games that political and economic actors play, as well as how new institutions might emerge or be established through repetition of those games. For example, a game played repeatedly may generate stable and mutually beneficial patterns of outcomes, if players can realize long-term benefits from maintaining a reputation for fair-dealing. In short, existing institutional arrangements structure games, and new institutions can emerge from those games.

NIE scholars focus their attention on the emergence of new institutions that can be characterized as self-enforcing equilibria of recurring games (Eggertsson 1990). They are self-enforcing in the sense of being a Nash equilibrium: each party considers it in their own self-interest to behave as required for that outcome to recur, as long as everyone else continues to see advantages in not deviating from the current arrangement. When players have the option of considering new institutional solutions, NIE scholars limit their attention to proposed solutions that would be self-enforcing in this sense.

However, game players may explore other options that are difficult to specify within the formal constraints of any specific game. Players may work together to change the rules of the game before it comes up again, or establish a new collective actor or public authority with the responsibility of insuring more desirable outcomes. In addition to building new organizations, policy actors may influence the normative expectations shared by some or all participants, or they may work together to define entirely new games. Scholars in the Bloomington school tradition insist that policy actors always have access to at least some creative options.

NIE scholars also strive to move beyond the limitations of traditional game models. After demonstrating that in some models equilibria can emerge in which the state commits to protect property rights in ways that are credible enough to incentivize property holders to invest in the economy and control their inclination to seek excessive rents, some NIE researchers then turn to the historical record to understand how those kinds of equilibrium solutions were arrived at in particular cases, to better understand why some economic systems prosper while others remain mired in a morass of rampant rent-seeking.

In the method of analytic narratives (Bates *et al.* 1998), a game model and its associated equilibria solutions help frame the researchers' analysis and presentation of historical evidence. Used in this way, simple game models can inform convincing reconstructions of critical junctures in the evolution of political economic regimes, such as the rise of merchant capitalism in medieval Europe (Milgrom *et al.* 1990; Greif 1998, 2006). This mode of analysis can be used to support alternative explanations of particular events. For example, North and Weingast (1989) conclude that formal changes in institutions were the primary reason behind the Glorious Revolution in seventeenth-century England, whereas Pincus and Robinson (2014) stress the importance of informal changes in political leadership.[2]

The long trajectory of North's research agenda evolved from an early focus on how equilibrium institutions are shaped by changing technology and new economic opportunities, to later focus more explicitly on the historical development of political institutions that directly address commitment problems (Ménard & Shirley 2014). North's interpretation of the effect of the Industrial Revolution in England has been challenged by Mokyr (2014), who counters that cultural entrepreneurs who had earlier changed society's image of science and technology built the foundation for that transformative event. Similarly, Acemoglu and Robinson (2012) argue informal adjustments in de facto power relationships had a more significant impact on major regime changes in formal political institutions.

The NIE–public choice view of the state as acting in cahoots with rent-seekers is sharply at odds with the view of politics within the Bloomington school. Both Vincent and Elinor Ostrom expressed deep appreciation for the ability of groups of fallible but capable individuals to govern themselves, by coming together to form diverse kinds of groups, associations, and formal organizations to engage in respectful contestation as a means towards resolving common problems and realizing shared aspirations. Although Bloomington school researchers acknowledge potential abuses of public authority (V. Ostrom 1991a, 1997), they also recognize that authorities play legitimate roles beyond just the resolution of credible commitment problems (E. Ostrom 1996, 2006).

At this point it is useful to clarify the distinction between NIE as a subfield of "institutional economics" and Bloomington school research as a mode of "institutional analysis". NIE naturally focuses on economic measures of performance: efficiency, growth, and development. In contrast, institutional analysts pursue more encompassing and less precise goals of identifying, analyzing, and understanding the social foundations of self-governance. To understand the long-term sustainability of macro-level patterns of social order, analytical efforts need to extend well beyond the ways credible commitments can support the security of property rights.

---

2. Many other examples of this mode of analysis are discussed in Furubotn and Richter (2005), North *et al.* (2009), and Alston *et al.* (2018).

From the very beginning of their academic careers, both Vincent Ostrom (1953c) and Elinor Ostrom (1965) emphasized that political change and improvements in policy outcomes are driven by the efforts of public entrepreneurs (who may be public officials, community leaders, or individual citizens) to identify collective problems or shared aspirations, and to explore available options or invent new ones when necessary. Collective entities constructed and operated by public entrepreneurs interact with each other in complex configurations of competition, collaboration, or integration. Let this process run long enough, and a very complex array of interconnected centers of authority will emerge and will continue to evolve as circumstances change (Aligica 2014). Furthermore, contributions from a wide range of public entrepreneurs are critical to the long-term sustainability of the civic foundations of liberal democracy (Aligica 2019; Aligica, Boettke & Tarko 2019).

Ostrom, Tiebout, and Warren (1961) introduced the term "polycentric political system" to describe patterns of metropolitan governance as a complex tapestry of cooperative and competitive interactions among public authorities with overlapping areas of jurisdiction. Urban reformers saw this as wasteful and advocated regional consolidation, but these authors stressed the practical benefits of maintaining units for the production of public goods at multiple scales of aggregation, because different public goods are most efficiently produced at different scales. Empirical researchers later documented that there are indeed benefits to maintaining multiple levels of jurisdictions in metropolitan settings (E. Ostrom 1972, 2010a; McGinnis 1999b; Oakerson 1999; Oakerson & Parks 2011; Boettke *et al.* 2013).

In *Governing the Commons* Elinor Ostrom (1990) identified eight "design principles" that were satisfied, in one way or another, by all the cases she examined in which local communities had managed to sustain their shared access to critical resources. Beyond requiring that the user group has a minimal level of de facto autonomy to make and enforce rules for their own interactions, there is nothing in that list of conditions that refers to the guaranteed security of property rights or requires reductions in transaction costs. To the contrary, the key finding of Ostrom's research is that resource users should be directly involved in as many aspects of the whole process as possible: resource extraction, infrastructure construction and maintenance, rule-making, norm-setting, monitoring, sanctioning, and dispute resolution. For Ostrom the high transaction costs of political contestation in all these activities are investments in building that community's capacity for effective stewardship of the resources they need to remain self-governing.

NIE and the Bloomington school manifest contrasting responses to the duality of political institutions:

> Political institutions serve two very different purposes. On the one hand, they help mitigate collective-action problems, particularly the commitment and enforcement problems so debilitating to political exchange, and thus allow the various actors in politics to cooperate in the realization of gains from trade. On the other hand, political institutions are also weapons of coercion and redistribution. They are the structural means by which political winners pursue their own interests, often at the great expense of political losers.   (Moe 1990: 213)

Moe argues that NIE scholars, for the most part, treat politics as if it were merely "an extension of economics" by highlighting exchanges between the state and its rent-seeking supporters, but concludes instead that "Politics is fundamentally about the exercise of public authority and the struggle to gain control over it" (1990: 217, 221). Public authorities can force others to behave in certain ways, and this power can be abused, either directly or in thrall to private interests. Even self-governance will at times require means to enforce collective decisions on reluctant community members, but the foundational principle of liberal democratic governance is that communities must develop effective ways to limit abuses of political authority (Aligica *et al.* 2019).

A theme common to Williamson's micro-level investigations of alternative organizational forms and North's macro-level examination of property rights and economic growth is their identification of a single evaluative criterion: the efficiency of alternative organizational forms or the overall performance of the economy (Eggertsson 1990). In contrast, the design principles discovered by Ostrom (1990) demonstrate that more than economic efficiency is needed for the successful management of at least some public economies, especially over the long term.

In lieu of positing equilibria determined by optimization on any single criterion, Bloomington school scholars expect a high-performing system of polycentric governance will support endless innovations in technology, politics, economics, culture, and society as a whole. In her contribution to a 2010 conference on the legacy of Douglass North, Elinor Ostrom embraces this lack of optimality:

> Polycentric systems are themselves complex, adaptive systems without one central authority dominating all of the others. Thus, there is no guarantee that such systems will find the optimal combination of rules. One should expect all governance systems to [be] operating at less than optimal levels given the immense difficulty of fine-tuning complex, multitiered systems. Empirical research, however, has documented that polycentric systems frequently outperform either fully centralized

or decentralized systems when citizens are expected to contribute significant efforts to use resource systems sustainably ... Such systems
look terribly messy and hard to understand. The scholars' love of tidi-
ness needs to be resisted.   (E. Ostrom 2014a: 104)

In a very different vein, North, Wallis, and Weingast (2009) develop a broad-
ranging analytical mega-narrative centered around two distinctive types of
political-economic systems. In the "natural state" governments reward their
supporters with access to valuable rents while routinely infringing on the rights
of other sectors of society. Conversely, in societies that have made a successful
transition to an "open access" regime, states protect the rights of all groups and
enhance their opportunities for advancement. The authors use examples from
several geographical regions and historical eras to demonstrate that open access
orders can achieve and maintain a long-term equilibrium with values of economic wealth and human rights significantly higher than in states that remain
in the natural state.

This contrast between social orders based on open versus limited access is
reminiscent of Vincent Ostrom's normative justification of polycentric governance (V. Ostrom 1972, 1991, 1997, 1999a), which he contrasts to a repressive
monocentric system in which all political power is ultimately concentrated in a
single authority, along the lines of Hobbes' *Leviathan* ([1651] 1965). Vincent's
conceptualization of polycentricity is typically seen as closely related to the
self-organized emergent order emphasized by Polanyi (1951), but a more apt
analogy may be to Schumpeter (1934, 1942), especially with respect to the latter's emphasis on creative destruction. For Schumpeter, a capitalist economy
is intrinsically dynamic, and can never be at rest. Innovators disrupt existing
monopolies or dominant sectors, and if an innovator's successors achieve a similar monopoly-like position, they will themselves be disrupted during the next
round of innovation.

Schumpeter's interpretation of a pervasively dynamic economic system deviates from the Northian ideal of a stable equilibrium that strongly protects the
security of property rights as currently defined. In a Schumpeterian system,
no dominant market position or valuable form of property can ever be truly
secure from the danger of disruption from the emergence of new technologies
that dramatically undermine the value of current forms of property. In a fully
polycentric system (V. Ostrom 1972, 1999a), any local or domain-specific concentration of power is similarly at risk, as long as rivals or innovators working in
other policy domains retain sufficient autonomy to disrupt dominant powers.
Schumpeter's logic of creative destruction is relentless, as is Vincent Ostrom's
vision of polycentricity, in that new forms of collective action will continue to
emerge to address new problems and to undermine past solutions that are no

longer effective (Aligica & Tarko 2012; Aligica 2014; McGinnis 2005, 2019). Polycentric governance is, by definition, open-ended.

This vision suggests that we should reconsider the primary goal of policy intervention in political economies. Given the critical contribution of innovation to economic growth and prosperity in modern economies, governmental efforts to facilitate innovations has become a key element of economic development policies. A recent overview of Schumpeter's influence on contemporary understanding of innovation systems concludes "innovation policy should be about facilitating the self-organization of innovation systems across the entire economy, not only in 'new' sectors" (Metcalfe 2007: 943). Similarly, the logic of polycentricity implies that the primary goal of government policy should be to strengthen the capacity of disadvantaged groups to self-organize as they strive to improve conditions governing their own existence. This goal would help societies follow Elinor Ostrom's advice to use policy to build institutional arrangements that "bring out the best in humans" (E. Ostrom 2010a: 664–5; see above).

Opportunities for closer integration: transaction costs, process narratives, and social foundations of order

Despite the decidedly different developmental paths they have followed since their common origins in the public choice movement, new institutional economics and the Bloomington school share a deep commitment to understanding the institutional foundations behind political and economic change. Scholars in these traditions continue to produce research of considerable interest to each other. Looking forward, these complementary perspectives may prove even more effective when wielded in combination.

NIE's focus on principal–agent problems emphasizes managerial problems faced by top-down control, while Bloomington school scholars emphasize bottom-up processes of joint participation in crafting, monitoring, enforcing, evaluating, and revising rules and the shared norms which support the legitimacy of those rules. The Bloomington school's aspirations of breaking up organizations into a complex network of mutually reinforcing institutional arrangements may make organizational analysis more unwieldly than necessary, while NIE's focus on formal organizations may bias analyses of social order in favor of overly simplistic managerial models of organizational behavior, at the risk of downplaying the critical importance of identifying (and building upon) the normative values and aspirations shared by the people playing leading roles within society as a whole, or within any single organization. Strategic utilization of their complementary strengths may help offset constraints inherent in either tradition when considered on its own.

This chapter concludes with a brief discussion of three promising directions for further collaborations: (1) explicit incorporation of transaction costs into analyses of the behavior of public organizations; (2) rigorous analytic narratives of path-dependent sequences of endogenous institutional change in polycentric systems; and (3) increased attention to the social and cultural foundations of social order.

Although the initial statement of polycentric governance (Ostrom, Tiebout & Warren 1961) was directed at public administrators and political scientists who study their behavior, this article did not attract much attention from contemporary policy-makers or mainstream policy scholars. Ironically, its core point about the need for complex networks of governing units is now understood as a commonplace occurrence and a central topic of research on public administration (McGinnis & Ostrom 2012). Looking forward, the need for polycentricity in governance may become even more broadly appreciated through the efforts of researchers using the institutional collective action (ICA) framework, in which the primary actors are public officials acting as agents for public, private, and community organizations operating at different scales (Feiock 2009, 2013; Feiock & Scholz 2009; Swann & Kim 2018).

Feiock (2009, 2013) uses a Williamson-type parametrization of the empirical sources of transaction costs to establish a taxonomy of different forms of collaborative arrangements among municipal authorities. As top officials in diverse agencies or other organizations contemplate moving beyond single instances of cooperative behavior to long-term contracts or formal consolidation with other agencies, they must learn to address new sources of risk and uncertainty. Feiock (2013: 408) argues that "collaboration risk in the underlying ICA dilemma reflects the risks of not being able to coordinate on a course of action (incoordination); not being able to agree to a division of costs despite agreeing on the action (division); or risk that once action is agreed upon, others may renege or free ride (defection)." By thinking through how these sources of risk interact in different configurations, different types of public agencies or collaborations emerge to match the nature of the problem being addressed. In this way the ICA framework provides conceptual clarity to the confusing variety of cross-sector collaborations found in metropolitan areas. It may also have important new policy implications – Swann and Kim (2018) use the ICA framework to draw practical lessons for public officials charged with the responsibility of managing fragmented governments. In sum, the ICA research program shows how a foundational aspect of NIE methods can be directly incorporated into a research project inspired by polycentric governance, a core concept from the Bloomington school.

In a second potential path toward cross-school collaboration, Bloomington school researchers who want to analyze the historical evolution of polycentric systems of governance might learn from NIE-style analytic narratives. As reviewed above, careful matching of game components to relevant aspects of the historical record can provide important insights into the often hidden logic of institutional development across time. In extensive form games, the sequence of choices is specified exogenously, and expected outcomes vary according to the order in which actors act and the timing of their receipt of information related to the choices of other players. Much the same might be accomplished by looking at how related action situations can be endogenously connected to craft historically informed narratives of the sequence of strategies, decisions, and outcomes in studies of the co-production of goods or public services, or the contributions of different kinds of public entrepreneurs to the resolution of policy dilemmas (McGinnis 2019).

Using path-dependence as a more explicit factor in models of policy settings could be especially useful for applications to recurring dilemmas. Consider, for example, the following comment from Elinor Ostrom (quoted in Tarko 2017: 32, 108): "Failure, in many cases, leads to adoption of another program – one often based, as was the first, on inadequate analysis of the strategic behavior of the different actors. Failure seems to breed failure" (E. Ostrom 1976: 7). I interpret Ostrom's comment here as a challenge to institutional analysts to develop carefully specified models of the circumstances under which cascades of policy failure may occur.

In *The Samaritan's Dilemma* (Gibson *et al.* 2005), Elinor Ostrom and her collaborators identified a recurring example of failure in the development assistance provided by the Swedish International Development Agency (SIDA) to poorer countries. The researchers combined concepts from the IAD framework and principal–agent models to formulate questions for interviews with SIDA officials in Sweden and in the recipient countries, and to organize their case studies of specific development projects. This research team concluded that members of recipient communities should be encouraged to be directly involved in all steps of the process from initial planning to proposal budgeting to construction (or co-production) and especially maintenance over the long term. They found that, ironically, local ownership of development projects had long been an avowed goal of top SIDA officials, but their own actions prevented them from achieving that goal. Routine patterns of employee rotation and advancement within SIDA itself gave project managers perverse incentives to spend the authorized money within the budgeted period, no matter what the conditions were on the ground, rather than to maintain attention to any particular project over the full range of time needed for its implementation. They concluded that the most influential actors in the whole process were contractors (mostly Swedish construction firms) hired to build and maintain these projects, rather than members of the recipient communities. A broader study of SIDA or other development agencies might benefit from careful attention to the hidden sources behind such sequential unfoldings of cascading policy failures.

Finally, new institutional economics might be enriched by a fuller appreciation of the influence of non-explicitly political or economic factors on the path-dependent co-evolution of political-economic-social-technological systems. Important steps along these lines have already been taken. In her summary of NIE's contributions to institutional analysis noted above, Elinor Ostrom (2007a: 243) remarked on NIE efforts "to expand the model of human behavior used to explain institutional behavior so as to be broadly consistent with important developments in cognitive science" (Denzau & North 1994; North 2005). In one of the works she cited, Denzau and North (1994: 4) highlight deep interconnections between institutions and the mental models that guide individual behavior: "mental models are the internal representations that individual cognitive systems create to interpret the environment; the institutions are the external (to the mind) mechanisms individuals create to structure and order the environment". Furthermore, mental models are deeply rooted in the cultural foundations of social order. As argued by Gehlbach and Malesky (2014), the failure of post-transition countries to fully benefit from the establishment of market economies after the fall of communism in Eastern Europe strongly suggests the need to dig deeper than mental constructs of self-interest or organizational structures.

Alexis de Tocqueville's *Democracy in America* deeply influenced how Vincent Ostrom came to understand social order as the ultimate foundation for the modes of institutional analysis required to build and sustain self-governing societies (V. Ostrom 1997). Recent works in the Bloomington school and beyond demonstrate the continuing relevance of Tocqueville's insights to the contemporary world (Craiutu & Geller 2009; Henderson 2015; Sabetti & Castiglione 2017; Schleifer 2018: 102–23). Although Tocqueville rarely used explicitly economic terms, I'm confident he would encourage us to recognize the high value of costly investments in encouraging widespread personal experience with self-governance in all kinds of communities. Future generations of institutional political economists would be well-advised to pay careful attention to understanding how self-governing citizens and public entrepreneurs can learn to make even more effective use of the essential institutions of markets, firms, property, and polycentric governance.

4

ELINOR OSTROM AS BEHAVIORAL ECONOMIST
Vlad Tarko

Vincent and Elinor Ostrom's work focused on how communities self-organize to solve collective problems. Together with their collaborators, they identified various institutional conditions that make self-governance possible and likely to lead to good outcomes (E. Ostrom 1990, 2005a, 2010a; V. Ostrom 1997; Aligica 2014; Cole & McGinnis 2015a,b; Tarko 2017). Their approach grew out of the public choice revolution, and, as such, is rooted in rational choice theory. However, they have never subscribed to a narrow view of rational choice, building instead on Herbert Simon's idea of "bounded rationality", i.e. the idea that people are broadly rational, but make decisions subject to imperfect information and time constraints (Grüne-Yanoff, Marchionni & Moscati 2014).

The vast majority of the behavioral economics literature focuses on individual cognitive failures, and the aggregate social issues that may emerge as a result (Ariely 2009; Kahneman 2011). Most of this literature is institutionally shallow, jumping to conclusions from individual cognitive biases to broad conclusions about social-economic consequences. Furthermore, a significant part of this literature has been affected by the replication crisis in psychology (Rizzo & Whitman 2019: ch. 6). For example, much of Kahneman's book, relying on priming effects, has turned out to be mistaken (Chivers 2019). Even effects once considered well-established, like the endowment effect, have recently come under serious doubt, and may reflect the choice of experimental procedures rather than the preferences of the participants (Plott & Zeiler 2005; Isoni *et al.* 2011, Loomes & Sugden 2011; Zeiler 2011).

In contrast with this, and similar to fellow Nobelists Vernon Smith (2007) and Richard Thaler (1991, 2008), Elinor Ostrom has emphasized not just our cognitive limits, but also the institutions that people create to overcome them. But, while Vernon Smith or Thaler still focus primarily on *private choices*, and the institutions within which such choices happen, for example, private financial or health choices, Elinor Ostrom has expanded the realm of inquiry by exploring how bounded rationality also enters the picture in collective action problems.

Part of what is at stake here is the recent reframing of paternalism. For instance, while Thaler has paid more attention to institutions than other behavioral economists, he has also been at the forefront of the "new paternalism", arguing that corporate and political decision-makers should engineer people's "choice architectures" in order to "nudge" them in better directions (Thaler & Sunstein 2008). As noted by Rizzo and Whitman (2019: 3):

> The conclusions of behavioral economics have been used to craft a new justification for paternalistic policies – that is, policies designed to influence, manipulate, or coerce individuals for their own good, as distinct from the good of others. Rational-choice models imply that, by and large, people act consistently with their own preferences and values. By challenging that claim, behavioral economics has opened the door to the possibility that some government interventions [with respect to private goods and outside the realm of regular market failures] might actually make us better off, even by our own lights.

Ostrom's work, by contrast, is very strongly anti-paternalistic, focused instead on people's abilities to self-govern. As she writes, "Leviathan is alive and well in our policy textbooks. The state is viewed as a substitute for the shortcomings of individual behavior and the presumed failures of community" (E. Ostrom 2000b: 5). This has serious consequences:

> [T]he image of citizens we provide in our textbooks affects the long-term viability of democratic regimes. Introductory textbooks that presume rational citizens will be passive consumers of political life – the masses – and focus primarily on the role of politicians and officials at a national level – the elite – do not inform future citizens of a democratic polity of the actions they need to know and can undertake. While many political scientists claim to eschew teaching the normative foundations of a democratic polity, they actually introduce a norm of cynicism and distrust without providing a vision of how citizens could do anything to challenge corruption, rent seeking, or poorly designed policies.
> (E. Ostrom 1998a: 3)

The fact that Elinor Ostrom is primarily interested in collective action, rather than private individual action, has also led her to a different perspective on the limits of rational choice models. For Ostrom, the simplistic rational choice collective action model, as developed in Mancur Olson's *Logic of Collective Action*, leads to wrong predictions about the conditions under which collective action happens (or doesn't happen), and, furthermore, biases the analysis in favor of paternalistic solutions for solving collective action problems, as illustrated in Hardin's analysis of the tragedy of the commons. The result of Ostrom's analysis is a richer concept of rational choice, which simultaneously (a) accepts that individuals will act opportunistically, possibly undermining collective action; and (b) acknowledges the capacities of groups to take advantage of richer behavioral features, like altruistic punishment, fairness, group loyalty, and intrinsic preferences, in order to enable self-governing collective action. This richer concept of human behavior also raises additional concerns about the problems of hierarchical paternalistic proposals, showing that tyranny and oppression can be even more robust than accounted for by the simple rational choice model, particularly when we consider group loyalty.

Table 4.1 illustrates different perspectives on the relationship between individual and collective action. Standard rational choice theory predicts that selfish and rational individuals will free ride in most cases of collective action, hence requiring top-down hierarchical solutions (for a good overview, see Miller 1992). Standard behavioral economics simply adds behavioral market failures to the regular market failures, and assumes the need for various paternalistic solutions to address these failures of individual rationality. The naïve holism of sociologists like Durkheim, of classical economists like Marx, and of old institutionalists like John Commons assumes that, while individuals are irrational, the collective is (more) rational. For example, workers' cooperatives are assumed to work without taking seriously the possibility of workers free riding. People are assumed to fall into very large classes with "class interests", again ignoring individual incentives (Olson 1965: ch. 4). The old institutionalist theory of "pressure groups" falls into the same category (Olson 1965: ch. 5).

Elinor Ostrom builds on Olson's critique of naïve holism, while at the same time observing the failed predictions of Olson's "logic". Free riding and opportunistic behaviors are indeed real and pose very serious challenges to collective action. Nonetheless, a "tragedy" does not necessarily happen if people are left to self-govern. Elinor Ostrom draws a distinction between the "drama" of the commons and the "tragedy" of the commons (National Research Council 2002).

Table 4.1 Varieties of behavioral model

| | | Collective action | |
		Drama of the commons	*Tragedy of the commons*
Individual action	*Rational*	Heuristics, self-governance (Gigerenzer, V. Smith, Ostrom)	Simple rational choice (Olson, Hardin, G. Miller)
	Irrational	Naïve holism (Durkheim, Marx, Commons)	Standard behavioral economics (Kahneman, Ariely)

This distinction draws from literary terminology. The tragedy is a type of play, commonly found in ancient Greece, in which the audience knows from the very beginning that there will be no happy ending. Tragedies are only a matter of seeing how the inevitable unfolds. By contrast, the drama is a modern type of literary work in which the audience is uncertain whether the end will be happy or not, and in which critical choices matter. Unlike tragedies, dramas are rooted in a concept of free will rather than in fatalism. In Ostrom's assessment, Olson's simple rational choice model leads to a fatalistic view of collective action, and she argues that a broader concept of rationality is needed for understanding the complex reality of collective action.

This being said, Ostrom's critique of existing rational choice theories are always aimed at improving the rational choice framework, rather than opting for some alternative. She agrees with Jon Elster that "all theories of social behavior implicitly assume individual rationality ... Any effort to try to understand others is an effort to learn about their goals and how they view the opportunities and limits of the settings in which they find themselves" (E. Ostrom 1991: 238). In her view, we need to "presume that individuals are rational and search for institutional structures to help explain behavior that appears to be irrational upon first inspection" (E. Ostrom 1991: 242). This progressive research program needs to identify and address "the limits of rational choice theories (1) as tools for normative analysis, (2) as tools for empirical explanation, and (3) the role of history, institutions, and cultural traditions" (E. Ostrom 1991: 238).

The limits of rational choice theory

We have three types of evidence about the limits of rational choice theory: (a) the empirical failures of mathematical microeconomics; (b) direct experimental evidence about people's biases; and (c) theoretical predictions from evolutionary psychology.

Mathematical microeconomics

Rational choice theory assumes that individuals have consistent preferences and beliefs, and that they choose whatever they expect to best satisfy those preferences. In the strictest versions of the model, preferences are also assumed to be stable or it is even assumed that everyone has the same fundamental preferences (Stigler & Becker 1977). In theory, rational choice allows for other-regarding preferences (i.e. generosity and altruism), but, in practice, people are usually assumed to be selfish. These additional assumptions about preferences (stability, uniqueness, selfishness) are made in order to restrict the arbitrariness of the model, and make the predictions more easily falsifiable.

Empirically, the most ambitious version of this project has not been very successful. Gary Becker, one of the key champions of this approach to rational choice, has himself noted that, "there is now a search for the most convenient [utility] function … consistent with behavior", but, so far, "[n]one of the functions [most commonly] suggested are consistent with behavior" (Becker 2007: 54–5).

One of the most potentially useful applications of rational choice is the theory of revealed preference (Chambers & Echenique 2016). The goal of revealed preference is to infer a person's utility function from observations of their past behavior, or from observations of other people's behavior (that are assumed to be representative more broadly). The key difficulty is the following: we always have only a finite number of observations, and, as a result, there are an infinite number of non-equivalent utility functions that fit (can rationalize) the observations, i.e. utility functions that lead to different predictions, but which are all compatible with the available observations. As such, we need some additional *theoretical* principles that would lead us to choose a family of utility functions that lead to a single, specific prediction, or, at least narrow the space of predictions. These are known as axioms of revealed preference and formalize the meaning of rationality. Unfortunately, all such principles proposed so far also conflict with the *observed* data.

As Jehle and Reny (2011: 97) put it in their textbook, "[u]nfortunately, consumption data usually contain violations of GARP [generalized axiom of revealed preference]. Thus, the search is now on for criteria to help decide when those violations of GARP are unimportant enough to ignore and for practical algorithms that will construct appropriate utility functions on data sets with minor violations of GARP". In other words, rather than searching for other principles that might fit the empirical data better than GARP, we are searching for criteria about when it is safe to ignore *the data* in favor of the existing abstract axioms.

There are three reactions to this empirical failure. First is to accept that people are irrational. The criteria mentioned by Jehle and Reny are criteria that would allow us to identify the circumstances under which people can be expected to act rationally, i.e. in accordance with GARP. The second approach is to continue to try to find some better models than our current utility functions and our existing axioms of revealed preference. This is Becker's preferred research direction, and it is also partially what drove Kahneman and Tversky to propose prospect theory as an updated and more accurate model of human behavior. Recent empirical studies have shown that prospect theory is indeed remarkably accurate (Heimer *et al.* 2020).

Finally, a third possibility is to embrace a more general concept of rationality, accepting both that people's preferences can change, and that limited memory and time to process information does not imply irrationality (Rizzo

& Whitman 2019; Shermer 2007). The Bloomington school understanding of people as boundedly rational fits in this latter category. Elinor Ostrom's position in particular was that (1) we should not abandon rational choice, because (a) this is the only way in which people's behaviors become intelligible, and (b) this is how we understand why failures of cooperation can and do occur as a result of self-interested rational behaviors; and (2) we should adopt a wide enough concept of rationality, such that people's cooperative behaviors in collective action dilemmas, which are also possible and do occur, are not seen as irrational.

Biases and heuristics

Psychologists and behavioral economists have found abundant empirical evidence of a large number of failures of our reasoning (Kahneman 2011; Pohl 2016). Some involve failures to calculate probabilities properly, for example, people often ignore prior probabilities, rather than applying Bayes' formula properly ("base rate neglect"), or mistake recent salient events for representative occurrences ("availability bias"). Some involve reasoning problems more broadly, such as motivated reasoning and confirmation bias – our minds acting as lawyers for the beliefs we'd like to be true, rather than as objective scientists (Mercier & Sperber 2011). Some involve problems with memory, especially that it turns out our memory works by inferring the past, rather than by simply getting memories out of "storage". Some involve apparent inconsistencies in preferences. For example, if you prefer A = {$100 now} to B = {$110 a year from now}, you "should" also prefer C = {$100 ten years from now} to D = {$110 eleven years from now}. Most people choose A over B, but D over C (which is known as "hyperbolic discounting"). Similarly, your preference of X relative to Y "shouldn't" be conditional on what you already own (the "endowment effect") – or at least that is not a factor included in regular utility theory, which clearly separates subjective preferences from objective endowments.

A key observation here is that all experiments showing the existence of some biases depend on a theoretical benchmark of "correct" rationality (Rizzo & Whitman 2019). For example, is the endowment effect irrational or is utility theory incomplete? Is hyperbolic discounting irrational, does it occur due to uncertainty (Sozou 1998), or is it a legitimate time preference? While Bayes' formula has a profound mathematical justification (Jaynes 2003), utility theory does not. This means that some biases, like base rate neglect, the availability bias or confirmation bias, are more clearly and uncontroversially biases than the others. Shermer (2007) argues that many of the empirical findings of behavioral economics are compatible with a broader concept of rationality, and Rizzo and Whitman (2019) note that adopting a broader concept of rationality also limits the interventionist policy implications of behavioral economics. Furthermore, policy-makers often target the more dubious preference-related biases, while they themselves suffer from serious biases related to reasoning (Thomas 2018).

Why do we have such biases? Gerd Gigerenzer notes that many (all?) of the biases of human cognition appear to be side-effects of our heuristics (Cosmides & Tooby 2006; Gigerenzer 2008; Gigerenzer, Todd & ABC Research Group 1999; Gigerenzer, Hertwig & Pachur 2011). Heuristics are rules-of-thumb that we use precisely because we don't have the time or the sufficient information to perform accurate, detailed calculations. Heuristics work well in most circumstances – which is why we have them – but it is always possible to find unusual circumstances when they will give mistaken results.

This is similar to how our visual perception is vulnerable to optical illusions. The cognitive apparatus behind our vision takes various shortcuts. Most of the time, these shortcuts enable much faster processing with no issues. But it is possible to create artificial circumstances that give rise of optical illusions. Similarly, our cognitive apparatus responsible for making probability estimates and other rational calculations, takes shortcuts – i.e. we use heuristics. The literature on behavioral economics can be seen as analogous to the study of optical illusions, but in a different cognitive realm. This raises a serious issue if we want to draw conclusions about the real world based on biases discovered under special circumstances in the lab. We should not, however, overstate the skepticism. Heuristics do imply occasional issues.

Evolutionary psychology

Evolutionary psychology builds on the heuristics perspective. The key stylized fact of evolutionary psychology is that "[o]ur modern skulls house a stone age mind" (Cosmides & Tooby 1997). This is a colorful way of saying that all our social and moral heuristics are adapted to our prehistoric life as hunter-gatherers, rather to modern life in extensive market economies and under large-scale political institutions (Ridley 1996). *Homo sapiens* appeared about 200,000 years ago, while the earliest settled agricultural communities are only about 10,000 years old, and it took many thousands of years for a sizable portion of humanity to switch to agriculture. This means that (a) for over 95 per cent of human existence, we were organized in very small roving communities (of about 50 people or less); and (b) at least some of our social and moral heuristics are likely to be poorly adapted to modern societies. For example, in small hunter-gatherer societies everyone knew everybody else, which drives our intuition to personalize political control and think in terms of "putting the good guy in charge", rather than in terms of institutions.

We can make sense of many of the findings of behavioral economics from an evolutionary psychology perspective (Haidt 2005; Shermer 2007). The focus is however different. Instead of comparing real-world behavior with an abstract standard of rationality, evolutionary psychology asks which of our intuitions are likely to backfire in the new context of the modern world. Additionally, this perspective focused on heuristics also has a positive contribution to make, telling us which of our social and moral intuitions can enable cooperation even in cases where the rational choice formal framework of microeconomics predicts cooperation is impossible (Bowles & Gintis 2011; Henrich *et al.* 2004). Interestingly, these two fields also partially share the same formal apparatus of game theory, which should enable greater integration (Gintis 2009). Elinor Ostrom's perspective on collective action took these foundations seriously, and even tried to connect her discoveries about the institutional "design principles" with such an evolutionary explanation (Wilson, Ostrom & Cox 2013).

Jonathan Haidt and his collaborators have developed the "moral foundations" theory, trying to identify the distinct components of our social heuristics, and map out the diversity of moral intuitions. Haidt further connects this theory to an explanation of politics, using the idea that different political ideologies appeal to different configurations of these moral intuitions (Haidt 2012). The six components identified by him, i.e. the underlining reasons why we call some things "good" or "bad", are:

1. *Empathy toward other people's suffering and a concern with welfare.* According to this intuition, what increases welfare is good, while suffering is bad. The evolutionary basis of this heuristic is that, in the small societies in which our moral intuitions evolved, most members were related to one another. The biological reason for this heuristic is obviously no longer with us in modern societies made up of a large number of unrelated strangers. In this case, the fact that this heuristic carries out, despite the disappearance of its original biological reason for evolving in the first place, is obviously beneficial.

2. *Fairness and equity.* According to this intuition, sharing is good, while inequality is bad. In the context of small hunter-gatherer societies, a concern for equality, fairness and sharing was crucial, given that many of their activities critical for survival, such as hunting, were collective and success was largely dependent on luck. Our strong egalitarian intuitions about the distribution of wealth backfire in the context of large-scale market economies in which the emergent distribution of income and wealth is a power law, and these intuitions struggle to make sense of how this modern economic reality might be emergent rather than simply corrupt.

3. *Respect for authority and status.* According to this intuition, respecting authorities and obeying status is good, while disrespecting them is bad. In

small-scale societies, in which people knew each other, authority and status were strongly connected to genuine qualities and demonstrated experience and skill. Moreover, respect for authority and status enabled learning, by identifying who to pay most attention to. Large-scale societies are made possible by institutions, often hierarchical, that create different formalized positions with different rights and obligations. The connection between genuine qualities and authority is significantly weakened, and our institutional hierarchies are less meritocratic than the informal relations in forager societies. As such, in the modern world, respect for authority often backfires, by providing extra support for undeserving and corrupt leaders and undeserving elites.

4. *Loyalty towards the group.* According to this intuition, being loyal is good, while being disloyal is bad. The flipside of this intuition is xenophobia: you should be more suspicious toward strangers than toward members of your own group. This heuristic evolved because the relations between foraging groups were much weaker than those within the groups, and violence often characterized these between-group relations. Moreover, because members of a group were related to each other, defending the group against others promotes ones own genes. In other words, the *same* biological phenomenon that favored collaboration inside the group also favored xenophobia. Obviously, this moral heuristic has often backfired with extraordinary costs to human life and welfare in the modern world of large-scale groups, enabling religious strife, racism, and nationalism. Once again, despite the fact that these groups are no longer made up of closely related people, the moral heuristic persists because the biology of our brains is still adapted to the life in the foragers groups. On the more positive side, loyalty makes it easier to monitor and enforce norms and rules, as breaking the norms and rules is perceived as an attack on the group and disloyalty toward what gives identity to the group. This leads to respect for traditions, which has mixed benefits.

5. *Aesthetics.* According to this intuition, beauty and awe are good, while ugly and disgusting things are bad. The original evolutionary mechanism at work here is protection against disease. For example, a rotting corpse or spoiled food is repulsive, keeping us away from an unseen health danger. This intuition has then been "hijacked" into the moral and social realm. For example, opposition to homosexuality is often framed in terms of repulsion and disgust. By contrast, awe-inspiring religious experiences and services are considered good.

6. *Freedom.* According to this intuition, being constrained is bad, while having the capacity to act unimpeded is good. This heuristic is the companion of fairness. Its function in the original forager social environment, was to prevent

anyone from gaining too much power in the group. While respect to authority has beneficial effects in terms of enabling learning, it can also create potential for abuse. Fairness and freedom act as a necessary counter-balance. Interestingly, in the modern context, fairness and freedom lead to usually diametrically opposed political intuitions.

Intrinsic preferences, norms, and nested social dilemmas

Elinor Ostrom (2000b: 8) noted that:

> At least some individuals in social dilemma situations follow norms of behavior – such as those of reciprocity, fairness, and trustworthiness – that lead them to take actions that are directly contrary to those predicted by contemporary rational choice theory. In other words, *the behavior of many individuals is based on intrinsic preferences* related to how they prefer to behave (and would like others to behave) in situations requiring collective action to achieve benefits or avoid harms. *Intrinsic preferences lead some individuals to be conditional cooperators* – willing to contribute to collective action as long as others also contribute. *Intrinsic preferences transform some dilemmas into assurance games* where there are two equilibria and not just one.
>
> (emphasis added)

This is not a new idea. But it is a neglected idea in the modern economic literature that overly narrowed the range of rational choice to focus exclusively on external material incentives.

> All long-enduring political philosophies have recognized human nature to be complex mixtures of the pursuit of *self-interest combined with the capacity of acquiring internal norms of behavior and following enforced rules when understood and perceived to be legitimate.* Our evolutionary heritage has hard-wired us to be boundedly self-seeking at the same time that we are capable of learning heuristics and norms, such as reciprocity, that help achieve successful collective action.
>
> (E. Ostrom 1998a: 2, emphasis added)

Other-regarding preferences

Consider a standard prisoner's dilemma game, for example, as shown in Table 4.2. In a one-shot game, the equilibrium is for both players to defect, as "defect" offers the highest payoff to either of them, regardless of what the other player chooses. Cooperation can be induced in such a game structure if the game is repeated, and the players credibly adopt some "trigger strategies", i.e. credibly commit to defect in future rounds if the other player defects in the present round. While the analysis of repeated games is indeed important, let us assume the worst-case scenario or a single round game, for the sake of illustrating the effects of other-regarding preferences. Moreover, we do have experimental evidence that people cooperate even in one-shot prisoner's dilemma.

Suppose that each player's *subjective utility* differs from the *objective payoffs* (the numbers in Table 4.2), and let us assume that a player's utility is partially dependent on the payoff received by the other player. Namely, each player has

Table 4.2 The prisoner's dilemma

		Player 2	
		Cooperate	*Defect*
Player 1	*Cooperate*	(7, 7)	(0, 10)
	Defect	(10, 0)	(5, 5)

Note: shaded area is the Nash equilibrium.

Table 4.3 Prisoner's dilemma with other-regarding preferences

		Player 2	
		Cooperate	*Defect*
Player 1	*Cooperate*	(7, 7)	$(10g_1, 10 - 10g_2)$
	Defect	$(10 - 10g_1, 10g_2)$	(5, 5)

Note: Nash equilibria depend on the size of generosities, g_1 and g_2.

Table 4.4 Assurance game

		Player 2	
		Cooperate	*Defect*
Player 1	*Cooperate*	(7, 7)	(4, 6)
	Defect	(6, 4)	(5, 5)

Note: shaded areas are the Nash equilibria.

a degree of generosity, between 0 and 1, $g \in (0, 1)$. If $g = 0$, the player is entirely selfish, i.e. the other player's payoff is irrelevant. If $g = 1$, the player is entirely altruistic, i.e. only the other player's payoff matters. In terms of utilities, Table 4.2 becomes Table 4.3 (see the appendix to this chapter for the algebra).

If g_1 and g_2 are large enough, the utility for defecting while the other player cooperates can become lower than the utility for mutual cooperation. This is because a generous player cares about the fact that the other player would receive zero. With the payoffs in Table 4.1, this happens if $g_1 = g_2 > 0.3$. In other words, it is not necessary for one person to assign *the same* value to the other person as they do to themselves, even a relatively small degree of generosity suffices. For example, suppose that $g_1 = g_2 = 4/10$. Table 4.3 becomes Table 4.4, which is an assurance game (a version of the stag hunt).

Importantly, the assurance game has two Nash equilibria, including one for mutual cooperation. Which of the two Nash equilibria will happen? It depends on the level of trust between the two players. With the payoffs from Table 4.4, the players will cooperate if they believe that the other player is more than 50 per cent likely to cooperate (see appendix for the proof).

What happened here is the following. Although the objective incentive structure is that of a one-shot prisoner's dilemma, which, supposedly makes cooperation impossible, the players might still choose to cooperate if (a) they have sufficiently strong other-regarding preferences (i.e. care about what the other is getting); and (b) they have sufficient trust in one another.

Fairness and equity preference

The same effect can be obtained without other-regarding preferences, but in the presence of a norm for fairness, i.e. if the players suffer some psychological harm if the distribution of payoffs is unequal. Assuming that players incur psychological harms if they observe unequal (objective) payoffs, Table 4.2 becomes Table 4.5 (see appendix for algebra). The two numbers f_1 and f_2, denote how much each player cares about fairness.

As before, the temptation to defect can be removed if the fairness norm is stronger than $f_1 = f_2 > 3/10$. For example, if $f_1 = f_2 = 4/10$, Table 4.5 becomes Table 4.6, which is another version of an assurance game.

Fairness norms can, thus, also lead to a mutual cooperation equilibrium, but they require a much greater degree of trust than other-regarding preferences. In our example, for the same objective payoff structure, and with comparable levels of generosity and fairness, relying on fairness requires a level of trust of over 90 per cent, while relying on generosity requires a level of trust of only over 50 per cent. The reason for this is that, while fairness leads one to care for those less fortunate (hence reducing the utility from defecting on a cooperator), it also

Table 4.5 Prisoner's dilemma with fairness norms

		Player 2	
		Cooperate	Defect
Player 1	Cooperate	(7, 7)	$(-10f_1, 10 - 10f_2)$
	Defect	$(10 - 10f_1, -10f_2)$	(5, 5)

Note: The Nash equilibria depend on the strength of the fairness norms, f_1 and f_2.

Table 4.6 Assurance game

		Player 2	
		Cooperate	Defect
Player 1	Cooperate	(7, 7)	(−4, 6)
	Defect	(6, −4)	(5, 5)

Note: shaded areas are the Nash equilibria.

leads to envy in the opposite situation (further reducing a cooperator's utility when being defected upon – hence the negative utility for that situation). By contrast, while generosity also reduces one's utility from defecting on a cooperator, it *increases* a cooperator's utility when being defected upon ("at least the other person got something"). For the same reasons, generosity makes one more vulnerable to being prayed upon by free riders, while fairness makes one more suspicious of free riders. In practice, both phenomena co-exist, and they co-exist within the broader logic of repeated games. As Elinor Ostrom (2000b: 9) put it, "[i]ntrinsic motivation needs to be backed up by institutions that enable those motivated to solve problems while protecting them from free riders and untrustworthy partners".

Nested social dilemmas: why external material incentives are not sufficient

What this analysis shows is that assuming some types of preferences, like other-regarding preferences or a preference for fairness, can lead to an increase in the predicted pro-social behaviors, *without exiting the rational choice framework*, although it does require a departure from the conventional uses of rational choice, and a departure from the typical restrictive assumptions. This matters for understanding both collective action and the results of lab experiments (E. Ostrom 1998a, 2000b). For example, a puzzling observation is that people

Table 4.7 Prisoner's dilemma with sanctions and rewards

		Player 2	
		Cooperate	*Defect*
Player 1	*Cooperate*	$(7 + R, 7 + R)$	$(0, 10 - S)$
	Defect	$(10 - S, 0)$	$(5, 5)$

Note: Nash equilibria depend on the size of reward R and sanction S.

cooperate to some extent even in anonymous one-shot prisoner's dilemmas. A common interpretation is that people are irrational – they either don't understand the game or have difficulty calculating the Nash equilibrium. But a different interpretation is that people maximize subjective utility, not the objective payoffs. They have a certain degree of generosity and fairness, and expect the other person to have them as well. As such, cooperation can be rational, i.e. the choice that maximizes expected utility.

Finally, cooperation can happen because communities create, monitor and enforce rules that change the objective payoffs structure. For example, rules may be established that reward cooperative behavior, while punishing defectors, as illustrated in Table 4.7. If R and S and are big enough, a prisoner's dilemma can, once again, morph into an assurance game (Tarko 2017: 93–9). As Ostrom (1998a: 8) put it, "individuals temporarily caught in a social-dilemma structure are likely to invest resources and innovate and change the structure itself in order to improve joint outcomes".

To summarize, a collective can escape a tragedy of the commons via several different mechanisms that complement and add on one another: (a) repeated interactions in which reputation is critical; (b) other-regarding preferences; (c) fairness; and (d) cooperating to change the structure of the game. As Elinor Ostrom (2000b: 5) put it, "it is necessary to adopt a broader theory of human behavior that posits multiple types of individuals – including rational egoists as well as conditional cooperators – and examine how the contexts of collective action affect the mix of individuals involved".

A common observation in the public choice literature is that option (d) is itself a collective action problem which may have the structure of a prisoner's dilemma, i.e. everyone wants to free ride on other people's efforts to monitor and enforce the rules (Buchanan 1994). Elinor Ostrom (2000b: 3–4) summarized these nested social dilemmas as follows:

> In the currently accepted theory of collective action, the temptation to free ride – to receive benefits without paying costs – prevents

individuals from voluntarily contributing to joint efforts in groups without selective benefits. And creating rules that induce contributions is itself a second-order social dilemma not likely to be solved by those mired in their inability to solve the first-order problem … Enforcing these rules would be a third-order social dilemma – costly to those who impose punishments on others and generating benefits of compliance that everyone, even free riders, would receive.

According to standard theory, "[t]he predicted outcome of any effort to solve a second-order dilemma is failure. Yet, participants in many field settings and experiments do exactly this" (E. Ostrom 1998a: 7–8). The explanation is that possibilities (b) and (c) enable the escape from these meta-prisoner's dilemmas and establishing norms and rules. Furthermore, so far, economics has considered only a rather limited concept of moral norms, namely other-regarding preferences and fairness, but, as described earlier, Haidt's moral foundations theory includes additional heuristics. These heuristics may further enable groups to escape tragedies of the commons. For example, Ostrom (1998a) notes that one of the many reasons "why communication facilitates cooperation" is that it helps "developing a group identity".

The role of intrinsic preferences and of beliefs about legitimacy of rules is essential. Without these, the nested social dilemmas could not be solved: "Without individuals viewing rules as appropriate mechanisms to enhance reciprocal relationships, no police force and court system on earth can monitor and enforce all the needed rules on its own. Nor would most of us want to live in a society in which police were really the thin blue line enforcing all rules" (E. Ostrom 1998a: 16).

Of critical importance for understanding collective action is understanding how those four mechanisms (and perhaps others as well) interact. Ostrom (2000b: 10) points out that "[i]nformation rules are as important (or more so) in solving collective-action problems than are changing payoff rules, but payoff rules have been the primary focus of considerable public policy". Why are information rules, i.e. institutions for making truth public, so important? This is because repeated games when participants can select their partners are a formidable way of creating cooperation. But, for this to work, "achieving some reliable information about trustworthiness of others is crucial" (E. Ostrom 2000b). The combination of intrinsic preferences (such as generosity and fairness) with repeated dealings is perhaps the most effective mechanism for enabling collective action.

The focus on adjusting the objective payoffs, i.e. on setting up external punishments and rewards, not only neglects this powerful mechanism, but it can interfere with it, leading to what Ostrom calls "crowding out citizenship".

Changing the payoffs *can* help: "External interventions crowd in intrinsic motivation if the individuals concerned perceive it as supportive." But the opposite happens all too often: "External interventions crowd out intrinsic motivation if the individuals affected perceive them to be controlling" (E. Ostrom 2000b: 9). A well-known example of this is that of an Israeli daycare center that introduced a small fine for parents being late for picking up their children:

> the fine didn't work well, and in fact it had long-term negative effects. Why? Before the fine was introduced, ... if parents were late – as they occasionally were – they felt guilty about it – and their guilt compelled them to be more prompt in picking up their kids in the future. ... But once the fine was imposed, the day care center had inadvertently replaced the social norms with market norms. ... Once the fine was removed, the behavior of the parents didn't change. They continued to pick up their kids late. In fact, when the fine was removed, there was a slight increase in the number of tardy pickups (after all, both the social norms and the fine had been removed). (Ariely 2009: 76–7)

In this case, the other-regarding intrinsic preferences of the parents were undermined by the change in external payoffs. This may have happened because the fine was too small, and it, hence, signaled to the parents that the cost they were imposing on the daycare center (by being late) was actually smaller than they had originally thought. A crowding-out phenomenon can also occur when rewards rather than punishments are used, if the rewards are perceived as a signal that something fishy may be going on and that some important negative information is not being disclosed. For example, Ostrom (2000b) points to a study in Switzerland in which support for having a nuclear facility in one's community dropped from 51 to 25 per cent when "substantial compensation" was offered. The bottom line of such examples is that "[w]hen intrinsic motivations are crowded out, substantially more resources are required to induce effort than when incentives support a sense of control and reliance on intrinsic as well as material incentives" (E. Ostrom 2000b: 11).

Between holistic theories and the "logic of collective inaction"

The foundation of the modern economic theory of collective action rests with Mancur Olson's *The Logic of Collective Action* (1965). As Elinor Ostrom often joked, a more accurate title would have been "the logic of collective *inaction*", as Olson's theory seemed to imply that large groups would find it nearly impossible to cooperate for common goals. She argued that:

We have not yet developed a *behavioral theory of collective action* based on models of the individual consistent with empirical evidence about how individuals make decisions in social-dilemma situations. A behavioral commitment to theory grounded in empirical inquiry is essential if we are to understand such basic questions as why face-to-face communication so consistently enhances cooperation in social dilemmas or how structural variables facilitate or impede effective collective action.   (E. Ostrom 1998a: 1, emphasis original)

Olson's theory is a theory of free riding and of the conditions under which free riding can be prevented. It uses a narrow concept of individual rationality, including the assumption of pure selfishness. As such, according to Olson, the members of a group manage to cooperate for a common goal only if they succeed in setting up a club good, i.e. they set up *selective benefits* that the members of the group can enjoy, in exchange to contributing to the group, while excluding the non-members from enjoying those benefits. When exclusion fails, collective action fails. However, Ostrom (2000b: 4) points out that "field research has ... challenged the now standard theory that without selective benefits no one in a large group will 'act to achieve their common or group interests'". Instead, "one is forced to conclude that Olson's initial negative result is not as general as he originally stated. Too many empirical cases exist where participants have voluntarily overcome the temptation to free ride on the provision of a collective good" (E. Ostrom 2000b: 5). "We now have enough scholarship from multiple disciplines to expand the range of rational choice models we use" (E. Ostrom 1998a: 2).

It is important to understand exactly what Ostrom's objection to Olson's theory is. She is not dismissing the focus on excludability. Indeed, creating boundaries between members and non-members is one of the "core design principles" that she highlights (E. Ostrom 1990, 2005a; Wilson, Ostrom & Cox 2013). The objection is that the focus on *selective benefits* is too narrow and can even backfire. The theory of selective benefits assumes that collective action fails unless it can be made profitable to narrowly selfish individuals. But, as discussed in the previous section, Ostrom thinks the success of collective action depends on stimulating and partially appealing to pro-social intrinsic preferences. In particular, the purely selfish theory of collective action has no solution to the problem of nested social dilemmas, in which to solve one social dilemma one needs to create and enforce rules, but creating and enforcing those rules is itself a social dilemma, which presumably would require the creation and enforcement of additional meta-rules, and so on ad infinitum. Intrinsic pro-social preferences allow us to break this infinite regress. And, as already discussed, the narrow focus on external material rewards (which would create the selective benefits) can undermine the intrinsic pro-social preferences, and, hence, undermine the success of collective action.

Elinor Ostrom's critique of Olson's theory should thus not be over-stated. Indeed, she is as far as one can get from the optimistic wishful-thinking fantasies of social harmony. As she pointed out, "[f]ield research has confirmed that free riding is a potential problem whenever individuals cannot be excluded from receiving the benefits of others' contributions to joint outcomes" (E. Ostrom 2000b: 4). Moreover, Olson's theory of selective benefits does provide an explanation for a wide range of observed social, economic, and political phenomena, from the operation of unions to rent-seeking, and Olson's account provides a powerful refutation of holistic theories of collective actions, such as Marxist class theory and the old institutionalist theory of pressure groups. The problem rests with thinking that selective benefits are the *only* mechanism for collective action.

Ostrom is even more critical of holistic theories than she is of Olson, noting that we cannot "simply retreat to the earlier view that groups will voluntarily organize when collective benefits can be achieved. Too many empirical cases exist where the problems of overcoming free riding have proved too substantial and collective action has failed to emerge or had faltered after initial success" (E. Ostrom 2000b: 5).

What is the alternative? She notes that one of the main intellectual competitors of standard rational choice theory is the claim that "behavior is primarily rule-governed *rather than* consequence-governed and that a logic of appropriateness is the way to theorize about human behavior" (E. Ostrom 1991: 238, emphasis in the original). However, this is also a problematic assumption. After all, how can we explain the origins, variation, and evolution of rules if we just take them for granted? This is still no better than the holistic theories.

Holistic theories follow a simple linear structure (E. Ostrom 1998a):

$$\begin{Bmatrix} \text{Structural} \\ \text{variables} \end{Bmatrix} \rightarrow \begin{Bmatrix} \text{Levels of} \\ \text{cooperation} \end{Bmatrix} \rightarrow \begin{Bmatrix} \text{Social} \\ \text{Benefits} \end{Bmatrix}$$

At best, this works as a purely descriptive account, which can be better or worse depending on which structural variables we are considering and what relationships between these variables we are postulating. But to understand the relationships between different macro-level structural variables, as well as the origins and changes to those relations, one needs to fall back on some rational choice and methodological individualist account. Elinor Ostrom's (1998) proposed "behavioral approach to the rational choice theory of collective action" follows a more complex pattern in which individual choice operates within the context of macro variables (such as the rules and norms):

Structural variables $\left.\right\}$ → $\left\{\begin{array}{c}\text{Reputation} \nwarrow \\ \downarrow \\ \text{Trust} \nearrow\end{array}\right.$ Reciprocity $\left.\right\}$ → $\left\{\begin{array}{c}\text{Levels of} \\ \text{cooperation}\end{array}\right.$ → Social Benefits $\left.\right\}$

Individual heterogeneity $\left.\right\}$

$\underbrace{\hphantom{Reputation Trust Reciprocity}}_{\substack{\text{rational choice} \\ \text{theory of norms}}}$ $\underbrace{\hphantom{Levels of cooperation}}_{\text{macro}}$

According to this account, "levels of trust, reciprocity, and reputations for being trustworthy are positively reinforcing", which "also means that a decrease in any one of these can lead to a downward spiral" (E. Ostrom 1998a: 13). The point here is that "[i]nstead of explaining levels of cooperation directly", as in the holistic approaches, "this approach leads one to link structural variables to an inner triangle of trust, reciprocity, and reputation as these, in turn, affect the levels of cooperation and net benefits" (E. Ostrom 1998a: 13).

Ostrom (1991: 239) argues that "[r]ather than conceptualizing rule-governed choice as more important than rational choice, a general approach would attempt to explain how both rules and anticipated consequences affect behavior and outcomes". We need a "synthesis" according to which "human action … is both rule-governed and rational" (E. Ostrom 1991: 242). In Ostrom's view, this synthesis involves two layers: first, rules determine the set of available choices, while rational choice determines which of these options is selected: "Choices made by rule-following individuals are from within the set of permitted actions" (E. Ostrom 1991: 239). It is rules that separate allowed from disallowed actions. Second, rationality extends to the choice of rules. What should or shouldn't be allowed? "To be rule-governed, the rational individual must know the rules of the games in which choices are made *and how to participate in the crafting of rules to constitute better games*" (E. Ostrom 1991: 242, emphasis added).

How are people going to rationally craft rules? A serious complication arises here due to the fact that the consequences of changes to rules cannot be easily predicted. "Given the nonlinearity and complexity of many action situations, it is challenging to predict the precise effect of a change in a particular rule" (E. Ostrom 2005a: 239), and, furthermore, "[g]iven the logic of combinatorics, it is not possible to conduct a complete analysis of the expected performance of all the potential rule changes that could be made in an effort to improve outcomes" (E. Ostrom 2005a: 243). This is the reason why Ostrom states that the correct theory of human action needs to assume that people are *both* rational *and* rule-governed. Rationality is not sufficient, because the consequences of rule changes can only be partially understood and predicted. Instead, her view is that "rational choice and institutional analysis are likely to be essential complements", and that "history, institutions, and cultural traditions will play a more significant role in the evolution of rational choice theories in the future than they have in the past" (E. Ostrom 1991: 242–3).

Elinor Ostrom believed that the reliance on the simplistic rational choice Olsonian model of collective action, rather than on a fuller model that accounts for people's capacity to collaborate to create and adjust rules, leads to a serious technocratic bias in policy-making, at the expense of self-governance and of the capacity of building institutions that crowd in intrinsic motivations. Olson's logic of collective *inaction* predicts that "only short-term selfish actions are expected from 'the common people'" (E. Ostrom 2000b), and assumes that the only solution to large-scale social dilemmas is to have top-down rules that set the proper material incentives in place. But this underestimates the complexity of most situations:

> The policy of assigning all authority to a central agency to design rules is based on a false conception that there are only a few rules that need to be considered and that only experts know these options and can design optimal policies. Our empirical research strongly challenges this presumption. There are thousands of individual rules that can be used to manage resources. No one, including a scientifically trained, professional staff, can do a complete analysis.   (E. Ostrom 2000b: 12)

This technocratic bias, stemming from underestimating the rationality of "the common people", paradoxically overstates the rationality of experts.

> The ... message contained in the policy literature is that citizens do not have the knowledge or skills needed to design appropriate institutions to overcome collective-action problems. Professional planners are, on the other hand, assumed to have the skills to analyze complex problems, design optimal policies, and implement these policies. Citizens are effectively told that they should be passive observers in the process of design and implementation of effective public policy. The role of citizenship is reduced to voting every few years between competing teams of political leaders. Citizens are then supposed to sit back and leave the driving of the political system to the experts hired by these political leaders.   (E. Ostrom 2000b: 12)

Needless to say, Ostrom did not think this was a correct view of citizenship, and instead decried the fact that "much of contemporary policy analysis and the policies adopted in many modern democracies crowd out citizenship", and undermine "the positive foundations of a free society by destroying the capacity of citizens to experiment with diverse ways of coping with multiple problems and to learn from this experimentation over time" (E. Ostrom 2000b: 13). This "[c]rowding out of citizenship is a waste of human and material resources and challenges the sustainability of democratic institutions over time" (E. Ostrom 2000b: 13). The alternative is to appreciate that self-governing arrangements are not helpless at solving the *drama* (rather than the tragedy) of the commons, and that rationality enables people to act pro-socially, thanks to intrinsic preferences for fairness and for increasing other people's (as well as one's own) welfare.

Conclusion

Elinor Ostrom's is in many ways a critique of the standard ways in which the rational choice framework is used in economics and political science, and builds on the work of behavioral economics, social psychology, and anthropology. However, unlike many other critics, she is not interested in dismissing the rational choice framework. In fact, she thinks rational choice is inescapable as a tool for understanding human behavior. But for rational choice to fully fulfil its role, we need to expand its range such that it becomes consistent with a "general theory of human behavior that views all humans as complex, fallible learners who seek to do as well as they can given the constraints that they face and who are able to learn heuristics, norms, rules, and how to craft rules to improve achieved outcomes" (E. Ostrom 1998a: 9).

Appendix: Utility functions with generosity

Utility functions with generosity

With generosity, the utility received by Player 1 in each case is:

$$\begin{cases} u_1(C_1, C_2) = (1 - g_1) \cdot 7 + g_1 \cdot 7 = 7 \\ u_1(C_1, D_2) = (1 - g_1) \cdot 0 + g_1 \cdot 10 = 10g_1 \\ u_1(D_1, C_2) = (1 - g_1) \cdot 10 + g_1 \cdot 0 = 10 - 10g_1 \\ u_1(D_1, D_2) = (1 - g_1) \cdot 5 + g_1 \cdot 5 = 5 \end{cases}$$

Similarly, the utility received by Player 2 is:

$$\begin{cases} u_2(C_1, C_2) = (1 - g_2) \cdot 7 + g_2 \cdot 7 = 7 \\ u_2(C_1, D_2) = (1 - g_2) \cdot 10 + g_2 \cdot 0 = 10 - 10g_2 \\ u_2(D_1, C_2) = (1 - g_2) \cdot 0 + g_2 \cdot 10 = 10g_2 \\ u_2(D_1, D_2) = (1 - g_2) \cdot 5 + g_2 \cdot 5 = 5 \end{cases}$$

The Aumann equilibrium in the assurance game from Table 4.4

The *expected* utility of Player 1, conditional on their subjective probability, p_2, that Player 2 will cooperate, is:

$$\begin{cases} E[u_1(C_1)|p_2] = 7p_2 + 4(1 - p_2) = 3p_2 + 4 \\ E[u_1(D_1)|p_2] = 6p_2 + 5(1 - p_2) = p_2 + 5 \end{cases}$$

Player 1 will cooperate if the expected utility of cooperation is greater than that of defection:

$$E[u_1(C_1)|p_2] > E[u_1(D_1)|p_2] \Longrightarrow p_2 > \frac{1}{2}$$

The same reasoning applies for Player 2. In other words, given the (subjective) payoffs in Table 4.2 and the levels of generosity, if the subjective expectation that the other player will cooperate is greater than 50 per cent (i.e. the players trust each other to cooperate more than half the times), these players will choose the mutual cooperation equilibrium.

Utility functions with fairness

Let us denote how much the players care about fairness as f_1 and f_2, and let us assume that Player 1's utility is:

$$
\begin{cases}
u_1(C_1, C_2) = 7 - f_1 \cdot |7 - 7| = 7 \\
u_1(C_1, D_2) = 0 - f_1 \cdot |0 - 10| = -10f_1 \\
u_1(D_1, C_2) = 10 - f_1 \cdot |10 - 0| = 10 - 10f_1 \\
u_1(D_1, D_2) = 5 - f_1 \cdot |5 - 5| = 5
\end{cases}
$$

while, similarly, the utility received by Player 2 is:

$$
\begin{cases}
u_2(C_1, C_2) = 7 - f_2 \cdot |7 - 7| = 7 \\
u_2(C_1, D_2) = 10 - f_2 \cdot |10 - 0| = 10 - 10f_2 \\
u_2(D_1, C_2) = 0 - f_2 \cdot |0 - 10| = -10f_2 \\
u_2(D_1, D_2) = 5 - f_2 \cdot |5 - 5| = 5
\end{cases}
$$

The Aumann equilibrium in the assurance game from Table 4.6

Repeating the same expected utility reasoning, we now obtain:

$$
\begin{cases}
E[u_1(C_1)|p_2] = 7p_2 - 4(1 - p_2) = 11p_2 - 4 \\
E[u_1(D_1)|p_2] = 6p_2 + 5(1 - p_2) = p_2 + 5
\end{cases}
$$

$$
E[u_1(C_1)|p_2] > E[u_1(D_1)|p_2] \Longrightarrow p_2 > \frac{9}{10}
$$

The same holds for Player 2. In other words, if the subjective expectation that the other player will cooperate is greater than 90 per cent, these players will choose the mutual cooperation equilibrium.

5

NEW ECONOMIC SOCIOLOGY AND THE OSTROMS: A COMBINED APPROACH

Alice Calder and Virgil Henry Storr

The Bloomington school and the new economic sociology both attempt to understand how and why people actually act and interact, rather than pursuing single explanatory factors to explain human behavior. Both posit that an individual's economic action is embedded in their social relations, their social context, their social norms, their community, but that people are *individuals* who think freely and deeply, reflecting on their choices, and are not guided entirely by formal and informal rules. Both schools also share an important intellectual foundation in the work of Alexis de Tocqueville. Bringing together thought from these schools will show what each can offer the other, strengthening their shared ideas and opening up areas of research where knowledge from both can be combined to explore new and old puzzles.

Economic sociology, as Emile Durkheim ([1909] 1978) described, is the application of the sociological perspective to the study of economic phenomena. Economic sociology, thus, approaches the study of economic phenomena with an appreciation that social factors, forces and structures can affect economic phenomena and that in turn economic phenomena can impact social factors, forces and structures. Max Weber (1949) has, similarly, explained that the field of economic sociology, or *Sozialokonomik* as he called it, is principally concerned with pure economic phenomena like prices, consumers and firms, economically relevant phenomena like religion which can shape the economic behavior of adherents, and economically conditioned phenomena like the family whose structure can be shaped by economic outcomes. Consider, for instance, Max Weber's ([1905] 1998) most famous work, *The Protestant Ethic and the Spirit of Capitalism*, where he explores how Protestantism offered an ethical foundation for the particular spirit of enterprise that animates modern capitalism in the West. More recently, Viviana Zelizer (1978) has explained how a shift in attitudes about life insurance, from something that was stigmatized to something that was celebrated, changed the prospects of that industry.

Most early political economists, such as Adam Smith and Karl Marx, could be quite accurately described as economic sociologists, although the term didn't come to be used until the late nineteenth century, with thinkers such as Emile Durkheim and Max Weber (Smelser & Swedberg 1994: 8). In the United States, however, the fields of economics and sociology remained quite separate until the 1950s, and even then, the combination was spoken of as "economy and society" rather than "economic sociology" (Swedberg 1991: 264). The "new economic sociology," however, began to emerge in the late twentieth century with the publication of Mark Granovetter's article "Economic Action and Social Structure: The Problem of Embeddedness" (1985), which is often seen as a key point in the development of the field, setting the trend for new economic sociology (Swedberg 1991: 268).

Starting from the foundational belief that all economic action is social action embedded within a particular structure, the new economic sociology attempts to understand the impacts of such social phenomena on the economic and vice versa (Swedberg 2004: 318). In so doing, it hopes to avoid the common pitfalls of both sociology and economics by advancing a middle way. Sociology sometimes adopts an over-socialized conception of economic actors who are entirely beholden to the norms and values of the social system they exist in (Granovetter 1985: 483). These over-socialized actors are, in a sense, social automatons whose actions are fully determined by the social factors. In neoclassical economics, however, the individual is seen as an atomized and so under-socialized decision-maker using utilitarian calculation to determine every choice (Granovetter 1985: 483). These under-socialized actors are socially isolated creatures. The new economic sociology hopes to avoid both an over- and an under-socialized view.

At its core, Granovetter and Swedberg (2001) explain, the new economic sociology advances three key propositions about the relationship between economy and society. First, economic action is social action. It is action in that it involves an effort to change something (however small) about the current state of the world. It is social in that it is oriented toward others. Second, economic action is socially embedded, i.e. economic action occurs within a context of ongoing social relations. Third, economic outcomes are socially constructed. This means that economic outcomes as well as the meanings we attach to economic outcomes are the products of human beings coordinating, cooperating, and competing with one another.

Economic sociology is not alone in its criticism of the oversimplified approach neoclassical economics takes to decision-making. The Bloomington school of political economy, established by the work of Elinor and Vincent Ostrom, shares many similarities with economic sociology.[1] Chief among them is a call for a more nuanced and real-world reflective approach to studying how people solve their problems. Rather than advancing "simple systems" to understand what is ultimately a "dichotomous world," scholars within the Bloomington school use "more complex frameworks, theories, and models to understand the diversity of puzzles and problems facing humans interacting in contemporary societies" (E. Ostrom [2010] 2016: 193). Rather than conceiving of humans as being self-interested, narrowly defined, the Bloomington school approach treats humans as having "complex motivational structures" which lead them to "establish diverse private-for-profit, governmental, and community institutional arrangements that operate at multiple scales to generate productive and innovative as well as destructive and perverse outcomes" (*ibid.*).

Herzberg (2015: 97) outlines several major themes that characterized the work of the Ostroms. As she (*ibid.*) explains, the Ostroms focused on "human capacity and self-governance; the need for empirically rich analysis of theoretical questions; the potential of polycentric and federalist structures; the core belief that institutions matter and the need to understand the institutions; and the development of a broad framework for Institutional Analysis and Design." Consider, for instance, Elinor Ostrom's (1990) work on common-pool resources (i.e. goods that are naturally rivalrous but non-excludable in consumption) which stresses the potential of local actors to develop effective governance structures which stand against the tendency of these types of resources to be overgrazed. Also, consider V. Ostrom's work on the potential of jurisdictional competition to promote more responsive government units. Together, their work has helped to illuminate various institutional and organizational forms and helped researchers better understand what is going on in public and private, collective and individual, voluntary and non-voluntary actions (Chamlee-Wright 2015: 156).

The new economic sociology and the Bloomington school make for easy bedfellows. Both are a reaction against over-simplified views of the world and how people act within it. The Bloomington school rejects the simple systems view that posits two optimal organizational forms (i.e. market or state), two types of goods (i.e. private or public), and a single model of the individual (E. Ostrom 2010a: 642). And, the new economic sociology rejects an over-socialized sociological perspective, or an under-socialized economic perspective (Granovetter 1985: 483). They share a few more specific similarities as well, which we will outline in this chapter. Firstly, they share Alexis de Tocqueville as a common intellectual ancestor. Secondly, they have a great deal in common, including an

---

1. The Bloomington school is so closely tied to the work of its founders the Ostroms that they and their school will be referred to almost interchangeably; Elinor and Vincent Ostrom spent their lifetimes creating this school of institutional analysis.

emphasis on embeddedness, an appreciation for polycentricism and bottom-up approaches, a focus on social capital and norms, and a mixed methods approach to empirical study. This chapter will attempt to make clear these similarities and demonstrate how the two schools may learn from one another and make the most of their shared forebears and intellectual themes. We believe there is much to be gained from bringing the two into conversation with one another.

Tocqueville as an important contributor to both fields

The distinction between economics and sociology is a fairly recent one. For much of intellectual history, ideas in both fell under the broad category of the social sciences, and the work of thinkers like Weber and Durkheim spanned economics, sociology, political science, and anthropology. As a consequence of this many now seemingly disparate fields share common ancestors, and tracing back these links can help us to find modern connections. Of particular relevance to both economic sociology and the Bloomington school is the work of Alexis de Tocqueville. Both Richard Swedberg (2009), one of modern economic sociology's most prominent thinkers, and Vincent Ostrom (1997), one of the founders of the Bloomington school, wrote books dedicated to Tocqueville's thought.[2] Swedberg (2008: 429) saw Tocqueville as an analyst of economic life who was keenly aware of its social importance, who understood the existence and importance of social factors at play in economic life. Ostrom (1997) frames his project on democracy as a response to Tocqueville's challenge. As Ostrom acknowledges, his "effort is to deepen the foundations implicit in Tocqueville's analysis so that we might recognize the theoretical merit of Tocqueville's achievements and begin to explore potentials for crafting democratic societies built on principles of self-governance" (V. Ostrom 1997: 30).

Tocqueville's work, especially his *Democracy in America* (1835) and *The Old Regime and the French Revolution* (1856), explores the connections between changing social conditions and various economic outcomes. Tocqueville's social science is similar to that of one of economic sociology's most popular ancestors, Max Weber, much more so than most of his contemporaries. He conducted a kind of cultural analysis of the societies he looked at, taking a similar approach to Weber's social economics (*Sozialökonomik*) (Swedberg 2009: 274).

---

2. See, for instance, Swedberg's *Tocqueville's Political Economy*, and Vincent Ostrom's *The Meaning of Democracy and the Vulnerability of Democracies: A Response to Tocqueville's Challenge*. This is not to suggest that all the key figures within economic sociology or the Bloomington school rely heavily or rely at all on Tocqueville. Instead, the point here is that Tocqueville anticipated a number of the concepts and arguments advanced by contemporary practitioners in these areas.

Although his work is often associated with political science, Tocqueville's descriptions and analysis of social and economic conditions in *Democracy in America* make it an important read in the field of economic sociology. In this work Tocqueville describes the economic culture of the United States in the early 1800s and attributes the young nation's success to three great causes: its geographic condition, its laws, and its *moeurs* (Swedberg 2003: 223). This concept of *moeurs*, or "mores", and their influence over economic phenomena, is of particular interest to economic sociology. Admittedly, mores are a slightly vague concept. Swedberg (2003: 223; 2009: 277) offers multiple ways of thinking about how Tocqueville viewed mores; first translating them roughly as "manners" or "customs" and later putting them into three categories, "values and emotions ('habits of the heart'), ways of the mood and public opinion ('habits of the mind'), and body routines and techniques ('habits of the body')". V. Ostrom used this same language in his work on democratic self-governance, that there were necessary "habits of heart and mind" for citizens to maintain for the system to endure and not fall to despotism (McGinnis & V. Ostrom [1999] 2012: 515).

Tocqueville was, thus, an early proponent of explaining economic phenomena by how they were related to and interacted with other phenomena (such as the social, cultural and political). However, unlike the new economic sociology, Tocqueville tried to explain the ways in which economic phenomena were merely *linked* to other phenomena, such as institutions and mores, rather than taking the approach of new economic sociology, that economic phenomena are *embedded* in social phenomena (Swedberg 2009: 277). Linking economic phenomena to institutions and mores, Tocqueville drew connections between things like industrial property and mores like habits of the body and mind, describing industrialization as brutalizing the bodies of the workers and weakening their intellectual capability (*ibid.*). Despite the difference between claiming economic phenomena are linked with, rather than embedded in, social phenomena, it is easy to see the similarities here to economic sociology, of taking a multi-faceted approach that avoids under- and over-socialized traps.

Another example of this approach is Tocqueville's discussion of rents and taxes in *The Old Regime and the French Revolution*. Only when the institutional arrangements of a society were such that the status of landlords was considered legitimate was tax collection seen as legitimate (Stinchcombe 1983: 160). If, as was often the case in pre-Revolutionary France, local policy was decided by a central government, and the landlord played no real role yet still demanded taxes for personal use, taxation came to be seen as extortion (*ibid.*: 161). Tocqueville described the growing resentment of the aristocracy that developed amongst the peasants as well as the rising tensions between the two classes that resulted from this shift.

One of the key elements Tocqueville related to a society's success was its governance, and he had a particular interest in democracy. As Boettke *et al.* (2013: 408) summarize, "what ultimately matters for the Tocquevillian project is the cultivation of citizens capable of democratic self-governance, and collective decision processes that respect the great diversity and desires of local communities." In *Democracy in America*, Tocqueville sought to answer the question of whether democracies are viable systems of order (V. Ostrom 1997: 5). In a similar vein, much of the work within the Bloomington school sought to answer similar questions about governance. As we shall explore later in this chapter, self-governance in particular is a focus of the Bloomington school, which defines democratic societies by their self-organizing and self-governing capabilities (*ibid.*: 84). Aligica (2019: 10), for instance, writes on how the Ostromian self-governance theorizing has deep roots in the Tocquevillian participatory democracy paradigm, where citizens' competencies are part of and shaped by the governance process, not outside of it.

Polycentrism, another foundation of the Bloomington school, also has its roots in the work of Tocqueville. In his discussions of democracy in America, Tocqueville makes several influential observations on associative life and the invisible mechanisms of social order (*ibid.*: 87). The Ostroms added to and updated Tocqueville's approach, that of linking institutions, politics and mores within the model of democracy, fleshing out the theory with studies on public entrepreneurship and citizenship.

Tocqueville has clearly had a great influence over both the Bloomington school and the new economic sociology, evidenced by the language and approaches each use. Given the importance of Tocqueville's work for each, it is therefore understandable that the two schools would share some key similarities, and tracing this influence back allows for an even more direct demonstration of this. In the next section, we discuss several of these similarities between the new economic sociology and the Bloomington school beyond their sharing at least one intellectual forebear.

Four commonalities in their approaches to social science

Both the new economic sociology and the Bloomington school (a) model humans as embedded within communities; (b) focus on social capital and social norms; (c) appreciate the possibility of polycentric governance systems and the potential of bottom-up solutions to collective challenges; and (d) embrace mixed methods in their empirical work.

Individuals are embedded in communities
(neither over- nor under-socialized)

In one of the most influential articles in sociology, Granovetter (1985) criticizes the common conception both sociologists and neoclassical economists have of economic actors. In Granovetter's view, the typical agent is either under-socialized and atomized (in economics), or over-socialized and atomized (in sociology) (*ibid.*: 485). The risk of the over-socialized view is that actors are seen as being overly obedient to the opinions of others and the norms of society, leaving no room for a conception of individual rationality (*ibid.*: 483). Conversely, relying too heavily on a theory of the rational economic actor can also lead to problems. As classical economists do, eliminating the social relations and structure from economic analysis assumes actors make purely utilitarian decisions with no regards for bargaining, negotiation, or social pressure (*ibid.*: 484). To avoid these twin concerns, Granovetter (*ibid.*: 487) proposes an alternative, one in which individual's economic action is situated within a social structure and "their attempts at purposive action are instead embedded in concrete, ongoing systems of social relations".

With the embeddedness approach, Granovetter (*ibid.*: 487) explains, "actors do not behave or decide as atoms outside a social context, nor do they adhere slavishly to a script written for them by the particular intersection of social categories that they happen to occupy". Recognizing that economic actors are embedded gives us insight into how mistrust and malfeasance are not rampant in markets. Social ties rather than generalized morality or institutional arrangements are "mainly responsible for the production of trust in economic life" (*ibid.*: 490). That there is a "widespread preference for transacting with individuals of known reputation," Granovetter (*ibid.*: 490) suggests, speaks to the potential of "concrete personal relations and structures (or 'networks') of such relations in generating trust and discouraging malfeasance". The diamond trade in New York City, which is dominated by ethnic trading networks who rely on familial ties and community enforcement as they sell goods and services, is a classic example of how personal relations and social networks can be effective checks on malfeasance (Richman 2017).

The concept of embeddedness was first popularized by Karl Polanyi who argued that "man's economy, as a rule, is enmeshed in his social relationships" (Polanyi 1957: 46). Polanyi argued that embeddedness was even more apparent in pre-modern societies, as with modernity came an increasing emphasis on the individual over the group. With Granovetter, however, the concept of embeddedness has become a foundational idea for the new economic sociology, and the core of many studies in the field since, as well as a target for criticism and revision. Uzzi's work, for instance, has employed the concept of embeddedness to study and explain the success (or lack thereof) for firms with differing social ties, such as garment manufacturers in New York. His studies present a nuanced view of social ties in such contexts, of how they can hinder as well as help (1996, 1997, 1999). Similarly, in her work Maurer (2012) praises the theory of embeddedness for its role in the revival of economic sociology but seeks to improve the concept by connecting it more strongly to institutional arguments. The concept of embeddedness has also been used to explore how social structures affect economic life within immigrant communities (Portes & Sensenbrenner 1993); the importance of embeddedness in buying situations that require trust (Buskens & Weesie 2000); the effectiveness of intergovernmental organizations at facilitating trade (Ingram *et al.* 2005); the emergence of the life insurance industry in China (Chan 2009); and, the dangers of (dis)embeddedness in the remote gig economy (Wood *et al.* 2019).

The lens of embeddedness highlights the importance of focusing on social contexts to understand individual behavior. Although they do not explicitly invoke the term embeddedness, members of the Bloomington school do emphasize how social structure frames economic action. This is certainly the case in studies by Elinor Ostrom and others of how communities overcome the challenges associated with common-pool resources. As Hardin (1968) explains, individuals who encounter a common-pool resource, like a field for grazing cattle that is in the public domain or a collectively owned lake that has fish, have an incentive to overuse it. Unlike with private resources, individuals do not have an incentive to conserve a common-pool resource for future use, since they can be almost certain that they will not benefit from conservation efforts. Elinor Ostrom's (1990) work documents how community members work together to find ways to govern common-pool resources that neither require privatizing the good nor rely on external authorities to regulate the use of the good.

In the Ostroms' work on common-pool resources, they sought to get away from the under-socialized view of humans and attempted to explain why in so many cases communities overcome problems that neoclassical economics says should cripple them (E. Ostrom 1990: 29). Starting from the common-sense viewpoint that people across the world find solutions to common-pool resource problems all the time, the Ostroms looked at what variables within a community, such as size, ability to monitor one another, and community bonds, effected their ability to manage resources. The theory of embeddedness complements this work as the collective action involved in common-pool resource problems is socially and culturally embedded.

Elinor Ostrom's discussion of the potential of polycentric systems to be more responsive to the demands of local populations than monocentric systems also speaks to her appreciation of embeddedness. Consider, for example, her research on whether or not Indianapolis residents were better off under consolidated or polycentric police departments (Ostrom *et al.* 1973a,b).[3] These studies found that residents under localized police departments were more satisfied with their police services than residents under the jurisdiction of larger more centralized police departments. Several other studies showed that smaller police departments were no less effective and had certain advantages over larger police departments (Ostrom *et al.* 1978; Parks 1985). Local police departments are able to benefit because they are embedded within their communities; "police and citizens engaging in coproduction of public safety could serve as a mechanism sufficient to overcome the collective action problem of maintaining public safety" (Boettke *et al.* 2013: 416). As Elinor Ostrom (2011b: 372) has summarized, "citizens are treated differently when you live in a central city served by a metropolitan police department. Many of the officers in very big departments do not see themselves as responsible to citizens."

The importance of local connections in increasing trust and performance as well as reducing malfeasance has been a recurrent theme in both the new economic sociology and the Bloomington school.

A focus on social capital and social norms

The second common theme of the new economic sociology and the Bloomington school is that of social capital. Social capital is an essential concept in both traditions and, as an important part of both frameworks, serves to bring the two intellectual traditions together. Social capital can be thought of as the resources that an individual can access through her social connections and the value and quality of those resources (Bourdieu 1986). Bourdieu believed that social capital could be a substitute for other forms of capital (financial, cultural, etc.).

Coleman (1988) stressed that social capital was a particular kind of resource. Rather than being something that an individual might value for its own sake, Coleman conceived of social capital as a productive asset, a tool. Social capital, for instance, can take the form of goods and services that you acquire and use by virtue of your ties, but it could also be less tangible. Norms (i.e. rules that govern the behavior of members of the social network) are another form of social capital. Social capital in the form of social norms, informal rules and regulations can constrain actors just as much as formal institutions, guiding the actions of individuals by way of implicit social pressure and rules that have developed over time in communities. Social norms help to explain the relationship between institutions and networks and provide a framework and structure for economic phenomena (Nee & Ingram 1998: 19). The rules governing economic actions

---

3. See Boettke *et al.* (2013) for an excellent overview of these studies.

may not be explicitly stated and often rely on approval and disapproval to monitor and enforce behavior.

Coleman highlighted several aspects of the nature of social capital that are worth reiterating. Social capital, Coleman (1988) explains, is not completely fungible. A given form of social capital might be useful for certain actions and useless or even harmful for others. Co-workers, for instance, might be very useful in offering advice on a good restaurant or hotel but probably will not help you to take care of an ailing spouse. Likewise, family members and close friends would likely be very useful in helping to take care of an ailing spouse, but family members might not be the best place to go for a restaurant recommendation. Coleman also stressed the importance of closure. A social network exhibits closure when a person's connections are independently connected with each other. If social capital in the form of norms are to be effective, and defections are to be punished, the relevant social networks must exhibit closure.

Several other definitions of social capital are worth reviewing. Putnam (1995: 67) describes social capital as the "features of social organization such as networks, norms and social trust that facilitate coordination and cooperation for mutual benefit." Putnam's essay, and later book *Bowling Alone* (2000), played a large part in popularizing the idea and the downfalls he perceived of a declining social capital. Communities in possession of large amounts of social capital have the ability to cooperate in a mutually beneficial way, across a wide range of activity, whereas the opposite is true of those with low levels (Fukuyama 1995; Putnam 1995). For Portes and Sensenbrenner (1993: 1323), social capital is defined as "those expectations for action within a collectivity that affect the economic goals and goal-seeking behavior of its members, even if these expectations are not oriented toward the economic sphere". It has been attributed to both individuals and communities. Originally, Portes (2000: 3) explains, social capital was a feature of communities that benefitted the individual but in later work, particularly when the concept was exported into other disciplines, the benefits of social capital were said to go to the community itself.

The ideas at the heart of the term social capital have been essential to economic sociology dating back to Durkheim and Marx, but social capital as a concept gained popularity in recent decades with the revitalization of the field, particularly with regards to its applications for policy-making (Portes 1998: 2). The new economic sociology built as it is on the importance of networks of personal relationships in structuring diverse economic exchange (Nee & Ingram 1998: 22) has ideas of social capital and social norms at its center. Social norms have many important functions that influence economics, such as inhibiting crime and improving education (Coleman 1988: §104). They can also have large effects on determining the types of economic phenomena that are allowed to occur.

Social capital has proven to be very useful when talking about collective action. This link between social capital and collective action is what unites this theory with that of the Bloomington school. Perhaps not surprisingly then, Elinor Ostrom (1994, 2000a) has devoted some attention to the concept of social capital and has utilized it quite profitably in her studies. She (2000a: 176) defines social capital as "the shared knowledge, understandings, norms, rules, and patterns of interactions that groups of individuals bring to a recurrent activity". For her, social capital is a resource that community members draw on and utilize as they work together to accomplish some joint activity. In discussing social capital, Elinor Ostrom (*ibid.*: 179) highlights several features of social capital that distinguish it from other forms of capital but make it nonetheless a critical concept for understanding collective action. Perhaps most importantly, she (*ibid.*) observes that "social capital differs from physical capital in that it does not wear out with use but rather with disuse". Deploying social capital can actually build mutual trust and shared understanding, increasing the stock of social capital available for future joint ventures. As Tocqueville has suggested, community members working together to solve small problems are better equipped to confront larger challenges.

Elinor Ostrom (1994: 559) suggests that individuals frequently "invest" in social capital in the process of bargaining over the rules that determine the allocation of costs and benefits in collective action. Social capital in this context is created over time just like other forms of capital, although it is far harder to detect and prone to destruction from external actors who do not understand the systems in place (E. Ostrom 1994: 528). This role that social norms play in governing behavior means the concept has a particular relevance for the common-pool resource problems studied by the Ostroms. In arguably her most famous work, *Governing the Commons* (1990), Elinor Ostrom looks at numerous case studies that show how polycentrism works in everyday life such as water provision. In *Governing the Commons*, Ostrom found that some efforts to solve commons problems succeeded and some did not. She outlines the factors that affected the institutional choices and arrangements available to communities and identifies eight design principles of stable local common-pool resource management.[4]

---

4. These eight design principles are (E. Ostrom 1990: 90): clearly defined boundaries; congruence between the resource environment and its governance structure or rules; decisions are made through collective-choice arrangements most affected individuals can participate; rules are enforced through effective monitoring by accountable monitors; violations are punished with graduated sanctions; conflicts and issues are addressed with low-cost and easy-to-access conflict resolution mechanisms; higher-level authorities recognize the right of the resource appropriators to self-govern; nested enterprises (for CPRs in larger systems).

In these situations, the successful institutions are ones that have been able to overcome issues of free riding and shirking (E. Ostrom 1990: 15). This is often achieved through informal means that are not legally binding but involve commitments by the members to act and use resources in a certain way, and to monitor one another (*ibid*.: 18). The question then arises, how are these rules enforced? The usual solution is external coercion (Schelling 1984) but in many common-pool resource situations this is not present. In Elinor Ostrom's study of numerous common-pool resource cases, she looks at the *de facto rules* used by the members of these communities, finding that it is these social rules and norms that often guide, constrain, and enforce behavior. As she (1990: 51) explains, "The difference between working rules and formal laws may involve no more than filling in the lacunae left in a general system of law. More radically, operational rules may assign de facto rights and duties that are contrary to the de jure rights and duties of a formal legal system."

In successful communities these rules are changing and evolving over many years with the society, in many cases conformance is remarkable given the relatively low level of severity of sanctions compared with the potential reward of defection, yet people still conform, showing the power that social norms can hold (*ibid*.: 59).

Both the new economic sociology and the Bloomington school have profitably used the concept of social capital in their studies.

An appreciation for the possibility of polycentric governance systems and the potential of bottom-up solutions to collective challenges

A key aspect of the Ostroms' work focused on how communities solved the challenges that they face within polycentric orders. More specifically, collective challenges are *more likely* to be solved within such orders rather than in monocentric ones. A polycentric system is composed of "(1) many autonomous units formally independent of one another, (2) choosing to act in ways that take account of others, (3) through processes of cooperation, competition, conflict and conflict resolution" (V. Ostrom 2014: 46). Polycentric orders can be political systems, but they can take many other forms such as market structures comprised of multiple firms, or networks of traders in competition with and cooperating with each other. The idea was first introduced by V. Ostrom, Tiebout and Warren (1961), who were attempting to answer whether the diverse variety of public and private agencies in charge of providing public services were as chaotic as many scholars thought.

Polycentricity became a key area of study for the Ostroms, who undertook fieldwork that showed how in many cases rather than being a chaotic force, polycentric orders were productive, i.e. that complexity was not the same as chaos (E. Ostrom 2010a: 644). Throughout her life Elinor Ostrom studied countless examples of polycentric systems, one of the most famous was that of the Central and West Basin Water Replenishment District of California (E. Ostrom 1990: 133). Rather than one central government authority, the replenishment district interacts with numerous other agencies in the management of water in the area, resulting in restored water levels and improved infrastructure for the area. Polycentric governance is quite common, and the ideas around the subject generated by the Ostroms are useful in analyzing many governance systems across the world. These ideas have inspired scholars across disciplines. Murtazashvili (2016: 156), for example, in her study of informal order in Afghanistan, found that the notion of polycentric governance was an appropriate lens through which to understand how villages interacted with one another and solved problems in rural Afghanistan.

This focus of the Bloomington school, on how communities *actually* govern themselves, complements that of the new economic sociology. Rather than a simple model of monocentric governance, or one that assumes just because a state has set up rules and institutions that these are what people follow, this approach studies how the complex institutional arrangements in communities interact and the type of governance this produces.

Perhaps the clearest evidence of the new economic sociology's appreciation for the polycentric nature of many social orders is their discussions and comparisons of various social networks. Burt's (2004) discussion of structural holes, for example, highlights the benefits of poycentrism within an organization. Examining the social structure within a large firm, Burt revealed that it was comprised of a series of tightly connected clusters (think business units) that were connected to each other by a few bridges. This picture of the firm did not neatly conform to the official organizational chart of vertical and horizontal ties within the organization. According to Burt (2004: 349) people in the firm standing next to structural holes, or rather who are connected to multiple clusters, are more likely to have good ideas than people without inter-cluster ties. Granovetter's (1973) work on the strength of weak ties and their importance in facilitating information transfusion is, similarly, a discussion of the benefits and weaknesses of polycentric networks. Also, Granovetter (1992: 8) used the example of immigrant communities to illustrate how various organizations comprised of close-knit groups that vary in size, structure, and legal structures work to coordinate investment and production across numerous industries and firms. And, Biggart and Guillen (1999) show how differences in the structure of social organization in automobile industries in South Korea, Spain and Taiwan, drastically effect development outcomes.

Both the Bloomington school and the new economic sociology recognize the polycentric nature of private and public governance systems.

Embrace of mixed methods

Both the Bloomington school and economic sociology embrace a mixed methods approach that is reflective of their interdisciplinary roots. The Bloomington school is characterized by rigorous qualitative and quantitative empirical work involving fieldwork and experimental studies combined with a theoretical approach that embraces economics, political science, organizational theory, and public administration. In fact, Elinor Ostrom wrote a volume, *Working Together: Collective Action, the Commons, and Multiple Methods in Practice* (2010; with Poteete & Janssen) that can be read as a methodological defense of the Bloomington school's mixed methods approach which involved game theory, lab experiments and extensive fieldwork for understanding collective action.[5] As Elinor Ostrom (2010a: 641) describes:

> I studied the efforts of a large group of private and public water producers facing the problem of an over drafted groundwater basin on the coast and watching saltwater intrusion threaten the possibility of long term use. Then, in the 1970s, I participated with colleagues in the study of polycentric police industries serving US metropolitan areas to find that the dominant theory underlying massive reform proposals was incorrect.

In many ways, their work was highly theoretical, and they developed intricate frameworks to analyze self-organizing and self-governing common-pool resources. Elinor Ostrom (1990: 183), however, recognized that merely saying the world is more complex than some models present it is obvious and not very useful, so she also sought to develop theory that would help identify variables essential in explaining and predicting when communities are more likely to self-organize to solve common-pool resource problems, and when this would be successful.

Similarly, the new economic sociology has always embraced mixed methods. Granovetter's (1973) work on how individuals search for and attained a job relied on fieldwork conducted in Newton, Massachusetts. Knorr and Bruegger (2002) make use of embeddedness theory in their ethnographic study of the social system in the realm of global investment bank trading. Locke (1995) explores how variation in socio-political networks and industrial relations have a far larger impact on economic success in a country than national institutions using the example of the success of the Italian economy, which lacked the

---

5. See Boettke *et al.* (2013) for a useful discussion of the contributions that E. Ostrom made through her fieldwork. And see Ahn and Wilson (2010) for a useful discussion of E. Ostrom's contributions through her experimental studies.

national features of many other successful economies. Uzzi's work on the garment industry combined ethnographic study with quantitative methods. Zelizer (2011) relied on qualitative analysis of a variety of primary sources in newspapers and magazines, legal records and memoirs. Network analysis has, similarly, proven to be a useful tool (Swedberg 2004: 321).

Both the Bloomington school and the new economic sociology have embraced multiple methods. This has allowed them to explore what is happening in specific social and economic contexts, to study what people actually do and think, rather than relying solely on generalized models that lose the details of circumstance and environment.

Conclusion

The Bloomington school and the new economic sociology share both intellectual roots and common themes that make them highly compatible fields. Both are attempting to develop theories to explain phenomena that do not neatly fit into classic dichotomies, like market versus state or like the economy or society. Tocqueville plays a vital role in the intellectual history of both. The work of the Ostroms built heavily on foundations laid down by Tocqueville in his analysis, developing a science of citizenship and exploring the potential of democracies crafted from self-governance (Aligica 2019: 99). For economic sociologists, Tocqueville's early cultural analyses of social and economic phenomena and the connections between the two make him a clear forbearer to their work.

The two schools are also united in their rejection of the neoclassical economist's view of individuals and their behavior. Rather than isolated actors, both schools recognize that the economic action of these individuals is embedded in their social context. In the same vein as this under-socialized account they also both reject the over-socialized view of individuals that many sociologists hold, that all choice is directed entirely by social norms that are internalized without question. Granovetter's theory of embeddedness works around this problem of actors behaving either as atoms outside a social context or slavishly following a social script (Granovetter 1985: 487). Linked to embeddedness is the idea of the importance of social capital, another commonality of economic sociology and the Bloomington school. Social capital, referring to features of social organizations such as networks, norms and trust, can facilitate coordination and cooperation (Putnam 1993b). Social capital is at the core of much economic sociology, and the emphasis of the Ostroms' on collective action and bargaining makes much use of the concept.

Whereas embeddedness and social capital are elements of economic sociology that lend themselves so well to the Bloomington school, there are also concepts that economic sociologists are using but where their theory could be improved by drawing on the already established knowledge of the Ostroms. Polycentricity as we have talked about here, which is so closely associated with the work of E. and V. Ostrom, refers to any system with many centers of decision-making that are formally independent of each other (V. Ostrom *et al.* 1961: 831). As the Ostroms show, rather than neat centralized systems, polycentrism is what really occurs in the world, and this is reflected in the studies undertaken by economic sociologists, and what theory on social networks and social capital would predict.

The numerous areas of intersection of these two schools in their approach, intellectual histories and themes suggest that there is much to be gained from scholars from either background studying the other and approaching new issues with a robust knowledge of both. There appear to be various areas of potential crossover study, issues in the field of economic development would appear to benefit greatly from this combined approach. In economic development, solutions are likely to be complex and top-down, technical solutions are unlikely to work (Easterly 2013). The Bloomington school focuses on careful, culturally aware fieldwork of the complex interface between public and private arenas, with an emphasis on bottom-up rather than top-down. Similarly, economic sociologists shun a broad one-size-fits-all approach, and instead study the highly specific situations of communities with highly specific variations in social capital, networks, norms and rules. Both approaches lend themselves well to complex issues of development. In economic sociology social capital becomes a useful analytical tool to study economic development; Woolcock (1998, 2000) has written on how the social relations that form the backdrop of social and economic life matter greatly, an aspect too often ignored by policy-makers and development economists, and provide a significant avenue through which sociologists can contribute to this field.

Given the novel contributions each has to make, a combined approach would seem rich in possibility for new contributions to the field.[6] Beyond this, anywhere ideas of social capital and self-governance cross over would seem to have the potential for a cross-theoretical approach – any community problem such as dealing with crime, providing public goods or community improvement in general.

---

6. One area that has profitably drawn on the shared insights of the new economic sociology and the Bloomington school is the study of community recovery after disasters; see, for example, Storr *et al.* (2015).

6

FOUNDATIONS OF SOCIAL ORDER: THE OSTROMS AND JOHN SEARLE

Adrian Miroiu and Adelin Dumitru

The impressive work of Vincent and Elinor Ostrom is commonly regarded as relevant for practitioners of policy analysis and also for more theoretically-minded scholars who are concerned with the functioning of institutional arrangements in small or larger communities. In recent years their accounts of phenomena like polycentricity and co-production came to enjoy a central place in discussions about the nature and the working of government and of contemporary democratic societies.

However, their views and reflections on more abstract, foundational issues – epistemological (what is the structure of scientific inquiry?), ontological (what does the stuff of our social world consist of?) and methodological (in what sense do individualistic assumptions matter?) – are less prominent among scholars who have studied their work. In our view, these issues – particularly questions related to ontology – are of crucial importance for a correct understanding of the Ostroms' intellectual inheritance. Ontological issues pertain to the very core of all theoretical approaches to social reality and invoke deep philosophical presumptions, of which Vincent and Elinor Ostrom were well aware. Their good acquaintance with the political philosophy of Thomas Hobbes, David Hume and Adam Smith grounded some of the positions they adopted. Other sources of their views can be traced back to American pragmatism (Aligica 2014: ch. 6) and to the comprehensive theoretical conception of politics of Lasswell (Lasswell & Kaplan [1950] 2014). Some different, albeit extremely pertinent insights came from the philosophy of language (Barwise & Perry 1983; Searle 1969, 1995, 2002). Vincent Ostrom was particularly impressed by John Searle's work. He greatly admired Searle's account of the role of language in the constitution of social reality and used it in setting the foundation of his own perspective on it. Having recognized the foundational role of language in the way humans think, communicate, associate, and work with others, he developed his social theory of institutional order as a language-based knowledge process (Aligica & Boettke

2011). Elinor Ostrom (2006) followed Vincent in acknowledging the influence of Searle and elaborated a profound and specific analysis of the way language informs our thought as well as the social reality we live in.

In this chapter we shall discuss three topics. In each case we shall focus on the Ostroms' views and try to correlate them with Searle's philosophy. We shall argue that, even though correspondences are remarkable, significant differences between the Ostroms' views and Searle's social ontology still exist. First, we shall analyze the nature and role of the distinction between "brute" and "institutional" facts. We shall argue that it has a significant bearing in the methodological dispute on methodological individualism and the role of group agents. Second, we shall go into more detail and discuss a couple of concepts that are central in Ostroms' view on institutions: common knowledge and shared community of understanding. They are crucial for understanding both the foundations of human cooperation and the creation of order in society. Finally, we shall concentrate on the institution of language. In line with Searle, who insisted that language has a foundational functioning in human life, the Ostroms studied at length and sometimes in an extremely technical manner the structural characteristics of both ordinary language and formal languages used in scientific inquiry (see, e.g., V. Ostrom 1997; E. Ostrom 2005a; Crawford & Ostrom 1995).

Institutional and non-institutional facts

Both Vincent and Elinor Ostrom recognized the influence of Searle's social ontology on their understanding of the social world. The root idea, argues Elinor Ostrom (2006), is to accept the significant difference between the social world and the biophysical world.

Vincent Ostrom (1980) once explained how he came to recognize this difference. Early on, he had worked with the presumption that social phenomena (particularly those concerning public administration) were similar to natural phenomena. Consequently, the methods of the natural sciences also apply to social phenomena. However, he gradually came to conclude that the study of public administration should not be treated as strictly natural phenomena, with the same methods as in natural sciences. Specifically, it was inappropriate to understand scientific inquiry as a linear process beginning with the development of theory as basic knowledge and only then considering applications of the theory. The main reason why the analogy does not work is that administrative tasks and administrative arrangements are different in type from natural phenomena. A better approach would be to treat them as similar to works of art or to artifacts. In social sciences objects are artifacts, "created by human beings with reference to the use of learning and knowledge to serve human purposes"

(V. Ostrom 1980: 309). The investigators do not discover phenomena, but rather create them. Their task and the processes involved in the creation of an artifact is artisanship. The study of social phenomena can then be more appropriately described as a scholar-artisan creating an artifact in their attempt to understand the social world.

Searle (1969, 1995, 2002) conceptualized the difference between attempts to understand the natural and the social world by highlighting the distinction between those features of reality that are intrinsic (for example, the "brute" fact that hydrogen atoms have one electron) and those that are observer-relative (for example, being a twenty dollar bill). As he put it:

> there are portions of the real world, objective facts in the world, that are only facts by human agreement. In a sense there are things that exist only because we believe them to exist. I am thinking of things like money, property, governments, and marriages. Yet many facts regarding these things are 'objective' facts in the sense that they are not a matter of your or my preferences, evaluations, or moral attitudes.
>
> (Searle 1995: 1)

In other words, Searle considers it an "objective" fact that one is a citizen of that state, or that one owns some piece of property in that city, or that one has in her pocket a five or a twenty dollar bill. The overwhelming part of social reality consists of these, humanly created institutional facts. What are the characteristics of the process that moves us from the world of "brute" (intrinsic) facts to the human social reality, consisting of "institutional" facts?

For Searle, the fundamental feature of social reality is that there is an enormous variety of different modes of social existence. However, he claims, the principles that underlie the constitution of social reality are few in number; thus, the underlying logical structure is rather simple. The social-institutional reality can be understood at its most fundamental level by resorting to only three primitives: (1) collective intentionality; (2) the assignment of function; and (3) constitutive rules and procedures (Searle 2006: 56). Each of these concepts plays an important role in explaining the way in which the social world is constituted.[1]

Collective intentionality refers, first, to the human capacity to engage in cooperative behavior. Examples of such cooperative behavior abound: conversations between two participants, a rock band playing a song, or two men playing

---

1. Besides Searle's account of collective intentionality, many other approaches are relevant to the topics we discuss here. Searle (2010: 45n2) himself mentions that he draws inspiration in his account of social ontology from previous works of Margaret Gilbert (1989) and Raimo Tuomela (2007), among others.

a tennis match. Second, collective intentionality requires "not only that they engage in cooperative behavior, but that they share intentional states such as beliefs, desires, and intentions. In addition to singular intentionality there is also collective intentionality. Obvious examples are cases where *I* am doing something only as part of *our* doing something" (Searle 1995: 23).

The assignment of functions refers to the capacity of humans to endow certain aspects of the world with "observer-relative functions": we assign functions to objects, where the object does not have the function intrinsically, but only in virtue of this collective assignment. A simple example is the following: how can we distinguish between plants and weeds? The distinction stems from the fact that the latter are plants that are not useful (yet) for humans. Or consider a twenty dollar bill. The function this piece of paper performs is not in virtue of its *physical* structure, but in virtue of our collective attitudes towards it. In Searle's words, "functions are causes that serve a purpose" (Searle 2010: 59).

Collective intentionality and the assignment of function are complemented by the assignment of status functions to an object (or a phenomenon). In the money example, an object is given a certain status; but this status cannot be performed solely in virtue of the intrinsic physical features of the object in question, without the collective acceptance of that status: "This assignment creates a new fact, an institutional fact, a new fact created by human agreement" (Searle 1995: 46). We have a quite simple means to recognize such assignments of the new status function to an object: the appeal to the formula "X counts as Y in C." By this formula we agree to count the object named by the X term as having the status and function specified by the Y term in the context C. Crucially, the occurrence of the expression "counts as" shows that object X can perform the function Y only in virtue of our (collective) agreement or acceptance that it be performed.

Searle argues that status functions represent veritable "vehicles of power" in our society. By accepting them, we also accept a long list of associated "obligations, rights, responsibilities, duties, entitlements, authorizations, permissions, requirements," which he condenses under the name "deontic powers" (Searle 2006: 57–9). It is in these deontic powers that the compatibility with Ostroms' institutional analysis and development (IAD) framework is most prominent. The IAD framework has been developed as a comparative method of institutional analysis which can be employed to understand a wide range of action arenas (Hess & Ostrom 2007). In turn, action arenas represent social spaces "where participants with diverse preferences interact, exchange goods and services, solve problems, dominate one another, or fight" (E. Ostrom 2005a: 14).

The analysis of action arenas requires the appeal to what Elinor Ostrom called "institutional statements." These statements describe opportunities and constraints that create expectations about other actors' behavior. An example is this:

"All villagers are forbidden to let their animals trample the irrigation channels, or else the villager who owns the livestock will have to pay a fine." This statement includes two types of components: descriptive and deontic. The descriptive components determine (a) to whom the statement applies (all the villagers); (b) the particular actions the actors may take (let their animals trample); (c) the conditions in which the action is performed (the irrigation channels); and (d) the institutionally assigned consequence for not following a rule (paying a fine by the owners of the livestock).[2] The deontic component determines the institutional status of the action performed in the particular circumstances: in our example, the action is institutionally forbidden. In general, a "deontic" is a holder for one of the following three modal verbs: "may" (permitted), "must" (obliged), and "must not" (forbidden). Thus, an action is permitted, forbidden or obliged by a norm or a rule.[3] Elinor Ostrom (2005a: 144) clearly acknowledges that her analysis of the deontic component of the syntax of a language which includes as core components institutional statements is inspired by Searle: to say, for example, that a rule assigns a "may" to an action is the equivalent of what Searle (1969) called "constituting" that action.

Consider the following example. In some Japanese villages in which villagers "were required to perform collective work to enhance and maintain the yield of the commons, such as the annual burning or specific cutting of timber or thatch. Each household had an obligation to contribute a share to such efforts" (E. Ostrom 1990: 67). A simple action such as burning a part of the common-pool resource can either be required as part of the operational rules-in-use (the rules effectively followed by a group of individuals) or sanctioned. Thus, the action of burning is endowed with what Searle called a status function. Burning a part of the CPR by someone who is not a member of the community or outside the specified timeframe for doing that is a matter of litigation. But burning a part of the CPR at a specified time is a requirement for the members of the community. The actions taken in an action arena thus take various meanings, and in order to determine when an action is permissible and when not, we need to resort to what is or is not collectively accepted or agreed.

Let us turn back to the realm of things (money, for example) that are both observer-relative, and so subjective, but at the same time contain observer-independent components. They are not a matter of "mine" or "yours," yet they

---

2. Elinor Ostrom (2005a: 140) calls these four components "attributes", respectively "aim", "conditions" and "or else."

3. The definition of a rule requires the occurrence of a deontic: "by rules I mean that a group of individuals has developed shared understandings that certain actions in particular situations must, must not, or may be undertaken and that sanctions will be taken against those who do not conform" (E. Ostrom 1998a: 9–10).

are anchored in the subjectivity of values and preferences. In his attempt to give an account of this institutional reality Searle concentrated on the role of collective intentionality in human interactions.

However, Ostroms' investigations prepared the path for a different way of dealing with this problem. To explain how humans cross the bridge from the conceptual, mental, and psychological to the social and institutional, they focused on special interactions and cooperative behaviors. Aligica and Tarko (2013) forcefully argued that one possible path on that bridge is Ostroms' concept of co-production. The structure of empirical interactions in co-production requires and at the same time makes possible joint intentions and collective beliefs. In co-production the collaboration between those who supply a service and those who use it is the factor determining the effective delivery of the service. Examples of this can be found everywhere: police need clues from citizens in order to catch criminals; teaching is effective only if the student is willing to learn; doctors need inputs from patients in order to come to a correct diagnosis and provide an effective treatment, etc. Usually these interactions are not centralized, and are characterized rather by a polycentric structure (Aligica & Boettke 2011; Tarko 2017). By working together in arenas in which the empirical and historical realities take center stage, people contribute to the creation of common intentions and beliefs, as well as of "valued states of affairs from as many normative perspectives as possible" (Aligica & Tarko 2013).

Here we reach the point where more complex concepts come to the fore. As argued in the next section, fundamental methodological claims are extremely relevant for understanding the nature of institutions.

Individualism and holism

Coming from the tradition of public choice, both Elinor and Vincent Ostrom were deeply attached to an individualist methodology in social sciences. Relying on Lasswell's view, Vincent Ostrom (1997: 105–106) took methodological individualism to attach a fundamental role to the "acts performed by individuals who are not merely biological entities but persons who have an individual 'ego' and a social 'self' embedded in a cultural heritage". For him, methodological individualism is not bound to assume the extreme rationality assumptions of microeconomic theory.

Vincent Ostrom considers two differences from the standard assumptions in public choice to be especially important here. First, individuals are treated as complex actors, who are characterized by both personal and social selves. Second, they never function in a vacuum, but in a social and cultural context of normative processes, i.e. in an institutional environment. But, although the role of the social and cultural context in which collectivities exist and their members live is acknowledged, this does not lead to the conclusion that methodological individualism must be abandoned. "Collectivities", writes Vincent Ostrom (1997: 106), "may act in concert and function as actors, but group actions are always to be understood as patterned forms of individual actions." So the primitive idea is that of an individual action, while group concepts can be analysed in institutional terms, i.e. in terms of induced patterns of individual actions.

The question is, however, in what sense Searle's ideas of institutional facts as opposed to brute facts, and of collective intentions as opposed to individual ones, are relevant to the methodological individualism of the Ostroms. The question has two facets. The first concerns the way in which Searle is positioned in the dispute of individualism versus holism. The second is how his concepts can be integrated and make a difference in the methodological framework developed by the Bloomington school.

A basic tenet of Searle's thought is that collective intentions of the members of a group of people cannot be reduced to the sum of the individual intentions of its members. But, as many scholars noted, this does not entail that the individualist assumptions are dispensed of. "Society consists of nothing but individuals", writes Searle (2002: 96), affirming an ontological individualist position. As Wendt (2004: 301) notes, Searle is a physicalist. For him, the constitutive relations between individuals and groups are one-way and bottom-up. In this sense, his realism about collective intentions is not metaphysically mysterious. Wendt adds to this a very significant commentary: for Searle, "individuals can still be seen in liberal terms as the basic building blocks of society". The bottom-up construction of collective intentions is given by the fact that Searle's account appeals to the concept of supervenience[4], and therefore he is close to the view that collective intentions can in one sense be reduced to individual ones. No surprise, Baier (1997) argued that Searle's theory is only "superficially different" from Bratman's (1992, 1993). For Bratman, collective intentions (what we intend to do) can be reduced to a very complex way of meshing individual but "interlocking" intentions.[5]

---

4. The concept of supervenience was introduced to account for relations between different kinds of properties of things. In a very simple formulation, a set of properties B supervenes upon another set A just in case no two things can differ with respect to B-properties without also differing with respect to their A-properties. For example, mental properties supervene upon physical properties of the brain. In our example, collective intentions supervene upon the individual intentions of the members of the group.

5. Bratman's proposal is this: with respect to a group consisting of you and me, and concerning a joint activity J, *we intend to* J if and only if:

Gilbert (2013: 89) also locates Searle in the camp of those authors who do not accept a genuine appeal to groups taken as wholes. She argues that, like Bratman, Searle does not employ the concept of joint commitment. Joint commitment is holistic in the sense that it cannot be analyzed in terms of a sum or aggregate of personal commitments.[6] But Searle accepts this holistic account only in a very weak sense: although for Searle each individual personally may ascribe an action to groups, their shared intentions reduce to their thinking, "We intend".[7] His account is to "reduce collective intentionality to a set of 'We-intends' in the minds of individual human beings. For *them* to intend is for *each of them* to think a particular thing"[8] (Gilbert 2000: 157). Consequently, although Searle allows for institutional facts and collective intentionality, his position is not much promising as a ground for attempts to construct a concept of genuine group agency, as authors like Tuomela (2013) or List and Pettit (2011) tried.

Starting from this root coherence between Searle's and Ostroms' view on social reality, in the next sections we shall investigate in more detail how institutional facts, collective intentions and, crucially, language are helpful in configuring Ostroms' institutional approach.

Shared communities of understanding

Given the presuppositions of methodological individualism, the individual interests people hold are the primary elements in the analysis of decision

---

(1) (a) I intend that we J and (b) you intend that we J;

(2) I intend that we J in accordance with and because of (1) (a), (1) (b), and meshing sub-plans of (1) (a), (1) (b); and you intend likewise;

(3) (1) and (2) are common knowledge between us.

As we shall immediately see, the concept of "common knowledge" can also be defined in terms of iterated individual knowledge (Bratman 1993).

6. A joint commitment involves two or more people. Their decision to do something cannot be reduced to their personal commitments. "A joint commitment, by its nature, may be said to tie or bind its participants together into a unit or whole" (Gilbert 2000: 3).

7. There are many passages in Searle's papers that support this interpretation. For example: "In collective intentionality, it cannot be required of each individual's intentionality that he knows what the intentionality on the part of others is. In complex forms of teamwork or collective behavior, one typically does not know what the others are doing in detail. All one needs to believe is that they share one's collective goal and intend to do their part in achieving the goal" (Searle 2010: 45).

8. See in this sense Searle (2002: ch. 6), where he defines what is for an agent who is a member of a group to "we-intends" to do an action.

situations. However, they must be put together to yield commonalities. How does this process work? Elinor Ostrom (1986) strongly argued that common interests, as well as common beliefs and collective actions, are not constituted by a simple summative appeal to unanimity. Rules are often the results of more sophisticated aggregation procedures. Different rules may bring about different results and different patterns of behavior.

But second, rules are not the only interfering factor between individual and common interests. Since individual interests are diverging, their aggregation requires processes of pooling, rearranging, and compromising (V. Ostrom 1997: 147). In other words, reconciling diverse interests requires processes of conflict resolution. These processes generate common knowledge and shared communities of understanding,[9] which are also fundamental elements necessary for the analysis of collective decisions. We shall first describe these concepts and their role in Ostroms' account. Then we shall show how they are connected with Searle's social ontology.

The first concept is that of common knowledge. Common knowledge is usually assumed in game theory. Note that it cannot be identified with an individual's knowledge of a state of affairs, not even with the mutual knowledge of all the members of a group about a state of affairs. In a way, it describes not the individual knowledge of the members of the group, but their collective knowledge. With reference to the definition given by Aumann (1976), Elinor Ostrom (1990, 2005a) used common knowledge as a technical term: by definition, the members of a group have common knowledge about x if each member of the group knows x, and each member of the group knows that each of the other members knows x, and each member of the group knows that each of the other members knows that each of the other members knows x, and so on ad infinitum.

Common knowledge is not an abstraction or a mere ideal assumption made by game theorists. Elinor Ostrom (1990: 125) argues that it closely approximates real-world situations. The example she gives is that of Raymond Basin, West Basin and Central Basin, where negotiated settlements concerning groundwater

---

9. Vincent Ostrom usually discusses the concepts of common knowledge and shared communities of understanding in conjunction with two other concepts: patterns of social accountability and mutual trust. Together these provide the "basis for assigning autonomy to individuals to exercise responsibility for the actions they take in the governance of their own affairs and in relating to others" and are "essential for self-governing communities of relationships and to the achievement of the conditions of peace and other public goods" (V. Ostrom 1997: 96, 100). However, here we shall focus only on the first two concepts. As V. Ostrom argues (1997: 207), their functioning implies the accountability for what is being asserted and also mutual trust.

production were established. In the following decades, the parties developed extensive monitoring, sanctioning rules and got easy access to accurate information. As a result, each pumper came to know that his or her own groundwater extractions will be known by all others. More importantly, the appeal to "common knowledge" is essential for the definition of rules: it must be presupposed if rules are to work in a group: "One should not talk about a 'rule' unless most people whose strategies are affected by it know of its existence and expect others to monitor behavior and to sanction nonconformance. In other words, working rules are common knowledge and are monitored and enforced" (E. Ostrom 1990: 51). This has a crucial implication: since in situations in which people have to make decisions market exchange cannot directly provide all necessary knowledge, other criteria are necessary. Common knowledge of the participants in a collective activity is then of "fundamental importance for coordinated activities in human societies" (V. Ostrom 1997: 108).

We can easily see that the appeal to common knowledge in the attempts to describe collective activities on which groups of people embark is in no conflict with methodological individualism. Common knowledge is just a complex way of asserting iterated individual beliefs or intentions.[10] It resumes expectations one has in common with the other participants about her relationships with her world.

But this is only one part of the story. For achieving common knowledge does not happen in a spontaneous way; it requires "intelligibility and skill on the part of human beings who know how to think and use their rational facilities to solve problems and constitute mutually productive relationships with one another" (V. Ostrom 1997: 147). In order to act, individuals need to share many things, common knowledge included: for they need to have shared expectations about the other participants' view about the world. So, we come to accept a social dimension of the self.

This brings us to a second, essential concept largely used by the Ostroms: shared communities of understanding. It is involved whenever one tries to analyze collective decision-making processes. Consider again the example of rules. Rules must be common knowledge in a group of individuals, and using them entails that, first, the group has developed shared understandings about what types of actions must, must not, or may be undertaken in particular situations;

---

10. The analysis of convention formulated in Lewis (1969) can also be understood as involving (possibly iterated) individual beliefs; see Crawford and E. Ostrom (1995). As we mentioned in an earlier note, Bratman's individualistic account of collective intentions also appeals to the concept of common knowledge. Searle (2010: 46), while acknowledging the reductionist nature of common belief, argues that it is not sufficient to produce a direct reduction of "We intend" statements to "I intend" statements.

and, second, that sanctions will be taken against those who do not conform (E. Ostrom 1998a). While in the case of an internalized norm sanctioning is an internal cost (e.g., guilt, anxiety, lowered conception of self-worth), in the case of shared norms "sanctioning for nonconformity comes from others who are part of the same group and exhibit social displeasure if a norm is broken" (E. Ostrom 1990: 206).[11]

Although expressions like "shared strategies", "shared rules", "shared norms", "shared meanings" or "shared communities of understanding" are used often in the works of both Vincent and Elinor Ostrom, we face a difficult task when try-ing to give a clear and precise definition of what it is for something to be shared by the members of a group. A starting point in analysis is to acknowledge that when a given community has a shared understanding of a situation, it must have in common more than common knowledge. But what does this "more" consist of? One answer was sketched earlier, when we noticed that in the case of a shared norm we need to take into account not only the knowledge the mem-bers of the community have about the situation they are in, but also their will-ingness to have certain attitudes (imposing punishment, for example) toward those participants who break the norm. Second, shared meanings exclude cases when those who must repeatedly interpret the meaning of a rule within action situations arrive at multiple interpretations. Shared meanings provide the basis for the stability of rule-ordered actions (E. Ostrom 2005a: 37). So, shared mean-ings are related not only to knowledge, but also to actions. A third related point concerns the way in which shared meanings are achieved. Since this is central in our comparative perspective, we shall investigate it in more detail.

V. Ostrom (1997: 164) defines shared communities of understanding as shared expectations about standards of judgement (e.g. warrantable knowledge, standards of fairness, and other normative considerations) that help individuals acquire knowledge about their world and act. Members of a community will then form beliefs and attitudes about their world and behave in ways that are related to social standards; behavior becomes patterned. So shared communi-ties of understanding are instruments to produce order in society[12] and deter-mine how rules and norms work.

---

11. Elinor Ostrom argues that this distinction (which she attributes to James Coleman) is difficult to draw in fieldwork. Note that when a norm is shared we need to take into account second-order beliefs and attitudes of the members of the group concerning their willingness to sanction those who do not comply with it.

12. V. Ostrom (1997: 109) observes that money functions as a good in two different ways: money as a medium of exchange has the characteristic of a private good, while money as a unit of account in a monetary system is a public good. Similarly, in an action situation, individuals hold shared understandings as a private good that informs their behavior. But shared understanding as a characteristic of the community is a public good.

The Ostroms' concepts of common knowledge and shared communities of understanding connect in interesting ways with Searle's account of collective intentions and actions. First, like V. Ostrom, Searle views the concept of common knowledge[13] as necessary, but not sufficient to explain cooperation in a group. Collective intentionality presupposes the existence of cooperation among the members of a group: "Cooperation implies the existence of common knowledge or common belief, but the common knowledge or belief, together with individual intentions to achieve a common goal is not by itself sufficient for cooperation" (Searle 2010: 49). Second, compare Ostroms' analysis of the concept of shared community of understanding and Searle's analysis of the concept of collective intentions. For the Ostroms, putting together individual beliefs and actions is not sufficient to explain group decision; for Searle (2002: 91–7), attempts to explain collective intentions by either a summation[14] of individual intentional behavior or by I-intentions supplemented with beliefs, including mutual beliefs, about the intentions of other members of a group are bound to fail. Third, the Ostroms retain an individualist methodology. Similarly, as already noted, Searle is reluctant to appeal to mysterious entities like group minds, the collective unconscious, etc., in explaining collective intentions and actions. He argues that we only have to accept that individuals who are acting as part of the collective have intentions whose form is: "We intend that we perform act A". Finally, the Ostroms locate shared communities of understanding at a special higher level[15], which requires the acceptance of standards of judgement. These standards are socially constituted as results of the cooperation between the members of the community. On his part, Searle (2002: 104) concludes that the features that make collective intentionality irreducible are entailed by structural aspects of cooperation: "Collective intentionality presupposes a Background sense of the other as a candidate for cooperative agency; that is, it presupposes a sense of others as more than mere conscious agents, indeed as actual or potential members of a cooperative activity".

The institution of language

A fundamental weakness of discussions about the nature of social reality, argues Searle (2006), is that the existence of language is taken for granted: thinkers from

---

13. Surprisingly, there are no direct references to it in Searle's earlier books.
14. What "summation" is is not very clear, but we can assume that it covers many types of aggregations.
15. See also Searle (1995: 88), where he argues that collective intentionality is characterized by "the acceptance, recognition, etc., of one phenomenon as a phenomenon of a higher-sort by imposing a collective status and a corresponding function upon it".

Aristotle to Hume, Rousseau, Weber or Durkheim "presuppose the existence of language and then, given language, ask about the nature of society". This presupposition is prominent in social contract theories: Searle argues that they assume that communities of humans had a language and then got together to make an original contract which founded society. But to share a common language and to be already communicating with the other members of the community in that common language means that those people already had a social contract. This paradoxical situation lets us conclude that language has a specific and unique feature among all human institutions: "Language is the presupposition of the existence of other social institutions in a way that they are not the presupposition of language" (Searle 2006: 54). Furthermore, there is a strong connection between rules and language. To speak a language is already to be "engaged in a highly complex rule-governed form of behavior" (Searle 1969: 12). The explanation for this fundamental role given to language is that it is the vehicle of speech acts, the "minimal units of linguistic communication" (Searle 1969: 17). Searle mainly associated speech acts with Austin's (1962) illocutionary acts, i.e. the linguistic acts of "stating, asserting, describing, warning, remarking, commenting, commanding, ordering, requesting, criticizing, apologizing, approving, censuring, welcoming, promising, expressing approval, expressing regret" (Searle 1965: 221). Since our focus in this chapter is not on speech acts, suffice it to say that for Searle deontic powers emerge as a consequence of uttering illocutionary acts/speech acts. That is, institutional facts are dependent on language: "we can create boundaries, kings and corporations by saying something equivalent to *let this be a boundary!, let the oldest son be the king!, let there be a corporation!*" (Searle 2010: 100).

The Ostroms took the foundational role of language very seriously. For instance, Vincent Ostrom focused on Hobbes' contractualist approach. His question was, is it possible to describe the imagined state of nature as consisting of brute, non-institutional facts? Clearly, the role of the social contract is to "constitute" an institutional reality, and so the pre-contractarian state could only consist of brute facts. He argued (V. Ostrom 1997: 92) that the state of nature can be defined by the following characteristics, which together entail that individuals would end up fighting with one another: (1) individuals seek their own good; (2) in the presence of others; (3) in a world of scarcity; and, very importantly, (4) in the absence of speech (see also V. Ostrom 1991: 34). The absence of speech is the sign of non-institutional reality: "Hobbes's Man in a State of Nature is, I believe, a hypothetical thought experiment of presuming human beings to be devoid of speech and, thus, comparable to animals like lions, bears, and wolves" (V. Ostrom 1997: 92–3). But if language cannot be presumed in the state of nature, how can we explain the move to a contractual state and so to an institutional human reality?

Vincent Ostrom's view is that humans make use of a normative inquiry, grounded in the golden rule: "Do not that to another, which thou wouldest not have done to thy selfe" (Hobbes [1651] 1965: 121). This method of normative inquiry allows individuals to make interpersonal comparisons and helps them arrive at rules of reason. For Hobbes these rules of reason are accessible to all human beings. The argument, however, is puzzling, because it assumes again that individuals' behavior is mediated by the use of language. V. Ostrom (1997: 94) accepted this conundrum. His way out was to distinguish between different meanings of the words "nature" and "natural". As we saw above, the meaning of the expression "state of nature" does not require reference to language; but when we use the expression "laws of nature" we presume characteristics of human nature, i.e. we necessarily make reference to language and in general to cultural achievements.[16]

Elinor Ostrom took a slightly different route to conceptualize the problem and offer an answer. She argued that the Hobbesian state of nature could be expressed in two different ways. First, it can indeed be viewed as a situation where there are no rules; there are no rules requiring or forbidding any actions or outcomes. But, she observes, "The Hobbesian state of nature is logically equivalent to a situation in which rules exist permitting anyone to take any and all desired actions, regardless of the effects on others. ... a CPR situation in which no one is forbidden or required to take any action is logically equivalent to a CPR situation in which everyone is permitted to take any and all actions" (E. Ostrom 1990: 140).

These rules working in a Hobbesian state of nature satisfy "default conditions". For example, in an action situation, a position rule may require by default that only one person can occupy a certain role or office. Boundary rules define not only who is eligible to enter a position, but also the process that determines which eligible participants may enter (or must enter) positions, as well as how an individual person may leave (or must leave) a position. The default condition in this case is that anyone can hold these positions, etc. (E. Ostrom 2005a: 211).[17] Given this equivalence, the Hobbesian state of nature can then be conceptualized as intrinsically characterized by an institutional, normative component.

---

16. Another interesting solution to Hobbes' puzzle is Philip Pettit's analysis of the contrast between the state of the first nature and the state of the second nature. The state of second nature "is not the precultural state in which human beings are as other animals but the state in which they have already mastered language. It is not the state of first nature, prior to language ... It is the state to which human beings are reduced, as language and the mixed blessings of language become second nature to them" (Pettit 2008: 98).

17. If the default position condition is also in place, it follows that anyone can hold this single position.

Specifically, speech cannot be totally absent in the state of nature. It has to be assumed, at least as a general default condition that makes the very existence of rules, and so of basic human cooperation, possible.

"The institution of languages is the fundament of order in all human societies", i.e. in rule-governed societies, concludes Vincent Ostrom (1997: 86). This makes possible the move from this state to the "living realities" of social life. Therefore, language grounds not only our beliefs and intentions, but also human artisanship. Vincent Ostrom (1980: 310) highlights a crucial feature of artisanship: it has a reflexive character. "In Hobbes's words, human beings are both the 'matter' and the 'artificers' of organizations. Human beings both design and create organizations as artifacts and themselves form the primary ingredients of organizations. Organizations are, thus, artifacts that contain their own artisans."

This conclusion is clearly in line with Searle's insistence that language has a foundational and reflexive character. It is presupposed by all human institutions, including the institution of language: "institutional facts require language because language is constitutive of the facts. But linguistic facts are also institutional facts. So it looks as if language requires language" (Searle 1995: 72). This self-reference is not vicious, however. To see why, note first that language does not contain only expressions that stand for prelinguistic objects (the expression "the evening star" stands for the evening star), but also expressions that play a much more complex role. The label "This is a twenty dollar bill" does not represent some prelinguistic natural phenomenon. It stands for an institutional fact, already presupposing our language, and creates an institutional status by representing it as existing (Searle 1995: 74). The job of these expressions is done without the need to move behind language, in the same way that artifacts like organizations contain their own artisans.

Conclusion: epistemological implications

The issues we discussed in this chapter are of fundamental importance for understanding the nature of human reality and the processes that constitute it. At the same time they also raise significant methodological implications. Both Vincent and Elinor Ostrom expressed on many occasions a deep concern about a largely accepted epistemological view on political inquiry. According to that view, scientific investigations should start with facts and then attempt to make sense of them by appealing to some theoretical tools. Facts and thought are mutually independent: we have empirical phenomena, on the one hand, waiting to be known; and we also have theoretical tools to make sense of them, on the other hand. The Ostroms regarded this view as fundamentally wrong and misleading.

For one thing, Vincent Ostrom was extremely reluctant to the idea that we can have access to "brute"[18] facts and therefore that we can "see the direct light of Truth." All our knowledge is mediated through the conventions of language. "The fate of humanity is, in my judgment, confined to learning how to read the shadows on the walls of the Cave, to use Plato's metaphor. The shadows in Plato's Cave are the words we use to stand for, symbolize, or represent 'reality' and to relate thinking and acting to whatever it is that human beings achieve" (V. Ostrom 1997: 7).

Elinor Ostrom also rejected the claim that the description of the facts can be made independent of our language and of our conceptual tools. "The presence of order in the world", writes Elinor Ostrom, "is largely dependent upon the theories used to understand the world" (2016: 104).[19] Our theoretical tools constitute the world as a cosmos, an ordered and legible reality. We see the market as consisting of beneficial outcomes emerging from the independent contributions of many individuals pursuing their own interests within a set of agreed upon rules because this is how Adam Smith's lenses make us see the world; and we are induced to see order in society and the state's use of coercion as legitimate because this is what Thomas Hobbes' theory of order implies. To put it in a simpler and more concise way, linguistic conventions and theoretical blocks are already built in the empirical phenomena. Therefore, the focus of our inquiry should (at least partly) consist in uncovering theoretical concepts and assumptions buried in the very structure of the empirical world.

An important consequence of this observation is that from the very beginning we have a sort of "correspondence" between the empirical world and the theoretical constructions. "The challenge for institutional theorists," writes Elinor Ostrom (2005a: 7), "is to know enough about the structure of a situation to select the appropriate assumptions about human behavior that fit the type of

---

18. "Brute" is a word Vincent Ostrom met in at least two very different contexts. First, it occurs in Searle's definition of naturally intrinsic, non-institutional facts. Second, it occurs in the definition of an important methodological position: Ostrom (1988: 9) quotes laudatorily Lasswell and Kaplan (2014: xxiii) who stated that theorizing about politics "is not to be confused with metaphysical speculation in terms of abstractions hopelessly removed from empirical observation and control. ... But this standpoint is not to be confused, on the other hand, with 'brute empiricism' – the gathering of 'facts' without a corresponding elaboration of hypotheses". V. Ostrom agrees with their criticism of this methodological position. He also argued that W. Wilson supported the position of "brute empiricism" in his call to "to escape from theories and attach himself to facts" in studying government (V. Ostrom 1997: 282).

19. See also V. Ostrom (1997: 156): "Languages-in-use relationships are of fundamental importance to the constitution of order in human societies and to how we create bodies of knowledge to be shared with others".

situation under analysis." When the theorist chooses a framework, a theory or a model to deal with a specific situation, she already assumes a general under-standing of the structure of the situation. Our knowledge of the reality is at the same time a construction of it by appealing to conceptual tools and mediated by language.

7

ENVIRONMENTAL POLICY FROM A SELF-GOVERNANCE PERSPECTIVE

Jayme Lemke and Jordan K. Lofthouse

Environmental policy is an arena characterized by extremes. On one hand, there are calls to take decisive, global action to resolve daunting environmental problems. Global climate change potentially threatens billions of people. Many fisheries around the world are collapsing (Worm *et al.* 2006). Groundwater in many areas is being overexploited, and some scholars predict that water quality and depletion problems will become more acute and widespread (Shah *et al.* 2001). Deforestation continues at rapid rates across parts of the developing world, and air pollution poses health problems for people in industrializing economies (Miettinen *et al.* 2011; Ravindra *et al.* 2016). On the other hand, there are those who argue that some concerns are not as serious as they may seem, or that the economic and social impacts of environmental policy are too severe (Lomborg 2001). Regardless of one's view on the seriousness of any particular environmental problem, it is an undeniable fact that any proposed solution will have a cost. Both natural resources and the resources it takes to resolve environmental problems are scarce. Putting resources into addressing one environmental concern often means diverting them from other uses, including potentially from the resolution of other environmental problems. Consequently the decision as to whether or not the benefits of an environmental policy justify the cost thus represent an inevitable trade-off that demands serious consideration. These tradeoffs could include unintended consequences of misguided or poorly implemented policies, population control measures that impinge on human rights, and attempts to avoid potential environmental consequences that could wind up disproportionately harming the poor (Lewison *et al.* 2019; Hampton 2003; Bruegge *et al.* 2019).

The result of this tension is that environmental policy discussions can become more of a battle between two warring factions than a collaborative effort to understand the full complexities of the situation, taking seriously both the health of the environment and our world's natural resources while also taking seriously the human and social impact. However, as has been seen in earlier chapters, the Bloomington school is not generally inclined to extremes of any sort. Elinor Ostrom and Vincent Ostrom rejected dichotomies, including the belief – false, in their view – that complicated issues like environmental resource management can be resolved through easily identifiable, single-best solutions. As such, the Bloomington school approach to environmental and natural resource policy represents a balanced, democratic alternative to the extremes sometimes observed in other approaches to policy. The Bloomington approach can perhaps best be summed up as one that considers environmental concerns to be real and serious, but also diverse in their specifics, with any given solution potentially having a radically different impact on different communities. Environmental problems are real; the trade-offs inherent to environmental policy are real; and the individuals on the ground are the only ones truly capable of understanding and navigating these trade-offs.

The seriousness with which Elinor Ostrom and other scholars working in the Bloomington school tradition take the stewardship of natural resources is demonstrated through the depth of inquiry into a broad range of environmental issues, including water resource management, forest preservation, the prevention of overfishing, and global warming (E. Ostrom 1990; E. Ostrom & Cox 2010; E. Ostrom 2010b). In addition, their work acknowledges that environmental policy is further complicated by the fact that these difficult decisions, made under conditions of scarcity, are being made in a political arena. By taking an interdisciplinary approach that incorporates political economy into environmental studies, the Bloomington school developed an approach that combines the study of economics and politics to help scholars and policy-makers understand the root cause of these environmental problems and find real, viable ways to address them.

In this chapter, we begin by discussing Elinor Ostrom's research on common-pool resources. Ostrom won the Nobel Prize for her insights into the resolution of the common-pool resource situations which are often at the heart of major environmental problems, and this body of research is a useful lens through which to understand the Bloomington approach. Second, we examine how the Bloomington school approach applies to global environmental concerns, taking policy responses to climate change as an important case. Third, we look at the Bloomington school's analytical grounding in public choice and institutional analysis, focusing on how incentive and knowledge systems affect solutions to environmental problems. The final section concludes with a discussion of the implications for environmental policy-making that emerge from the Bloomington school's decades of research into complex problem-solving.

The environment as a common-pool resource

One of Elinor Ostrom's most significant scholarly contributions has been a radical re-imagination of the way common-pool resources (CPRs) and CPR management are typically thought of in environmental policy. A CPR is a resource or a good that is subtractable but not excludable. This means that, like private goods, one person's consumption of a unit of a resource means that the same unit cannot be utilized by anybody else. However, unlike private goods, it is difficult to exclude people from accessing the resource – hence, the "common" in common-pool resource (E. Ostrom 1990: 30). This combination makes CPRs the hardest case of resource management (Gibson, McKean & E. Ostrom 2000: 6). When subtractability and excludability are considered binary variables – meaning a resource is either subtractable or non-subtractable, and either excludable or non-excludable – there are four possible types of resources, as visualized in Table 7.1.

Table 7.1 Four types of resource

		Subtractability of Use	
		High	*Low*
Difficulty of Excluding Potential Beneficiaries	*High*	Common-pool resources (Groundwater basis, the atmosphere, irrigation systems, fisheries, forests, etc.)	Public goods (peace and security of a community, knowledge, weather forecasts, etc.)
	Low	Private goods (Food, clothing, automobiles, etc.)	Tolls/Club Goods (Theaters, private clubs, daycare centers)

Source: E. Ostrom (2010a).

Common examples of CPRs include oceans, aquifers, fish populations, unmonitored forest, the atmosphere, and pretty much any other major environmental resource you can think of. Consequently, many environmental problems have become associated with CPRs, including climate change, overfishing, deforestation, and groundwater depletion. This association between CPRs and environmental problems has led many to identify CPRs as inherently problematic. From this perspective, a typical recommended solution to a CPR problem is to transform it into either a publicly or a privately owned resource (E. Ostrom 1990: 1–18). Elinor Ostrom's contributions, including her influential book *Governing the Commons*, demonstrate that this traditional perspective overlooks the great diversity in both CPR circumstances and CPR problem solutions. Individuals and communities around the world have demonstrated their ability to effectively design rules to prevent the overdepletion of CPRs without resorting to either privatization or national control. In short, communities are capable of overcoming CPR problems in a much wider range of ways than is commonly recognized. Although the above two-by-two matrix is helpful for simple categorizations, Elinor Ostrom emphasized that subtractability and excludability are not truly binary variables. Instead, they are more accurately thought of as matters of degree. Resources are more or less difficult to exclude people from, and subtractability can take many different forms (Ostrom & Ostrom 1977; E. Ostrom 2010a). For example, the difficulty of preventing someone from fishing in a particular pond will depend on its location, surrounding geological features, and laws and local customs regarding ownership and trespass. And this is just the tip of the complexity iceberg that makes it difficult to fit either CPRs or potential CPR management strategies into tidy, one-size-fits-all boxes.

Knowing that a resource is a CPR does not in itself give policy-makers very much information. In addition to the great variety of resources and physical circumstances that exhibit CPR characteristics, CPRs are especially complex because of the variety of property ownership schemes that can be employed in their management. CPRs can be completely unowned or owned and managed as government property, private property, or community property, and each of these types of ownership could manifest very differently in its particulars (Bromley 1986). Property rights are a relationship among people about the ownership and control of resources, and there are many ways in which those relationships can be defined and modified. Owning a piece of property consists of several potential sub-rights, including the right to access, use, sell, inherit, rent, change, use as capital, and use as collateral. Different forms of property rights may include different combinations of these sub-rights (Anderson & McChesney 2003; Baron 2014).

The Ostroms emphasized the complexity of the world, and argued that each complex issue needs its own unique solution based on the circumstances (E. Ostrom 2007b; E. Ostrom, Janssen & Anderies 2007; E. Ostrom & Cox 2010). For example, the problems confronting fishers are quite different than those confronting irrigators, even though fisheries and irrigation systems both face collective action problems associated with CPRs (E. Ostrom 1990; Schlager & Ostrom 1992; V. Ostrom 1997). The complex nature of most social-environmental problems means that one-size-fits-all solutions are unlikely to work.

CPR management is often perceived as a social dilemma because of the way in which neoclassical models of individual rationality predict it will lead to unfortunate social consequences (Tullock 2005). The classic example of a CPR-related dilemma is a communal pasture for grazing. If you are a rancher near a communal field, it is hard to restrict others from grazing their cattle on the field. Consequently, each rancher has the incentive to graze their cattle as quickly as possible, an effect further exaggerated by the fact that every rancher expects everybody else to do the same. From the perspective of an individual rancher, showing restraint only increases the risk that the food will be gone by the time her cattle are able to graze. However – and this is why the situation is referred to as the *tragedy* of the commons (Hardin 1968) – when everybody grazes their cattle as quickly as they can, the grass in the field will be depleted to the point where it can no longer renew itself, and everybody's cattle starve. Thus, in this model, individual rationality leads to unfortunate social consequences.

By the logic articulated above, common-pool resource situations should all devolve into unmitigated disasters. However, as Elinor Ostrom showed repeatedly in *Governing the Commons*, real-life CPR situations are often not so tragic. The way out of tragedy is, in a word, rules. If ranchers use a communally owned field, they can mutually constrain each other through rules or institutions that align private incentives with their shared goal of not depleting the commons. The specifics of this mutual constraint, which the Ostroms term self-governance, will "depend on the particular configuration of variables related to the physical world, the rules in use, and the attributes of the individual involved in a specific setting" (E. Ostrom 1990: 47). The ranchers could turn the field over to a local government to manage it through laws and regulations, or they could turn the common grazing space into privately owned plots for each rancher. Alternatively, the ranchers could keep the land communally owned and agree on any number of different systems of rules that would be monitored and enforced by community members to avoid the tragedy of the commons.

None of this implies that solving a CPR problem will be easy. Creating a workable set of rules is often difficult and time-consuming. As Elinor Ostrom (1990: 39) argued, "At the most general level, the problem facing CPR appropriators is one of organization: How to change the situation from one which appropriators act independently to one in which they adopt coordinated strategies to obtain higher joint benefits or reduce their joint harm." Further, if people cannot be excluded from the benefits of effective self-governance, but the activities of designing and enforcing good rules for CPR management are costly to perform, each individual has a strong incentive to free ride by letting other people incur the costs. In some cases, a few people may work together to provide the collective good, but since some people will free ride, the group will produce a less-than-optimal amount of the collective good. This free-rider problem means that in addition to addressing the CPR problem itself, communities must also invest time and effort in encouraging adequate participation in the governance process, including by devising rules that punish free riders or reward active participants (E. Ostrom 1990).

Despite the possibility of free-rider problems, the Bloomington school criticized the idea that CPR-related problems required a top-down government solution. A critical insight from the Ostroms' scholarship is that successfully overcoming social dilemmas can only happen when people discover and implement rules that change the incentives of individuals so that they are aligned with social interests. Failure is much more likely to happen when a community cannot agree on what the problem is or what the outcome should be (Tarko 2017: 74). Consequently, the Bloomington approach is at its core deeply democratic in that it insists on deliberation, cooperation, and compromise as important tools for resolving social problems. This is just one of the ways that Elinor Ostrom's work on environmental policy connects to her and Vincent Ostrom's lifetime of inquiry into self-governance and democratic institutions, as we explore in greater detail later (Boettke, Palagashvili & Lemke 2013). Before doing so, however, we look at one particularly important common-pool resource case in greater depth: that of the global climate, and how the Bloomington school approach might be applied to such a vast and complicated problem while retaining its democratic character and commitment to acknowledging the trade-offs involved in all CPR situations.

Global environmental policy from a Bloomington perspective

Climate change is a notoriously difficult collective action problem. Since climate is by its nature a global phenomenon, devising, agreeing on, and implementing a unitary solution seems nearly impossible. The free-rider problems alone are seemingly insurmountable. When we add to this difficulty the fact that both climate change and its proposed correctives have very different impacts on people in different parts of the globe and at different levels of economic development, it's no surprise that the policy debates over climate change are often slow and conflict-ridden.

Perhaps the most direct link between the Bloomington school and the issue of global environmental policy is through their work on polycentric systems. Institutional arrangements that can best overcome the incentive and knowledge problems necessary to solve environmental problems are often polycentric, meaning that the relevant decision-makers are dispersed throughout many autonomous decision centers which are "formally independent but functionally interdependent" (Tarko 2017: 64). In her writings on the topic of climate change, Elinor Ostrom argued that a polycentric approach would be more capable of combating the massive collective action problem of climate change than a one-size-fits-all global solution (E. Ostrom 2012). A polycentric approach to climate change allows public and private institutions to experiment at different levels. This experimentation then allows people to develop different ways of weighing the costs and benefits of different kinds of approaches to combat climate change. In particular, Elinor Ostrom (2014b: 99) argued, "To solve climate change in the long run, the day-to-day activities of individuals, families, firms, communities, and governments at multiple levels – particularly those in the more developed world – will need to change substantially."

Although Elinor Ostrom unfortunately died before it was enacted, the logic of her argument can be illustrated through discussion of the 2015 Paris Agreement, one of the most recent attempts to create a large-scale plan to combat climate change. The 195 signatory countries agreed to three main goals. First, participating countries agreed to keep the global average temperature rise below 2°C and to limit temperature increase to 1.5°C above pre-industrial levels. Second, the agreement states that countries will increase their adaptability to the adverse impacts of climate change. Third, the agreement allows financial flows to achieve low greenhouse gas emissions and climate-resilient development (United Nations 2015). Although the United States left and then rejoined the Paris Agreement, it remains one of the largest efforts to address climate change at the global scale (Shear 2017).

The logic of self-governance in a polycentric system holds two important implications for such large-scale agreements for the management of CPR situations. First, the Bloomington school approach suggests that global solutions are unlikely to succeed unless they are accompanied by national, regional, and local solutions to the same problems. Polycentric systems have many decision-makers and multiple, overlapping layers of decision authority. In the international arena, countries cooperate and compete among themselves. There is no world government that can force countries to do one thing or another (V. Ostrom 1991a). This means that creating long-term solutions to climate change involves changing the day-to-day activities of individuals, companies, communities, and governments at multiple levels. Even without formal US participation in the Paris Agreement, Americans – working individually and together in industry and in non-profit organizations – can find innovative solutions through technology and institutions, including by adopting at a more local level the goals and prescriptions of the Paris Agreement (Cooper 2018). Elinor Ostrom wrote, "If only one country in the world tried to solve climate change – even one of the wealthier countries of the world – this would be a grossly inadequate effort;" however, she also noted, "Waiting for a single worldwide 'solution' to emerge from global negotiations is also problematic" (E. Ostrom 2014b: 98). Climate change policy must be polycentric because there has been a "decades-long failure at an international level to reach agreement on efficient, fair, and enforceable reduction of greenhouse gas emissions" (E. Ostrom 2014b: 99).

Second, diverse contexts require diverse solutions. These solutions can only be discovered if learning is allowed to take place in a decentralized, democratic way. Enabling localities to adopt a variety of different approaches will help us to learn which sets of actions, technologies, and institutions are the most effective at reducing the threats of climate change (E. Ostrom 2014b). Individual localities can experiment, and both they and all those watching have the benefit of learning from the result of those experiments. Research conducted in laboratory settings or in the context of an advanced economy will only go so far towards addressing the problems that a severely resource constrained community may face in their attempts to curtail emissions. As such, creating the maximum amount of opportunity for communities to be able to learn for themselves and from each other is of particular importance.

Article 7 of the Paris Agreement nominally gives credence to a polycentric approach, stating that the signatory countries "recognize that adaptation is a global challenge faced by all with local, subnational, national, regional and international dimensions." Article 7 also states that adaptation action should follow "the best available science and, as appropriate, traditional knowledge, knowledge of indigenous peoples and local knowledge systems." Article 11 asserts adaptation and mitigation actions need to include national, subnational, and local levels of governance (United Nations 2015). However, merely stating that a system needs to be polycentric is very different from finding a workable polycentric solution. A Bloomington school perspective on institutions prioritizes participant buy-in and democratic decision processes as critical to being able to generate effective solutions (V. Ostrom 1997; E. Ostrom & V. Ostrom 2004; Aligica 2019; Levi 2010). As Vincent Ostrom (1991a: 58) stated, people will need to "draw upon a science and art of association in learning how to put polycentric systems of order together." Polycentric systems are often self-organizing and democratic, which means that a command from global or national leaders to find a polycentric solution may not work. People on the ground must feel that they are a part of the decision-making process and that goals reflect their priorities, otherwise a polycentric solution will not emerge.

Solving global environmental problems is a puzzle with many pieces. As Elinor Ostrom (1998a: 17) argues, "National governments are too small to govern the global commons and too big to handle smaller scale problems." Institutions made by and adapted to local conditions can be pieces to solving a larger global puzzle:

> The advantage of a polycentric approach is that it encourages experimentation by multiple actors, as well as the development of methods for assessing the benefits and costs of particular strategies adopted in one setting and comparing these with results obtained in other settings

… Rather than only a global effort, it would be better to self-consciously adopt a polycentric approach to the problem of climate change in order to gain benefits at multiple scales as well as to encourage experimentation and learning from diverse policies adopted at multiple scales.

(E. Ostrom 2010b: 555–6).

One of the defining features of polycentricity is its adaptability to problems at various scales. Since polycentric systems are divided among many decision-makers, they are better equipped to address issues at a variety of different scopes and scales. Polycentricity means that citizens can fix a wide variety of problems by organizing together in the public and private spheres and at different levels (E. Ostrom, interviewed by Aligica 2003; Tarko 2017: 30–31). Polycentric systems allow for small-scale administrative units to organize when necessary to address some larger scale problems. For example, a few towns may create a temporary administrative unit to overcome an environmental problem that they share. Or, a few states may create a temporary administrative unit to solve a common problem. This approach may not work for every problem that arises, but it is something for policy-makers to consider to take advantage of the benefits of polycentricity (Tarko 2017: 41).

The concept of polycentricity is especially important for environmental problems because polycentric systems tend to be more resilient. This resiliency can take many forms. For example, in polycentric systems, the multiple centers of decision-making means that errors only affect a small part of the system, not the entire system. This means polycentric systems are better able to absorb the shock from one mistake without impacting the entire system. Polycentric systems may also recover faster from problems because people in the various parts of the system are able to experiment with a diversity of solutions. Trying many different approaches to solve the same problem facilitates learning because many different experiments can be done simultaneously. In a monocentric system, only one solution can be tried at a time, and if the solution fails, it could mean disaster for the whole system.

Polycentric and monocentric systems also have different properties in terms of the extent to which entrepreneurship in policy will be encouraged and entrepreneurial solutions adopted. In polycentric systems, there are opportunities for entrepreneurship at all different levels in the system. Not only can ideas be proposed at different levels, but different decision-makers can respond to them differently. This means a larger number of opportunities for learning and experimentation. Successful ideas can be imitated and improved upon in other areas of the system (Tarko 2017: 118). In monocentric systems, changes can only be adopted at the highest level, which means that there are inherently fewer opportunities for entrepreneurs and innovators to have their ideas considered.

Therefore, while broad, systematic changes can be easier to make in monocentric systems, those changes will be made in an environment where policy-makers and policy entrepreneurs have had less opportunity to learn what works.

Another benefit of polycentric systems is that viable solutions can emerge without top-down plans or large-scale coordinated efforts. Polycentric systems may seem chaotic because they include many activities and policies occurring in both the private and public sectors at multiple scales and at different times. For example, policy makers, scholars, and pundits disagree about the best way to address climate change, such as cap-and-trade policies or carbon taxes. Other disagreements arise over how much funding should be allocated and who that funding should be allocated to. Despite what appears to be chaos at first glance, a viable solution can emerge spontaneously from a polycentric approach because of the combination of the various approaches and policies. As Elinor Ostrom (2014b: 116) argued, "The likelihood of developing an effective, efficient, and fair system to reduce greenhouse gas emission that can be rapidly initiated at the global level appears to be very low. Given the severity of the threat, simply waiting for resolution of these issues at a global level, without trying out policies at multiple scales because they lack a global scale, is not a reasonable stance." Thus, we can leverage complex, multi-level systems to cope with a complex, multi-level problem.

An objection to managing any environmental problem through a polycentric system is that it could lead to redundancy, with multiple units in the polycentric system performing the same function. Indeed, it is the case that the possibility of multiple units duplicating the same efforts and investments is an inherent feature of polycentric systems. Polycentric systems also have the potential to move more slowly and less decisively than monocentric systems, and they by design lack the capability for a single powerful decision-maker to impose and enforce a solution (Coyne & Lemke 2011). However, under the right circumstances, redundancy can be a productive feature of a system rather than a bug. For example, there are hundreds of companies that make shoes. This might sound wasteful, but in reality, multiple shoe producers mean not only greater diversity, but also competitive pressure that keeps shoes affordable and greater assurance that shoes will still be available even if one producer meets with misfortune. In the scientific community, redundancy is important because multiple people can make new discoveries and verify or disprove old ones.

In the realm of government, redundancy can be beneficial because it encourages innovation, as well as providing a protection against institutional failures. Elinor Ostrom (1976: 8) argued,

> In an imperfect world where institutions are filled with weakness, redundancy in organizational arrangements may prevent the failure of

any one set of decision rules from seriously handicapping us, as citizens, in accomplishing some of our goals. A multiplicity of arrangements also enables us to test the relative performance of different types of institutional practices and thus evolve new solutions to different kinds of problems.

Polycentric systems have flaws, but they may be the best option to overcome complex environmental problems. As Elinor Ostrom (2010b: 552) said elsewhere, "No governance system is perfect, but polycentric systems have considerable advantages given their mechanisms for mutual monitoring, learning, and adaptation of better strategies over time."

Another important tool from the Bloomington school that has potential to be productively engaged in environmental policy-making are the design principles, identified over decades of research as the most important factors in determining whether a system of rules will be effective and sustainable (E. Ostrom 1990: 180; Cox *et al.* 2010). Each of these principles are general, broad considerations for policy-makers to consider when creating or reforming institutions. The principles are not simply a recipe that can be used to make workable rules and institutions for social cooperation, but they can help analysts and policy-makers understand which institutional arrangements are more likely to succeed.

- Are there clear boundaries between legitimate users and non-users of a good? Are there clear boundaries for the resource that is being protected versus not protected?
- Are the rules and institutions tailored to the specific cultural and environmental context in which they are implemented?
- Do the people in a society perceive that the benefits and costs to various actors in a society are fairly distributed?
- Are monitors and enforcers of rules held accountable for their actions?
- Are rule-breakers punished according to the seriousness, frequency, and context of the offense?
- Do people feel that conflict resolution provides decisions perceived as fair? Do governmental authorities allow local people to devise their own institutions?
- Are social institutions formed in polycentric layers?

When communities keep all these design principles in mind, there is a much higher likelihood that rules and institutions will be robust and resilient. If some of the design principles are missing, rules and institutions may still be workable, but they are more fragile and prone to failure. If too many of the design principles are missing, there is a higher likelihood that rules and institutions will fail to achieve the desired goal.

Institutional solutions to incentive problems and knowledge problems

The Ostroms rejected the presupposition that centralized government control was always necessary to solve environmental problems. The people facing the problem often have better incentives and knowledge to find solutions than outside experts who are familiar with the abstract model that a problem is most like, but unfamiliar with the particular manifestation (E. Ostrom 2005a: ch. 9; Tarko 2017: 16). Further, for a solution to be sustainable, it needs to be compatible with the lives of the people who are expected to change their behavior. Consequently, real-world evidence shows that communities around the globe have often devised rules and institutions for themselves that have solved environmental problems in a self-sustaining and self-enforcing way (E. Ostrom 1990, 2010a).

This emphasis on the importance of community-created rules challenges the assumption that people are trapped helplessly in social dilemmas. If government policy-makers believe that people cannot get out of social dilemmas by themselves, then the only option is to bring in an outside force. Government intervention becomes essential. However, if people are innovative and entrepreneurial, then they can create new rules and institutions to overcome social dilemmas (E. Ostrom 1990: 14). When we factor in the real-world implications of creativity, innovation, and entrepreneurship, the role of government is fundamentally different in solving complex social-environmental problems (E. Ostrom 1998a). Rather than presuming the necessity of governmental intervention, the analytical problem becomes one of analyzing the comparative performance of community and external problem solving.

The foundations of the Bloomington school are based in public choice theory, which assumes that voters, politicians, and bureaucrats act to pursue diverse and at times conflicting goals, for reasons that are determined individually and subjectively (V. Ostrom 1993; Boettke & Snow 2014). This idea is sometimes described as behavioral symmetry; in short, the idea is that people are people wherever they go, flaws and all. Acknowledging this human-ness is critically important to being able to understand behavior in political contexts, making public choice theory particularly useful for public policy analysis (Tullock 2004).

Elinor Ostrom emphasized the fact that solving environmental problems means that scholars and policy-makers must understand how real-world institutions in practice enhance or restrict the building of mutual trust, reciprocity, and reputations. Trust, reciprocity, and reputation form a core relationship that affects the level of social cooperation. These three concepts are interrelated and positively reinforce each other. If a society has high levels of trust, reciprocity, and reputation, then the members of that society will cooperate more frequently, and there will be higher net benefits resulting from the cooperation (E. Ostrom 1998a). When groups lack trust in one another or they lack low-cost means of communication, their rules and institutions for overcoming social dilemmas are more likely to fail. Trust and communication are two key components for institutional innovation and the creation of monitoring and sanctioning rules. The creative, entrepreneurial talents of local communities have a higher chance of success when there is a culture of trust and communication (V. Ostrom 1997; E. Ostrom 1998a). Building trust and finding focal points for coordination facilitates institutions that can lead to continued cooperation over time. Further, trust, communication, and coordination are necessary factors to make rules and institutions self-enforcing, meaning that the people within an institutional environment are incentivized to take actions that preserve rather than erode the institution (Tarko 2017: 100). If rules and institutions are not self-enforcing, individuals have an incentive to break the rules for their own personal gain. People will then use their creativity and entrepreneurial spirit to find ways of breaking rules instead of upholding them.

One of the most important insights from the Bloomington school is the distinction between rules-in-form and rules-in-use. Rules-in-form are the way that rules look on paper, but in the real world, there are often a different set of rules that govern how people actually behave. "Working rules may or may not closely resemble the formal laws that are expressed in legislation, administrative regulations, and court decisions ... In many [common-pool resource] settings, the working rules used by appropriators may differ considerably from legislative, administrative, or court regulations" (E. Ostrom 1990: 51). People who are attempting to solve complex social-environmental problems may simultaneously follow de facto as well as *de jure* rules. Thus, analyzing people's behavior and shaping public policy become tricky because of the complicated nature of how rules unfold in the real world (E. Ostrom 1990: 55).

Even with trust and communication, people may make mistakes. Humans are, of course, fallible. As such, a critical question for policy is whether or not a particular rule, law, or practice is robust and adaptable enough for people to be able to learn from their mistakes. If institutional incentives discourage people from learning about and fixing mistakes, the society will be less likely to successfully overcome social-environmental problems (Ostrom & Ostrom 2004). Elinor Ostrom (1990: 14) wrote, "Instead of presuming that optimal institutional solutions can be designed easily and imposed at low-costs by external authorities, I argue that 'getting the institutions right' is a difficult, time-consuming, conflict-invoking process."

The importance of getting the institutions right led Vincent and Elinor Ostrom to argue that mainstream policy analysts should avoid over-simplifying the policy choice into either "governments" or "markets." These binary concepts are not very useful and can be misleading because they neglect real-world nuances (V. Ostrom 1997). Instead, the Ostroms argued that the most effective systems would often be hybrids of private and public, specifically tailored to fit local cultures and environments. Such hybrid, community-driven solutions have often been used to overcome seemingly insurmountable problems (Tarko 2017: 82).

The key to understanding the nature of the public–private collaborations the Ostroms had in mind lies in the distinction between top-down and bottom-up action. Even when collective action is necessary to solve an environmental problem, that collective action need not take the form of a top-down, bureaucratically-implemented solution. Instead, governance can be bottom-up, carried out through a process within which individuals and local groups – like civic associations, businesses, community non-profits, and local governments – cooperate, compete, and mediate arguments over how best to approach the resolution of problems facing their community (V. Ostrom 1991b). Local people directly involved in these institutions and contracts have the strongest incentive to monitor each other if they fail to live up to the rules and agreements. A government regulatory agency is not self-enforcing in the same way. Regulatory agencies must hire their own monitors to make sure that rules and agreements are upheld, creating abundant opportunity for principal–agent problems. Further, given their greater distance from the social-environmental problem, a central authority in a regulatory agency is less likely to have the time-and-place information needed to exercise good judgement. For example, a government regulator is unlikely to have accurate estimates of "both the carrying capacity of a [common-pool resource] and the appropriate fines to induce cooperative behavior" (E. Ostrom 1990: 17–18).

If large-scale cooperation is determined to be an important part of solving a particular environmental or resource problem, then organizations across many different communities might work together, and they might even enlist state and federal governments to facilitate coordination. For example, sometimes local communities cannot cope with rapid environmental changes because they do not have enough time to adjust their local institutions to address the new problems. In such cases, a community may be locked into suboptimal outcomes. If those situations arise, external authorities can facilitate cooperation on larger scales so that communities can better cope with new problems (E. Ostrom 1990: 21). Government authorities may have important roles to play in addressing environmental issues, but government authorities must also acknowledge that they have imperfect knowledge and may create perverse incentives. The critical point is that government is not presumed either necessary or unnecessary, but instead involved to the extent that individuals on the ground determine that government action is the most effective way to proceed.

Elinor Ostrom, combining public choice theory with institutional economics, argued that "advice to centralize control … is based on assumptions concerning the accuracy of information, monitoring capabilities, sanctioning reliability, and zero costs of administration" (E. Ostrom 1990: 10). In other words, whether or not state or federal involvement makes sense depends on the specifics of how that particular government can reasonably be expected to actually operate. When these institutional specifics are not considered carefully, politicians or bureaucrats may attempt to force top-down solutions on smaller communities out of a misguided surety in the superiority of their capabilities. For example, politicians or bureaucrats may lack the on-the-ground knowledge about the scale and scope of collective action problems, which means that the policies meant to address the problem may miss the mark. Bureaucracies may also lack the capability to monitor the implementation of a policy properly, rendering the policy largely ineffective. The administration of government policies is often costly, and when costs are high, enforcement may become inconsistent and subject to favoritism or discrimination.

The Bloomington school's insights about the differences between local, bottom-up decision-making processes and large-scale, top-down decision-making processes suggests that government officials and policy analysts need to be intellectually humble about the extent to which they can design effective policies:

> [O]fficials and policy analysts who presume that they have the right design can be dangerous. They are likely to assume that citizens are short-sighted and motivated only by extrinsic benefits and costs. Somehow, the officials and policy analysis assume that they have different motivation and can find optimal policy because they are not directly involved in the problem ... All too often, these 'optimal' policies have Leviathan-like characteristics to them.   (E. Ostrom 2005a: 256)

This danger is one of the reasons why figuring out the proper role for government in environmental policy-making is complex. Elinor Ostrom (2010a) argued that we should move away from presuming that government must solve all environmental problems, but we cannot neglect the important role that government has to play in solving some of those problems. The most effective solutions are likely to be those where national officials, local officials, non-governmental organizations, and local groups of citizens cooperate to find the most workable and effective solutions.

Overall, the Bloomington school's research has found that people in a wide variety of settings have the capacity to overcome dilemmas. The research has shown that societies create effective governance far more frequently than most other social scientists presumed. Two of the most important factors for whether a group would overcome a social-environmental dilemma depended first, on the structure of the resource itself, and second, whether the rules-in-use were linked effectively to the resource's structure (Blomquist et al. 1994).

Concluding words for policy-makers

The idea of democratic self-governance is fundamental to the Bloomington school. Democracy, in the Ostroms' view, is not just a system of voting; it is a system of how people relate to one another as equals. A society of free and responsible individuals is the purpose of a self-governing, democratic society. Citizens have the ability and responsibility to set up their own institutions to solve collective action problems. Consequently, one of the reasons the Ostroms advised against increasing the scale and scope of national government was because it was displacing activities that had previously been the responsibility of voluntary civic associations and state and local governments (Bish 2014). Elinor Ostrom explained, "My hope is ... that the examination and analysis of [common-pool resources] in the field, in the experimental laboratory, and in theory, contribute to the development of an empirically valid theory of self-organization and self-governance" (E. Ostrom, interviewed by Aligica 2003).

When people are given the ability to engage in self-governance, they can harness the gains from peaceful social cooperation and productive specialization. Communities can and have devised a wide range of institutional solutions to environmental collective action problems that often contain a mix of private action and government action. The Ostroms provided a diverse set of evidence that top-down government solutions are not necessary to overcome environmental problems because local people often have the knowledge and the incentives to make a successful, self-enforcing system.

There are many implications to the Bloomington school's approach that can help solve policy problems into the future. Using the concept of polycentricity and the design principles, government officials and regular citizens can devise ways to create self-governing institutions that help resolve collective action problems without the limitations of one-size-fits-all government policies. New environmental problems emerge every day, so scholars and policy-makers should seek for the most effective and efficient way to address them. The Bloomington school's approach provides the framework for figuring out what the most effective and efficient ways are. The Bloomington school's approach adds the nuance and realism that is necessary for tackling even the most daunting problems. Policy-makers can look for ways to decentralize decision-making authority to lower levels and allow polycentric solutions to emerge. If policy-makers can create multiple jurisdictions with considerable autonomy at the local level, they can allow for more simultaneous experimentation within those separate jurisdictions. "[B]ecause polycentric systems have overlapping units, information about what has worked well in one setting can be transmitted to other units. And when small systems fail, there are larger systems to call upon – and vice versa" (E. Ostrom, interviewed by Aligica 2003: 13).

This reasoning has important implications for commonly accepted policy wisdom. For instance, it is often taken for granted that global problems require global organizations to resolve them. However, Elinor Ostrom criticized the idea that global environmental problems require a global administrative and regulatory body. She argues that an alternative way of thinking involves organizing the incentive structures at lower levels that would generate the desired global public good as an emergent outcome. "An important lesson is that simply recommending a single governance unit to solve global collective-action problems – because of global impacts – needs to be seriously rethought" (E. Ostrom 2010b: 552). Policy-makers may be tempted by a pretense of knowledge where they assume that they have the knowledge necessary to comprehend and plan an entire social organization (Hayek 1988, 1989). This potentially dangerous line of thinking can turn even the most well-meaning policy-maker into a social engineer where people in a society can be treated like "pieces upon a chess-board" (Smith [1759] 1793: 77).

Policy-makers would do well to remember that people are innovative, entrepreneurial, diverse, and constantly changing. People with on-the-ground knowledge and experience can facilitate polycentric solutions to environmental problems, and they can do this if policy-makers give them the freedom to experiment with different institutional arrangements. With this freedom, societies can leverage the power of spontaneous order. Policy-makers must take care that too much conscious planning does not actually impede the solution to environmental problems, and they must acknowledge their own limits. Based on the evidence from other polycentric systems, outcomes are likely to be better able to cope with change and less subject to political corruption (Tarko 2017).

8

LEARNING FROM THE SOCIALIST CALCULATION DEBATE: IS EFFICIENCY IN PUBLIC ECONOMICS POSSIBLE?

Peter J. Boettke

Vincent Ostrom's *The Meaning of Democracy and the Vulnerability of Democracies* (1997) is in many ways his scholarly manifesto, and as such provides a window into his world view and the scholarly task he set for himself throughout his career. Critical to his effort was a quest to understand the human condition, and in particular the conditions that would make possible a self-governing democratic society. Democracy for Ostrom was not primarily about the mechanisms of political selection, that would no doubt be part of the machinery that would be analyzed, but about ways of relating to one another as free, equal, and dignified individuals. Citizens in a democratic society would need to shoulder the burden of the "cares of thinking" and the "troubles of living", as Tocqueville put it, in order to be capable of self-governance. But institutions of governance must also be structured in such a manner that they exhibit neither dominance, nor acts discriminatory. "Democratic ways of life," Ostrom tells us at the very beginning of his book, "turn on self-organizing and self-governing capabilities rather than presuming that something called 'the Government' governs" (1997: 3–4). Democratic societies are at risk, Ostrom states clearly, when relationships are grounded on the "principles of command and control rather than on principles of self-responsibility in self-governing communities of relationships" (*ibid.*: 4).

It is often forgotten in the aftermath of Elinor Ostrom's Nobel Prize, how their respective projects shared this fundamental commitment to the exploration of self-governing democratic society. They embarked from the mid-1960s onward on their "long polycentric journey" as she put it on more than one occasion. This included not just the more philosophical explorations of Vincent's meaning of democracy, and the relationship between political theory and policy analysis, but the nuts and bolts of institutional arrangements that made self-governance possible even in the face of difficult initial conditions. This was most famously seen in the acts of public entrepreneurship associated with managing common-pool resources, but it was also evident in the local provision of public goods such as roads, police, schools, etc. There is a necessary machinery that must match with the governance of democratic societies. And this led them to jointly and separately explore the various types of goods not produced in the market economy that must be produced in order for individuals to live better together than they ever could in isolation of one another.

Stating the mere fact of the desirability of such goods, does not necessarily inform us about how these goods will be produced, what goods will be produced, and for whom these goods will be produced. The answer provided by the price system in a market economy is by definition not available in the situations examined by the Ostroms. Instead, the very process of working through collective action is expected to provide the required guidance. But can we be so sure?

Vincent Ostrom raises the question, which I will focus on, deep in *The Meaning of Democracy and the Vulnerability of Democracies* (1997: 207–208) in his discussion of technical feasibility and economic feasibility (or the better term I would suggest would be viability). Answering can it be done must be followed by asking whether it is worth doing. And that leads to the deeper question about operational feasibility. Whatever endeavor we are discussing, whether in private or public choices, requires that we think through carefully these feasibility questions. Resources will be expended to achieve goals, and if we don't sort out from the array of technologically feasible projects those that will be economically and operationally feasible, we run the risk of destroying the viability of social order. The idea of viability without feasibility is a non-starter.

The famous socialist economic calculation debate touched directly on this question of technical, economic and operational viability. What monetary calculation does in a market economy is provide a guide to decision-makers in sorting out from the array of technologically feasible projects those that are economically and operationally feasible. This is accomplished through relative prices and the accounting of profit and loss. This insight owes its origins to the writings of Ludwig von Mises. But Ostrom picked up where Mises left off.

Mises in both his essay "Economic Calculation in the Socialist Commonwealth" and his subsequent book *Socialism: An Economic and Sociological Analysis* admits to the limits of monetary calculation. Monetary calculation cannot price, Mises states, the beauty of a mountain or a waterfall. But within its limits, the critical role that monetary calculation plays within an economic system is all that one could practically demand of it. It enables economic actors to sort out among the technologically feasible those projects that are economically and operationally feasible. What about though, those projects beyond the limits of monetary calculation? Can we find some mechanism that accomplishes what monetary calculation does when we don't have recourse to it?

In this chapter, I will discuss the implications for public economics of the socialist calculation debate. As Vincent Ostrom puts it: "If people are to rule, members of society should know how to govern themselves." They cannot assume that government knows how to exercise dominion over society and direct it in the most desirable path. If the strategic opportunism initiated by command and control is allowed to run rampant, "the cumulative result would be the trampling of civilization underfoot." Hope only resides in individuals learning to become citizens working with other citizens in open and free relationships and thus becoming capable of self-governing. "The challenge in democratic societies," he states, "is to extend the horizons of knowledge and skills by learning to work with others in ways that enhance error-correcting capabilities, rather than fabricating patterns of deception and self-deception to tranquillize, tease, and terrorize the mind into states of helplessness" (1997: 271).

The institutional framework determines the outcomes of the invisible hand

There is much confusion about the essential message of Adam Smith and classical political economy. Contrary to popular opinion, Smith never argued that individuals pursuing their self-interest will always and everywhere result in an outcome that served the public interest. Instead, his argument explicitly stated that the individual pursuit of self-interest within a specific set of institutional arrangements – namely well-defined and enforced private property rights – would only produce such a result. Absent that institutional context, the pursuit of self-interest will not result in serving the public interest, but would more likely than not produce socially dysfunctional and destructive outcomes. Consider Smith's comparative institutional analysis of both college teaching in Oxford, where the professors were paid out of an endowment, and those teaching in Glasgow, where the professors were paid by direct student fees. In both environments, the professors were pursuing their self-interest, but the manifestation of that self-interest and the consequences of that self-interest was institutionally contingent.

The great British economist Lionel Robbins argued that: "You cannot understand their attitude to any important concrete measure of policy unless you understand their belief with regard to the nature and effects of the system of spontaneous-cooperation". The system of spontaneous-cooperation, or economic freedom, does not come about absent a "firm framework of law and order". The "invisible hand," according to the classical economists, "is not the hand of some god or some natural agency independent of human effort; it is the hand of the lawgiver, the hand which withdraws from the sphere of the pursuit of self-interest those possibilities which do not harmonize with the public good" (Robbins 1965: 12, 56). In other words, the market mechanism works as described in the theory of the "invisible hand" because an institutional configuration was provided for by a prior non-market decision-making process. The correct institutions of governance must be in place for economic life to take place (within those institutions).

Social life always exists inside of an *institutional framework*. Whether social life exhibits Adam Smith's human propensity to "truck, barter, exchange" or Thomas Hobbes's human capacity to "pillage and plunder" is a function of the institutional framework within which social life is played out. It is the *framework* that determines the marginal benefit/marginal cost calculus that individuals face in pursuing sociability. If the rewards for productive specialization and peaceful cooperation exceed those of predation and confiscation, then the Smithian expansion of commercial and civil society will follow. But if the calculus tends the other way, then the Hobbesian depiction of life as being "nasty, brutish and short" will materialize. As Elinor Ostrom stressed in *Governing the Commons* (1990: 22) "institutional details" matter, and that the biggest errors in social analysis might follow from the habit of pursuing "institution-free" analysis.

The pursuit of productive specialization and peaceful cooperation requires security and stability of possession, the keeping of promises, and the transference of property by consent (see Hume [1739] 2000: Bk III, Pt 2, §II–IV, 311–31). Where property is insecure, promises aren't kept, and violent taking characterizes the social situation; human sociability will be truncated and the Hobbesian propensities will prevail. On the other hand, when the social situation is characterized by property, contract and consent, the Smithian propensities triumph and peace and prosperity prevail.

Smith's argument in *The Wealth of Nations* ([1776] 1976) must be understood in this two-stage manner. Yes, the greatest improvements in the material conditions of mankind are due to the refinement in the division of labor. But, as Smith pointed out, the division of labor is limited by the extent of the market. The process of development follows from the expansion of the market, and thus the refinement of the division of labor. That fundamental cause of development, however, are the ideas that give rise to the *institutional framework* that in turn makes savings and capital accumulation safe. As Adam Smith ([1776] 1976: Vol. II, Bk V, 232) put it:

> It is only under the shelter of the civil magistrate that the owner of that valuable property, which is acquired by the labour of many years, or perhaps of many successive generations, can sleep a single night in security. He is at all times surrounded by unknown enemies, whom, though he never provoked, he can never appease, and from whose

injustice he can be protected only by the powerful arm of the civil magistrate continually held up to chastise it. The acquisition of valuable and extensive property, therefore, necessarily requires the establishment of civil government.

This is the foundation for Smith's "tolerable administration of justice."

The early neoclassical economists in the wake of the marginal revolution in value theory did not see their task as all that radically different from Smith's. They simply had a new set of analytical tools to explain value, exchange and productive activity *within* the market economy. Many of the early neoclassical theorists, such as Alfred Marshall and Frank Knight, possessed a deep appreciation of the institutional framework within which economic activity takes place. However, most theorists of this period simply began their analysis by assuming well-defined and strictly enforced property rights, and then proceeded from that starting point. In other words, the institutional framework was fixed and given for analysis, and not an object of analytical study.

This "given" aspect of the institutional framework is critical because it soon led to the framework being ignored in analysis altogether as economic thought evolved in the twentieth century. This ignoring of institutions was most evident in the socialist calculation debate between Mises, Hayek and Robbins on the one side, and Oskar Lange, Abba Lerner and Abram Bergson on the other. The Mises, Hayek and Robbins side of the dispute stressed not merely the role of relative prices in the coordination of economic activity, but the institutional framework that made possible the configuration of the price system in the first place. As Hayek put it in the heat of the debate: "The fact is that it has never been denied by anybody, except socialists, that these formal principles [optimality conditions] *ought* to apply to a socialist society, and the question raised by Mises and others was not whether they ought to apply but whether they could in practice be applied in the absence of a market" (Hayek 1948: 183).

In the analysis of the market system, prices have a place of pride. Economic analysis flows from the recognition of scarcity and the fact that all choices are made within given constraints. For analytical tractability, the institutional context can be taken as part of the background conditions. Thus, during the first decades of the neoclassical refinements of economic theory, the analysis proceeded with a given institutional environment of fully defined and strictly enforced private property rights and freedom of contract embodied in the rule of law.

My point is simple: the classical political economists and the early heirs to that intellectual tradition saw economic activity as embedded within an institutional context and never as acontextual. Smith "derived" his famous "invisible hand" theorem from the self-interest postulate *via* institutional analysis.[1] The analytical devil was to be found in the institutional details.

Mises (1920) had issued the challenge that, due to the inability to engage in rational economic calculation, socialist planning could not deliver on its stated goals of rationalizing production. Absent private ownership in the means of production, Mises argued, there would be no prices established on the market that could form the basis for rational economic calculation. Economic calculation enables market decision-makers to sort out from an array of technologically feasible production projects those which are economically viable from those that are not. Economic calculation is a waste-identifier and eliminator. By definition, the socialist aspiration of the rationalization of production requires that the waste of resources and errors in investment be eliminated. Mises's criticism was decisive and cut to the core of the promise of socialism.

This was also purely a point of positive economics. Mises did not question the socialists' ends. At the time of his original article, socialism meant something – the rationalization of production through the abolition of private property and commodity production. Mises simply asked if abolition of private property and commodity production was coherent with the rationalization of production, and he demonstrated it was not. Technological efficiency is not enough to answer the economic question of the efficiency of resource use. Prices without property rights are an illusion.

In an ironic twist of argument, Lange (1936: 55) actually accused Mises of being an institutionalist for making this point. But the fact that Lange said this should alert you to the changes that were taking place in the economic theorist's self-understanding from 1900 to 1930. Since math is math and institutions don't matter, if someone invokes institutional differences to explain comparative performance, then he has failed to appreciate the universal nature of economic theory. But to Mises, it was precisely the universality of economic theory that enabled him to understand why institutions matter for economic performance.[2]

Monetary economic calculation works by constantly revealing errors in decision-making, and the complex apparatus of market signals will continually prod and cajole participants to make less erroneous decisions than before. Adjustment and adaptation is unending in the market as the production plans of some must mesh with the consumption demands of others for the advanced coordination of economic activities through time.

---

1. See *Living Economics* (Boettke 2012), where I make the distinction between "mainline" economics and "mainstream" economics. Also see Boettke, Haeffele-Balch and Storr (2016), Mitchell and Boettke (2017).

2. Also see Lange's (1937: 127) theory that incentive arguments belong to the field of sociology and not economy theory.

But what happens when we move outside the realm of the market economy? Public administration begins where the realm of rational economic calculation ends. As Ludwig von Mises ([1949] 1966: 311) puts it: "Where economic calculation is unfeasible, bureaucratic methods are indispensable". To put this in a concrete way, the rules of bureaucratic management are going to have to attempt to do for governmental services what property, prices and profit and loss does within the market setting. And, make no mistake, governmental decision-makers are going to have to weigh trade-offs, and they will face – however imperfectly – budget constraints. Again, as Mises ([1949] 1966: 309) points out: "There is no doubt that the services rendered by the police department of the City of New York could be considerably improved by trebling the budgetary allocation. But the question is whether or not this improvement would be considerable enough to justify either the restriction of the services rendered by other departments – e.g., those of the department of sanitation – or the restriction of the private consumption of the taxpayers." But *how* are government decision-makers going to accomplish this?

The allocation of resources in non-market settings

It is precisely at this point where Vincent Ostrom's work on public administration enters into the analysis. To stress the point, public administration begins where the realm of economic calculation through the market process ends. So how precisely are public choices to be made in a way that has any semblance of a procedure that enables them to sort from the socially desirable to the technologically feasible to the economically viable? As Vincent Ostrom puts it in *The Meaning of Democracy* (1997: 207):

> Questions of technical feasibility at an engineering level turn on a response to a question of whether alternatives can be brought to realization: Can it be done? Technical feasibility, in turn, depends on establishing economic feasibility: Is it worth doing? Another aspect pertains to operational feasibility: Can the necessary resources and efforts be mobilized to bring an endeavor to realization?

The market economy and the price system, as we previously discussed, has a built-in mechanism for answering these questions through profit-and-loss accounting, and the entire process of rational economic calculation based on monetary prices. Operational feasibility in this sense entails understanding financial viability of the enterprise. By definition, though, public administration cannot rely on the market mechanism to direct the allocation of resources. As Vincent and Elinor Ostrom put it:

> A decision to buy a particular good or service reflects willingness to forgo all other opportunities for which the money could have been used. An expression of demand in a market system always includes reference to what is forgone as well as what is purchased. The articulation of preferences in the public sector often fails to take account of forgone opportunities. ... Because most public goods and services are financed through a process of taxation involving no choice, optimal levels of expenditure are difficult to establish.   (E. & V. Ostrom 1991: 185)

Alternative processes of coordinating the supply and demand of public goods must be found and the organization of collective action within any given public space. Any theory of public finance must postulate a basic political theory from which it commences its analysis, precisely because the question of the scale and scope of governmental activities must be addressed prior to determining governmental expenditures. In delineating the basic functions and responsibilities of government, the rule of thumb should be that the size of the externality to be dealt with through collective action should match with the decision unit. Simply put, we rely on local government to pick up our garbage, but national government to provide military protection from foreign invasion. This is a core proposition of federalism, and critical to understanding public finance theory. And, to avoid the problem of the "fiscal commons" in our public finances, the institutions of governance should be arranged such that the revenue decision is not to be divorced from the expenditure decision. If it is divorced, then political decision-makers can impose costs on others who do not benefit either directly or indirectly from the expenditure. In public finance this is known as the "benefit principle" – namely that taxation should mimic what the "willingness to pay" criteria ensures within the context of a market economy even though by definition the public sector is eschewing the market mechanism for a variety of reasons. Vincent and Elinor Ostrom recognized this problem and emphasized its critical importance:

> Costs must be proportioned to benefits if people are to have any sense of economic reality. Otherwise beneficiaries may assume that public goods are free goods, that money in the public treasury is "the government's money", and that no opportunities are forgone in spending that money. When this happens, the foundations of a democratic society are threatened.   (E. & V. Ostrom 1991: 186–7)

In short, citizens should pay taxes that match the benefits they receive from public goods and services. The theory of fiscal equivalence ties both the subsidiarity principle underlying a theory of federalism and the benefit principle underlying a theory of taxation to propose a general theory of centralization and decentralization in governmental responsibilities.

The Ostroms' deployment of the idea of polycentricity has two purposes in light of this discussion. First, it was deployed to describe the various governmental decision nodes that were in operation within metropolitan areas, and how they functioned to deliver essential goods and services to their respective constituencies. Second, it was deployed as a foundational idea in a political theory with implications far greater than the organization of the public economy of metropolitan areas relating to the operational functioning of a self-governing democratic society. Polycentric political systems are more adaptable, adjustable and ultimately more responsive to diverse citizens compared to monocentric systems.

In the wake of the classic paper by Ostrom, Tiebout and Warren (1961) critical responses took either one of two shapes: (1) restate their argument as little more than a naïve "market model" of government, with its supposed attendant corollaries of atomistic individualism, perfect knowledge/perfect rational, and laissez-faire ideology, and dismiss their argument as irrelevant to problems of organizing local public economies, or (2) brand the argument as "conservative" because it was used to explain why the status quo was more orderly and less in need of structural change than reformers desired. These explanations were assumed to carry a normative weight for their positive analysis of the "order" rather than "chaos" of functioning, overlapping and competing jurisdictions. Reformers preached "efficiency and economy" and argued that while there were many governments in operation in metropolitan areas, there was too little government. These decentralized and overlapping set of governmental bodies, the argument went, were the primary reason for institutional weakness and institutional failure in metropolitan areas. Duplication of services and wastefully inefficient provision of services plagued these areas. But this was not what Ostrom, Tiebout and Warren saw when they studied the operation of governmental decision bodies within metropolitan areas.

Ostrom, Tiebout and Warren (1961) challenged the reformers presumptions at each stage of their argument. They defined polycentric political systems as having many decision-making nodes that were formally independent of each other. And they argued that the primary business of local government was the production and provision of public goods and services to their respective communities. Rather than chaotic and wasteful, Ostrom, Tiebout and Warren argued that polycentric systems were offering similar but differentiated services that serviced diverse interests of varying communities. Responsiveness to citizen demands was more critical than merely looking at the technological efficiency in production of public goods and services for determining the success or failure of a local public economy. The polycentric system, they argued, provides much of the same flexibility and responsiveness to citizen preferences that market organization has toward consumer preferences but within the setting of a public service economy. Of course, they argued there are problems with polycentric governance, and that close scrutiny must always be in operation, but consolidation and establishment of monocentric systems of governance logically move us away from flexibility and responsiveness almost by design. Monocentric systems, they argue, may exhibit some economies of scale in organization of public services, but at the cost of a single dominant decision center becoming "insensitive and clumsy in meeting the demands of local citizens for the public goods required in their daily life" (1961: 41).

The 1960s and 1970s saw the consolidationists in metropolitan reform win the argument. The Ostroms – both Vincent and Elinor – were the outliers and challengers in various studies looking at the provision of local public goods, such as police, roads, and schools. In *Understanding Urban Government: Metropolitan Reform Reconsidered* (1979), Robert Bish and Vincent Ostrom argued that discussion of the efficiency of the provision of public goods and services "without reference to citizen preferences makes no economic sense" (1979: 20). The last decade had seen a trail of disappointed policy reforms, as each effort at consolidation was met with rising frustrations as the newly structured city governments were unable to cope with the elementary problems that must be addressed for citizens to live their everyday lives. These governmental reforms "failed to produce desired consequences but instead make matters worse" (1979: 5). Time to rethink, they argued, the ever-present demand to merge and consolidate local governmental units into a single unit of government with jurisdiction over the entire metropolitan area. At a minimum, the criteria utilized should include along with efficiency, responsiveness and fairness or equity in the provision of public goods and services (1979: 21). And responsiveness to citizen preferences ought to be given a priority in these deliberations within a democratic society. "Citizen demands," Bish and Ostrom write (1979: 24), "can be more precisely indicated in smaller rather than larger political units, and in political units undertaking fewer rather than more numerous public functions".

This argument is much broader than the metropolitan reform debate, as already mentioned. In his work, *The Intellectual Crisis in American Public Administration* (1973), Vincent Ostrom laid out his fundamental opposition to the centralizing bureaucratic vision of public administration most clearly identified with Woodrow Wilson, and contrasted it with the more democratic vision of public administration associated with the founding fathers such as James Madison, but also as documented in the musing of Alexis de Tocqueville. This debate is already close to a century old. The Ostroms were innovators by importing economic reasoning into public administration and political science to tackle tough questions about the nature of democratic society, and the institutional machinery necessary for self-governing democratic societies to function.

The information rationale of polycentricity

In *The Public Economy of Metropolitan Areas*, Robert Bish (1971: 14–15) contrasts the "synoptic" approach with the "public choice" approach to public administration. "Underlying assumptions of the synoptic model," Bish writes, "are very similar to those made by some economists who recommend omniscient benevolent despot solutions: that the individual at the top of the controlling political hierarchy will be both knowledgeable and benevolent in his direction of public activities". But from a Madisonian perspective such a concentration of power could not be entrusted to those in political authority. Such an accumulation of power, it was argued, whether through political structure, through self-appointment, or through election, was a quick path toward tyranny. So the American political and economic system was institutionally structured to avoid concentration in a single center. It was this fragmented, and decentralized system that Tocqueville saw as one of the key sources of vibrancy in the American system of democratic self-governance.

But the synoptic model has several related problems that must be laid bare for us to make progress in understanding the Ostroms' contribution. First, this synoptic or "seeing like a state" model tends to ignore the fundamental problem of political externalities. The philosopher king is not out to exploit others, but to serve the public interest. To achieve that, they must be empowered to achieve this goal. Bish (1971: 37–42), however, building on the pioneering work of Buchanan and Tullock's *The Calculus of Consent* (1962) argues that any theory of public economy must take into account both the decision costs with collective action, and the political externality costs of collective action. Once these costs are taken into account, then the appropriate conceptual cost-benefit analysis of alternative institutional arrangements for the provision of public goods and services can begin.

Second, the synoptic model, because it postulates an all-knowing and benevolent social planner (and the attendant social welfare function for them to maximize), is blind to how coordination of the public economy can be coordinated in the absence of (a) the market, and (b) a central governmental authority. This way of characterizing the world leads theorists to think in strict dichotomies within two-dimensional space; i.e., state or market. The reality is that the complex organization of a modern metropolitan public economy requires "varieties of political units and coordinating mechanisms" to efficiently guide public decision-makers in the provision of "the variety of public goods and services" and satisfying "diverse preferences of individuals" (Bish 1971: 78).

As Vincent Ostrom states in *The Meaning of Democracy and the Vulnerability of Democracies*, "The application of economic reasoning to public choices cannot be advanced very far using the postulates of perfectly informed actors participating in competitive markets operating in unitary States directed by a single center of Supreme Authority" (1997: 115–16). Elinor Ostrom in *Governing the Commons*, refers to the synoptic view as an "intellectual trap", and one that provides practitioners with "the false confidence of presumed omniscience" which results in "proposals to governments that are conceived in their models as omnicompetent powers able to rectify the imperfections that exists in all field settings" (1990: 215).

A better approach had to be found so that the intellectual crisis of public administration could be avoided. That intellectual crisis results from the high expectations set by the synoptic approach to righting public wrongs in the policy space, and the hard reality of unintended and undesirable consequences. Part of this better approach is to scale back expectations from the public sector, and increase expectations of the ability of individuals in their private and public spheres to act creatively to solve social dilemmas. And, the Ostroms sought to construct a science of public administration that was consistent with the practice of a self-governing democratic society.

Critical to that exercise was the practice of public entrepreneurship within democratic self-governance. "Viable democracies," Vincent Ostrom (1997: 114) writes,

> are neither created nor destroyed overnight. Emphasis on form of government and the binding character of legal formulations are not sufficient conditions to meet the requirements of democratic societies. The moral and intellectual conditions of those who constitute democratic societies are of essential importance. This is why building common knowledge, shared communities of understanding, patterns of accountability, and mutual trust is as essential as producing stocks and flows of material goods and services.

It is *public* entrepreneurs that do that construction of common knowledge, etc. And, our theories must be capable of addressing the phenomena of change; of adaptation and adjustment; of discovery and creativity. And as Vincent and Elinor Ostrom stressed, that theory will not be found within the orthodox or mainstream application of price theory to the public sector. Instead, it requires a theoretical framework that seeks to better understand the basic anomalies, social dilemmas, and paradoxes involved in non-market decision-making. "The future of Public Choice," Vincent Ostrom (1997: 115) writes, "will be determined by its contributions to the epistemic level of choice in the cultural and social sciences and to the constitution of the epistemic order with which we live and work."

In short, we must first move away from assumptions of omniscient and benevolent social planners. This would also entail a move away from postulating the stable and coherent social welfare functions that the planners are supposed to utilize in selecting optimal policies. "The typical assumptions," Elinor Ostrom (1990: 214) writes, "of complete information, independent action, perfect symmetry of interests, no human error, no norms of reciprocity, zero monitoring and enforcement costs, and no capacity to transform the situation itself will lead to highly particularized models, not universal theories." If we are to build a social science relevant for understanding public policy problems, she argues, we must change the intellectual terrain on each of these margins.

In changing that intellectual terrain, the Ostroms harked back to the classical political economy of Smith and Hume, and the political project of Montesquieu and Madison, as well as the property rights economics of Alchian and Demsetz, the law-and-economics analysis of Coase, the public choice economics of Buchanan and Tullock, and the Austrian economics of Mises, Hayek and Kirzner. It is in this consilience of these traditions in political economy that progress is made, and we will "see a new political science join a new economics and a new sociology in establishing the basis for a major new advance upon the frontiers of public administration" (V. Ostrom 1973: 5).

Conclusion

Vincent and Elinor Ostrom had a radical vision of local public economies and the appropriate methods for studying them. They put great emphasis on the citizen's capacity for self-governance, and for democratic ways of relating to one another. We are one another's dignified equals. And, thus, our public institutions and public authorities should *never* presume to govern *over* us, but instead always seek to find the most effective ways to govern *with* us. This means governments need to be responsive to the preferences of citizens – as diverse and divergent as they are, and in their respective communities.

Once stated in this way, the basic questions become clear: in governing, how do we come to decide *what* government is going to do, *who* is responsible for doing what must be done, and *how* is it going to be produced and paid for. Local public economies must have a way to answer the what, who and how questions. This is the classic problem of coordination of economic activities. Understanding the complexity of coordination begins with a recognition of the fundamental problem of rational economic calculation under socialism. Absent a private property order and a functioning price system, the social system of production in a modern complex economy will have to forgo productive specialization and peaceful social cooperation. But in order to achieve that private property system we need an institutional infrastructure that operates outside of the market process itself. Public administration begins, as we have said, where the realm of rational economic calculation ends. So complex coordination of the public sector must be achieved in a non-market manner.

The Ostroms' contribution was to focus on how overlapping, functional and competing jurisdictions provided the necessary feedback in the public sector to guide decisions and respond to the diverse preferences of people in a manner that minimized political externalities, and maximized the chance for the effective delivery of public goods and services to citizens. They developed a political economy for the non-market sector that sought to give priority to "seeing like a citizen" and in doing so, created a new science and art of association worthy of a democratic self-governing society. It is as inspiring a vision as it is bold.

9

PUBLIC ADMINISTRATION FROM "INTELLECTUAL CRISIS" TO CONTEMPORARY "GOVERNANCE THEORY"

Paul Dragos Aligica

The most consequential foundational contribution of the Ostromian research program to the field of public administration is the effort to introduce the apparatus of modern "political economy" to the core of the field. The other important contributions to the theories of governance and public administration are, in one way or another, based on, or derived from, that. Following the evolution of public administration as a field, and its relationship with economics since its inception in Woodrow Wilson's effort to institutionalize the new discipline, one realizes that the Ostromian perspective was a turning point. The Ostroms pushed for a change of paradigm, as the main advocates in the field of public administration of the public choice revolution fuelled by scholars such as James Buchanan and Gordon Tullock in the 1960s.

Public administration and political economy developed as two distinctive domains and traditions.[1] Yet, with the burst of the public choice movement in the academic arena in the 1960s, a convergence takes place. Elinor and Vincent Ostrom's contributions emerge as uniquely important in this respect because the two Bloomington scholars were the unquestionable architects of the intellectual junction point. Working in both traditions – public administration and public choice – they created an entire research program aiming at their integration

---

1. There are two related but different usages of the term "public administration": the first is for an activity, the real life organization and management of public affairs. Usually that is designated as "public administration". The second is for an academic discipline, an area of study and inquiry that explores both positively and normatively the processes, organizations and institutional arrangements associated to the activity of public administration. Usually the second is designated as "Public Administration" (capitalized). Irrespective of usage, the notion has major links to the problems of applied economics.

(Aligica 2015; Aligica & Boettke 2009). The attempt to promote public choice as the theoretical foundations in public administration, and public administration as the applied domain of public choice is undoubtedly a major contribution of the Ostroms to both the foundational and the applied social sciences in the twentieth century.

By the beginning of the 1970s Vincent Ostrom recognized an acute "intellectual crisis of public administration", which created the conditions for a potential new start and a novel approach. The Ostroms' alternative was to use the new theory of public choice as the foundational theoretical framework for public administration:

> Fashioning the architecture for a system of democratic administration will require different concepts and different solutions from those that can be derived from Wilson, Goodnow, W. F. Willoughby, White, and Gulick. Instead, a new theory of democratic administration will have to be fashioned from the works of ... Buchanan, Tullock, Olson, William Niskanen, and many others ... The theory of externalities, commons, and public goods; the logic of collective action and public enterprise; the concepts of public service industries; and fiscal federalism will have prominent places in that theory. (V. Ostrom 1973: 114)

In what follows, this chapter concentrates on the Ostromian efforts to introduce the "political economy" way of thinking and the apparatus of modern economics to the core of the field of public administration. Once seen in the context of the larger picture of the evolution of the relationship between economics and public administration, the attempt to promote the public choice perspective in public administration, and the public administration perspective in public choice, emerges as a major contribution of the Ostromian research program, rich in both analytical and applied level implications.

Public choice as a foundation to the study of public administration

The insight behind Ostroms' contribution was rather straightforward: public administration evokes the idea of the institutionalization of public or collective action in allocation, organization and management of resources in governance. It is about the technology of human cooperation taking place through various arrangements of social coordination, cooperation, command, monitoring and control, all traditionally studied in various forms by economics and political economy. The public choice approach was upgrading and modernizing the traditional political economy perspective, and, as such, it was the ideal vehicle for a systematic reconstruction and relaunching of the theoretical apparatus of public administration. At the same time, the domain of public administration was presented as a natural ground for the applied, public choice approach. In both cases, the logic of economics was supposed to operate as the link between theory and practice, between the foundational and the applied level, while public choice could be seen as an attempt to express and materialize a form of "public reason" at the applied level.

In their article "Public Choice: A Different Approach to the Study of Public Administration" (1971), the Ostroms explain how public choice can help public administration solve its "crisis of identity." The perspective is, again, straightforward. The key element is embracing the economic way of thinking and then to apply it to public goods, collective action and the social dilemmas engendered by them. The territory is familiar to all those at home with the basics of economic reasoning.

A set of assumptions about individual actors are made (V. Ostrom 1971; Ostrom & Ostrom 1971: 204–5): first, individuals are self-interested such that each have their own set of preferences (which can differ between individuals) and these preferences affect decisions. Individuals will adopt maximizing strategies such that an individual will consistently choose the alternative that they believe will give them the greatest net benefit according to their particular preferences in accordance to their levels of information.

Second, a classification of goods is introduced. While there are purely private goods (goods and services which are highly divisible and can be easily excludable) and purely public goods (goods and services which are highly indivisible and cannot easily exclude individuals from using), there is also an "intermediate continuum" of goods that display varying levels of divisibility and exclusivity. These goods and services may have "spill-over effects or externalities that are not isolated and contained within market transactions" (Ostrom & Ostrom 1971: 210).

The analysis of individual choices, as they shape up in relation to the nature of the goods, sets the stage for collective and comparative analysis:

> Recognizing that the world is composed of many different goods and services that have these characteristics, and that such goods come in many different forms, we are confronted with the task of thinking through what patterns of organization might be used to accommodate these difficulties and yield reasonably satisfactory results. Just as we can expect market weakness and failure to occur as a consequence of certain characteristics inherent in a good or service, we can also expect problems of institutional weakness and failure in governmental operations as a consequence of the characteristics of certain goods and services. (Ostrom & Ostrom [1977] in McGinnis 1999b: 82)

In brief, the approach as aptly synthesized by Vincent Ostrom in his *The Intellectual Crisis in American Public Administration* has four elements:

(1) Use the individual as the basic unit of analysis; (2) use the theory of externalities, common properties and public goods to define the structure of the events relevant to public administration; (3) analyze the consequences of different organizational or decision-making arrangements on the output of public goods or services; and (4) evaluate these consequences by whether the outcome is consistent with the efficiency criterion or other measures of performers. (1973: 44)

The metropolitan reform debate

Decisive for our understanding of the more specific nature of the Ostromian contribution is to keep in mind the historical context of its emergence. This novel approach to the analysis and evaluation of public administration institutional arrangements and their performance took shape in the context of what was called the "metropolitan reform debate".

A vast literature around the mid-twentieth century claimed that there was a serious problem with the American metropolitan government. The "multiplicity of political units", "duplication of functions" and confusing "overlapping jurisdictions" gave governance in metropolitan areas the features of "a pathological phenomenon", an "organized chaos". A Committee for Economic Development report released in 1970, quoted by E. Ostrom ([1972] in McGinnis 1999b) synthesized the diagnosis shared by most mainstream public administration scholars and practitioners:

The present arrangement of overlapping local units is not serving the people well. Citizens in metropolitan areas are confronted by a confusing maze of many – possibly a dozen – jurisdictions, each with its own bureaucratic labyrinth. This baffling array of local units had made it difficult for citizens – the disadvantaged particularly – to gain access to public services and to acquire a voice in decision making.

(Committee for Economic Development 1970)

As E. Ostrom repeatedly noted, the diagnosis came with one core prescription: reorganization into larger units. An administrative system with a single dominant center was seen as the optimal way of administering and providing the public goods and services. The Ostroms were among the small group of scholars that questioned the validity of the mainstream approach both in diagnosis and solutions. The evidence, they wrote, pointed to a failure: despite the many initiatives fuelled by the reformers, no substantive progress was made.

The mainstream view was missing the functional logic underlying what they perceived as "a pathological phenomenon", i.e. an "organized chaos". A pattern of order was in fact at work. To identify it one needs the tools inspired by the economic way of thinking, which allow one to think more critically about the alleged absolute virtues of centralization. The logic of the economic way of thinking was opening the way and in that they did not hesitate to invoke and use Stigler's work, up to its applied level conclusions:

> If we give each governmental activity to the smallest governmental unit which can efficiently perform it, there will be a vast resurgence and revitalization of local government in America. A vast reservoir of ability and imagination can be found in the increasing leisure time of the population, and both public functions and private citizens would benefit from the increased participation of citizens in political life. An eminent powerful structure of local government is a basic ingredient of a society which seeks to give to the individual the fullest possible freedom and responsibility.   (Stigler 1962: 146)

The Ostroms went on to theorize that very "structure of local governance". They started to chart it conceptually and theoretically and to identify and explore its features. One of the first observations was that the multiplicity of governance units was functioning as a competition-generating structure. Thus, they begun the long journey of theorizing competitive governance as a key to understand public administration and public governance processes.

> The presence of more than a single producer of urban public goods within a metropolitan area may enable citizens to make more effective choices about the mix of services they prefer to receive than reliance upon voting mechanisms and a single producer. Multiple governments existing within a metropolitan area enable citizens to "vote with their feet". The presence of multiple producers within one metropolitan area may also reduce the cost for citizens of comparing the levels of output provided by different jurisdictions. Public officials who are representing one constituency in a bargaining process with other public officials over cooperative arrangements (such as contracting for services to be performed) may be able to bargain more effectively if alternative public producers are present in the area.
>   (E. Ostrom [1972] in McGinnis 1999b: 148)

To sum up, what was called "the political economy approach" questioned the mainstream reformers' assumption that centralized, large bureaucracies were more efficient in solving problems and in providing public goods and services than the decentralized systems based on competition or bargaining. Ultimately, the public choice perspective means that public administration can be viewed in terms of overlapping and competing "multiorganizational arrangements" rather a hierarchy of agencies (Ostrom & Ostrom 1971: 212). One rule or principle is not universally applicable, therefore one needs to be open to alternatives:

> We never intended to develop a strict market model for the supply of public goods and services to individual buyers. Nor did we intend to present an economic analogy based upon classical economic theory. On the other hand, we thought an indication that quasi-market mechanisms were operable in a public service economy would imply important new dimensions for a theory of public administration.
>
> (V. Ostrom [1972] in McGinnis 1999b: 54)

The allocation of resources without market prices

To fully grasp the nature and depth of the Ostromian contribution we need to take a step back and revisit the foundational problem of evaluation and prices in non-market settings. The starting point is the familiar observation that economic calculation covers effectively only things which can be sold and bought against money (Mises 1949: 214). For example, appraising the value of a business upon which has been laid a special regulation. The price or cost of the regulation can be derived by subtracting the price of the regulated business from the price of a similar but unregulated business. What makes this method of appraisal work is the availability of a transaction assumed similar in all but one aspect. More generally, the method works best when a set of transactions is available that taken together overlap to the bundled transaction in question sufficiently precisely that they isolate the aspect we are interested in, such that they make it derivable as a residual.

To be sure, the available surrounding transactions are each unique complex historical events concerning unique agents with uniquely contextualized preferences. But in the absence of the first best appraisal method, we are left with a set of surrounding transactions and with what Mises called an "understanding" (Mises 1949: 51) of the similarities between these surrounding transactions. Entrepreneurs interested in efficiency, who judge similarities between different market contexts (Kirzner 1997), and common law judges, who appraise transaction costs and the monetary value of certain disservices that are not the object of transactions (Posner 1993), all operate with this second-best domain.

The relevance for public governance is obvious. Public agencies interested in efficiency, and establishing a tax or a subsidy, encounter a version of the same challenge. Public goods and commons are dominating and defining the field. But there is a world of difference in precision between a common law judge aiming for efficiency, and who estimates the monetary value of a damage to a fairly common car model in a fairly common setting, and a government motivated by efficiency who estimates the value of a tax for a public service. The difference is given by the number of surrounding market transactions that afford guidance in value appraisal. The two price-setting decisions, the common law judge and the public agency are not equally arbitrary. The fewer the relevant transactions available for guidance, the more arbitrary the decision becomes.

If this is the case, then the only way we can inject rationality in the public good economy is to have a rich network of relevant transactions available. One can inject rationality in public good economy by introducing competitive rivalry in the provision and production of public goods. Competing rivals will perform an informational function (Lavoie 1985) by discovering ways to sell the same package to sets of smaller collective consumption units, or to unpack the bundles differently (Ostrom & Ostrom 1977, 1971). An increasing amount of available transactions and guiding prices in the public economy will lead to increasingly less arbitrary decisions.

A system having more than a single producer of urban public goods within a specific area, may enable citizens to make more effective choices about the mix of services they prefer to receive. Thus, following the logic of this argument and corroborating it with the empirical evidence from the American metropolitan governance cases, the Bloomington school come to introduce the correlated concepts of monocentricity and polycentricity:

> By conceptualizing metropolitan areas as polycentric political systems, we were suggesting that a system of ordered relationships underlies the fragmentation of authority and overlapping jurisdictions that had frequently been identified as "chaotic" and as the principal source of institutional failure in the government of metropolitan areas. We identified a polycentric political system as having many centers of decision making that were formally independent of each other. A "system" was viewed as a set of ordered relationships that persists through time.
>
> (V. Ostrom [1972] in McGinnis 1999b: 53)

To sum up, what was called "the political economy approach" questioned the view based on centralized bureaucratization of governance. Instead it focused on systems based on pluralism, decentralization, competition and bargaining, defined by multiple decision-making centers operating overlapping and competing jurisdictions. The nature of polycentrism and its application to governance and public administration has become a trademark of the Ostromian approach (V. Ostrom 1971, 1972, 1991a; McGinnis & Ostrom 1996; McGinnis 1999a,b, 2000).

Implications of thinking in terms of polycentricity

A polycentric order is one where many decision centers operate autonomously but share a set of rules (Polanyi 1951). Four basic assumptions are implied in this definition. First, a polycentric order is an "order", which means that patterns of cooperation are persistent. This distinguishes a polycentric order from chaos or violent anarchy. However, the degree of order, the efficacy of a common framework for cooperation, and conflict resolution is an empirical matter. Second, centers of decision in a polycentric network actually "decide": they actively exercise their different opinions and methods of operation. Third, agents operate "autonomously". Autonomy means decision centers are independent of one another and from agents present in different networks. Fourth, the condition that agents share a set of rules, whose similar content enables us to single out an analytical object of study (Aligica & Tarko 2012: 254).

Decision centers at a given level may resort to hierarchies, but do not usually act in their quality as subordinates. In many cases what appear to be higher levels of decision-making are networks whose rules nest the rules of the inside network in a way that offers support at will, instead of imposing direction as a matter of course. What appear to be hierarchies outside the polycentric network are agents appealed to or appointed by insiders to arbitrate or enforce a specific arrangement developed in the inner network. For example, the legal structure of the state of California allows water pumpers to organize, and enforces whatever rules they collectively devise (E. Ostrom 1990: 136).

One could combine these basic assumptions to draw implications. For instance, if we take the conditions of order and autonomy together, it follows that rules need to be compatible with agents' incentives. If orderly patterns are persistent, then order is self-reinforcing. Or, if we adopt an evolutionary perspective, then we draw the implication that competition between the methods of operation tried out by different decision centers will force these methods to become increasingly fit through natural selection.

We can also dig for the statements' presuppositions and add content to the concept. For example, if we understand agents in terms of their aims, then polycentric orders are classified as either featuring common aims or individual aims. If an order is identified by members' shared set of rules, then polycentric orders can be classified as ones with more or less constrained entry and exit.

Polycentricity can also be ascribed to organizations (a collective, a team with a common meaning, objective, concern and plan), and to spontaneous orders of interacting agents who do not form a collective, do not have common concerns or plans, and whose meanings bear at most family resemblances. Agents mutually adjusting in a polycentric order need not constitute a community of meanings or objectives. A market is a polycentric order where agents engage in exchanges without having to share meanings or common goals.

The Ostroms are theoretically interested in both ascriptions. The opening sentence of Ostrom, Tiebout and Warren's (1961: 31) seminal article notes that a polycentric order is not a legal entity, organization, or agent. A polycentric order is a web of orderly interactions. Similarly, a polycentric order is "one where many elements are capable of making mutual adjustments for ordering their relationships with one another within a general system of rules where each element acts with independence of other elements" (V. Ostrom 1972 in McGinnis 1999: 57). The chapter dedicated to theorizing polycentricy in *The Meaning of American Federalism* (V. Ostrom 1991a) defines it as "a structural basis for the emergence of self-governing arrangements". Its description by Ostrom and Ostrom (1977) captures both structure and process:

> Relationships are coordinated among collective consumption and production units by contractual agreements, cooperative arrangements, competitive rivalry, and mechanisms of conflict resolution. No single center of authority is responsible for coordinating all relationships in a public economy. Market-like mechanisms can develop competitive pressures that tend to generate higher efficiency than can be gained by enterprises organized as exclusive monopolies and managed by elaborate hierarchies of officials.
> (Ostrom & Ostrom [1977] in McGinnis 1999b: 99)

The notion of public economy was serving two purposes. First, to make clear that the concept of "public" should not be conflated with that of "the State" and "centralized systems of governance". Second, to emphasize the difference from the market economy:

> Local public economies are not markets. Nor are they hierarchical in structure. Individuals are not able to engage in a wide diversity of independent *quid pro quo* relationships with any vendor they choose. Decisions are made for collectivities of individuals who are then held responsible to provide tax revenue and user charges to pay for the provision of public goods and services. Like markets, however, there are regular relationships among entities in a local public economy.
> (Ostrom & Ostrom [1965] in McGinnis 1999b: 107–108)

Among the possible forms of relationships, rivalry and competition are pivotal. The greater the competitive pressure the better the performance, be it defined as costs-minimizing or as responsiveness to demands and needs.

> Competitive pressures are the key factors in maintaining the viability of a democratic system of public administration. The traditional principles of public administration imply monopoly organization applied to the entire public sector. Private enterprises as producers of public goods and services can significantly improve the efficiency of the public sector so long as competitive pressures can be openly and publicly maintained. The characteristics of public services and the important role for diverse organizations, including private enterprises, in the delivery of such services dictate the nature and structure of a public economy. The public economy need not be an exclusive government monopoly.   (Ostrom & Ostrom [1977] in McGinnis 1999b: 99)

The theoretical perspective built using the observation of empirical case studies of US metropolitan governance has thus led the Ostroms to advance the model of institutional system in which a citizen could opt depending on their preferences for geographical or functional jurisdictions that offer their favorite bundle of public goods and services. The more open to entry and exit jurisdictions are, the more competition is induced into the system. The more freedom citizens and officials have to define demand and supply of public goods and service, the more efficient the institutional arrangement is, leading to greater welfare for the community. The logic of economic reasoning thus leads to the following conclusion: when market prices are not available, public entrepreneurship emerges naturally to generate and organize change in public economies, being a force of institutional adaptation. The more a system encourages (or at least leaves room for) citizens' and officials' initiative and decision within the rules of the game, the more favorably it will be to the emergence of public entrepreneurship. Public administration becomes in this view strongly connected to public entrepreneurship (E. Ostrom 2005b; V. Ostrom 2006; Oakerson & Parks 1988; Kuhnert 2001).

It is pivotal in a process leading not to "a single, most efficient pattern of organization but to a continual search for more efficient ways to perform" (Oakerson & Parks [1988] in McGinnis 1999b: 320). E. Ostrom notes that the structure of such systems predicated on competitive governance and public entrepreneurship induce self-organization, initiative and institutional adaptation:

> While all institutions are subject to takeover by opportunistic individuals and to the potential for perverse dynamics, a political system

that has multiple centers of power at differing scales provides more opportunity for citizens and their officials to innovate and to intervene so as to correct maldistributions of authority and outcomes. Thus, polycentric systems are more likely than monocentric systems to provide incentives leading to self-organized, self-corrective institutional change. (E. Ostrom 1998b)

Voice, exit, competition and public entrepreneurship are thus the engines of polycentric systems. In the absence of public entrepreneurship, citizens' "voice" and "exit" are unable to operate effectively as a mechanism for "translating jurisdictional fragmentation and overlap into relatively efficient outcomes." Therefore, we should not be surprised, conclude the Ostroms, turning from theory to the empirical reality, that the American system, displaying since its founding a non-trivial measure of polycentricism, would fail to behave on the lines forced and predicted by the metropolitan reformers' plans.

The empirical validity of polycentricity

We have already noted that the Ostromian empirical analysis and evaluation of public administration arrangements and their performance, took shape in the context of the "metropolitan reform debate". As noted, the debate centered on the claim that there was a serious problem with the American metropolitan government with its "multiplicity of political units", "duplication of functions" and confusing "overlapping jurisdictions" generating "a pathological phenomenon" of "organized chaos". Was the core prescription (i.e. reorganization into larger units with a single dominant center) the way out of the crisis?

We have seen that the Ostroms were skeptical and questioned the validity of the mainstream approach, both in diagnosis and solutions. They went to the core of the issue: reform proposals were based on unrealistic theoretical assumptions and created unrealistic expectations not grounded in the empirical reality and the lessons of the existing experience. The problem, writes E. Ostrom, is that the elements of the metropolitan reform agenda "have rarely been clearly formulated and subjected to empirical research by those who recommend drastic change" (E. Ostrom [1972] in McGinnis 1999b: 140–42). "The changes recommended are presumed to lead to the postulated consequences without need for empirical investigation of the relationships involved". However, without empirical examination one could never know if the recommendations made by metropolitan reform advocates were feasible. In that case, it becomes plausible that "voters may have had a better intuitive understanding of the relationship among structural variables in metropolitan areas than the social scientists who have consistently made, and are still making, the same recommendations". The conclusion was evident: "Empirical research investigating the warrantability of the postulated relationships may be long overdue" (E. Ostrom [1972] in McGinnis 1999a: 119–20).

This is the point where E. Ostrom took the lead in shaping the research agenda by channelling it on empirical and applied level lines. She started by listing the theoretical differences between the two approaches to metropolitan governance (metropolitan reform vs political economy) and insisted that the mere comparative assessment of the two theories was inconclusive: the "differences in theoretical perspectives", the "different orientations to their subject matter", the "different concepts and languages" could not be decided "by discussion and deliberation alone". Specific empirical tests were necessary. "The theory that has the weaker explanatory capability presumably would give way in the course of time to the theory with the stronger explanatory capability" (E. Ostrom [1972] in McGinnis 1999b: 148).

And, thus, for the first time in the long history of the "metropolitan governance debate" the propositions implicit in the positions of the metropolitan reformers and the political economy scholars were articulated in testable forms. Once formulated in empirical relevant terms, the opposing claims became very plain and their testability more feasible.

For instance, the reformers' approach was based on propositions such as:

(a) Urban public goods and services are relatively homogeneous and similarly affect all neighborhoods within a metropolitan area. (b) Increasing the size of urban governmental units will be associated with higher output per capita, more efficient provision of services, more equal distribution of costs to beneficiaries, increased responsibility of local officials and increased participation by citizens. (c) Reducing the number of public agencies within a metropolitan area will be associated with more output per capita, more efficient provision of services, more equal distribution of costs to beneficiaries, more responsibility of local officials, and more participation by citizens. (d) Increasing the professionalization of public employees will be associated with a higher level of output per capita, more efficient provision of services, and increased responsibility of local officials.

(E. Ostrom [1972] in McGinnis 1999b: 148)

In a similar way, a group of alternative propositions may be derived from the political economy standpoint:

(a) Urban public goods and services differ substantially in regard to their production functions and their scale of effects. (b) Multiple jurisdictions with different scopes and scales of organization allow citizens to better make effective choices when selecting packages of services most important to them, to better articulate their preferences and concerns, and, if necessary, to move to other jurisdictions. (c) Producers who must compete for contracts are more likely to search for innovative technologies, to operate at close to optimal scales of production, and to encourage effective team production, as well as coproduction, so as to enhance their own performance. (d) Increasing the size of urban governmental units will be associated with decreased responsibility of local officials and decreased participation by citizens. (e) Whether increasing the reliance upon hierarchy as an organizing principle within a metropolitan area will be associated with higher output per capita and more efficient provision of services depends upon the type of public good or service being considered.

(E. Ostrom [1972] in McGinnis 1999b: 148)

The two parallel sets of propositions thus made possible a set of empirically grounded methodological comparisons. Building on all of the above, the growing empirical agenda advanced by the Bloomington school was a huge contribution to the field of public administration.

The objective of this chapter is not to explore how that empirical agenda evolved, or go into details regarding its substantive analytical results. The goal is to point out that it pushed the debate to a new level and that it forced things in a direction which went beyond the mainstream approach, by opening a solidly grounded empirical agenda which profoundly changed and challenged the status quo in the field of public administration.

In this respect it is important to note that Elinor Ostrom's leadership on the empirical front was decisive. First, she organized and coordinated an entire series of ground-breaking studies on the operational foundations laid on the lines described above (E. Ostrom 1983; McGinnis & E. Ostrom 2012; Oakerson & Parks 1988; McGinnis 1999a,b, 2000; Gibson *et al.* 2005; Sabetti 2004; Wagner 2005; Boettke *et al.* 2013). In doing that, she set up an example of how comparative and evaluation studies could be done in the field of public administration when it comes to contentious points, such as those salient in the metropolitan governance debate. Yet, at the same time, she set up an example of how the comparative institutional analysis advanced and advocated by the public choice revolution should be operationalized.

From the metropolitan debate to the study of the commons

As years passed, and as the development of the Bloomington school entered a new stage, the contributions made by Elinor Ostrom were not limited just to the fields of public choice and public administration, but touched multiple domains and disciplines, thus gaining a truly interdisciplinary dimension. The contributions to public governance continued nonetheless to be central to the agenda. Her common pool resources work, for instance, was not a deviation but a logical and natural step further in focusing and elaborating the research line defining the "metropolitan governance" phase of the Bloomington school. Commons and common goods were at the core of public governance theory and processes. The public choice dilemmas they generated were the sources of both challenges and institutional solutions in the public arena. Concentrating the research on them was decisive for better understanding of the structures of social interaction and the institutional arrangements defining the public sector. It is a very effective strategy of zooming in, isolating and analyzing specific classes of cases defined by a specific type of collective action dilemma. Focusing on the "commons situation" and studying it in depth, seen as a microcosm, as a paradigmatic case of governance and public administration situation, generates an array of insights relevant for other related situations or cases, and becomes a strategy that contributes both to the conceptual and theoretical approach to the study of public administration, as well as to its empirical basis.

And thus, one could get a better sense of the multiple dimensions of the well-known commons studies as well as of the fact that they were part and parcel of a larger intellectual project, evolving over decades, through several stages and spanning multiple themes and disciplines. Prior to Elinor Ostrom's contributions, there was a conventional wisdom on how to deal with common-pool resources (CPR) dilemmas, mostly consisting of government intervention and regulation. However, she noted that the "standard theory" was not fully satisfactory because it failed – among others – to focus on the appropriate level of decision-making in scenarios where CPR dilemmas had been mitigated or avoided (E. Ostrom 1989: 17).

To accommodate her observations and insights she modified the assumptions of the standard theory, contributing to the development of the "second generation rational choice theory" (E. Ostrom 1989, 1997, 2005). Her approach in this respect started from the theoretical apparatus to be used in analysis (E. Ostrom 1989: 14).

In order for a scenario to be considered a commons dilemma, it must meet four conditions (E. Ostrom 1989: 14–15): (1) resource unit subtractibility; (2) multiple appropriators; (3) suboptimal outcomes (from the perspective of the appropriators); and (4) constitutionally feasible alternatives (given constitutional and institutional arrangements, there are coordinated strategies that exist that are more efficient than what was decided, that the total discounted benefits are greater than total discounted costs of these alternative strategies, and there is a consensus in favor of the change). In her work she identified, conceptualized and theoretically elaborated these and similar aspects of the problems and phenomena in case.

For instance, while standard theory assumed omniscience, she changed that assumption (E. Ostrom 1989: 20–26). She introduced asymmetric information. She also examined the possibility of shared norms (as opposed to models without normative restraint). Instead of assuming a "no rules" scenario, status quo rules were added to broaden the applicability where rules that were established prior to the CPR dilemma affected entry and/or use patterns of appropriators. And very importantly, she added "level changing strategies" where social actors consider how to change the constraints that are under their control, "shifting" levels of decision-making, and thus self-consciously designing rules to change behavioral patterns in an operational situation. With these modified assumptions, Elinor Ostrom was able to examine how the external variables affected internalized choice and in general to set up more robust methods and approaches to the study not only of commons and their governance but to public governance in general.

These contributions are obviously crucial for both the theoretical and applied-level approach to public administration theory. The new theory of governance emerging towards the end of the twentieth century to inspire the views on "reforming the administrative state" and "reinventing government" were direct responses to the "crisis of public administration" diagnosed and analyzed by the Bloomington scholars in the second half of the twentieth century. These new views were a direct descendent of the efforts to respond to that crisis, by renewing both the theoretical apparatus and the empirical agenda of the mainstream field of public administration. Seen in this light, the Ostromian contribution is as relevant today as it was at the time the Bloomington scholars were promoting the new public choice approach to public administration.

10

RETHINKING FEDERALISM: SOCIAL ORDER THROUGH EVOLUTION OR DESIGN?

Rosolino A. Candela

The joint work of Elinor and Vincent Ostrom sought to address the possibility for individuals to establish a set of institutional conditions that would allow them to self-govern, rather than to be governed. Fundamental to their analysis was the idea that institutions are not only an *artifact* of deliberate human choice, but also that institutions facilitate *learning* about the behavior of individuals within society. Human beings must craft institutions in order to create reliable expectations for peaceful and productive interaction. In so doing, they are able to learn about the behavior of individuals within a set of institutions. Yet, individuals do not passively respond to their own constraints: they also learn how to better utilize those constraints for their own betterment, using their own particular and tacit knowledge. As a result, learning gives rise to the possibility for a greater variety of human behavior, the possibility of which can generate social instability. The role of institutions, then, in an Ostromian framework, is to order such adaptive human potential in such a way as to create reliable expectations about how others will behave and adapt to changing circumstances of time and place. Reflection and choice occurs *on the margin* with regard to institutional change. Individuals are grounded and shaped by the institutional framework within which they interact, but are nonetheless *artisans* that *both* tinker and adapt to the institutions that are the artifacts of their creation.

The particular focus of this chapter will be to analyze institutional change from an Ostromian perspective by analyzing the relationship between self-governance, polycentricity, and federalism. Throughout the work of Elinor Ostrom and Vincent Ostrom, there exist two consistent themes regarding the importance of federalism for polycentric governance. First, the Ostroms emphasized that the institutional conditions of federalism are a human artifact, based upon choice and deliberation. However, given their emphasis on processes of learning among human beings, this second theme suggests, as I argue in this chapter, a bi-directionality in institutional analysis. Although federalism and polycentric governance may be based on deliberate choice, such an institutional framework facilitates learning and the adaptive potential of human beings, leading to unintended innovative institutional changes to reinforce social cooperation between individuals.

The structure of this chapter proceeds as follows. In the first section, I illustrate the distinctiveness of the Ostrom research agenda, one that is rooted in the development of public choice in the 1950s, yet a distinct program that explores possible points of synthesis between James Buchanan and F. A. Hayek on institutional analysis. In the following section, I develop a broad overview of an Ostromian understanding of polycentricity and federalism. The distinction I explain is the following: federalism is a particular *manifestation* of polycentric order, one that guides learning in a positive-sum manner. In order for a polycentric order to facilitate interjurisdictional competition that is positive-sum, federal institutional constraints are required to promote the conditions of civil association not only within jurisdictions, but also between jurisdictions. The third section addresses how and why polycentric processes can be redirected towards negative-sum outcomes in the absence of federalist institutions. I show this through the example of the political absorption of Sicily into the Italian peninsula. The final section concludes with implications for understanding Ostromian political economy as a progressive research agenda.

Institutional analysis in Ostromian political economy: between James Buchanan and F. A. Hayek

Both Elinor and Vincent Ostrom were key pioneers in the development of public choice, or the analysis of individual decision-making in non-market settings. Ostromian political economy is fundamentally grounded in two interrelated concepts: (1) institutional diversity and the polycentric nature of the rules of the game, which emerge from (2) individual heterogeneity, the analytic precondition for both institutional problems as well as institutional solutions that foster social order. As Aligica states, "Institutionalism is not only about this or that specific institution, and its specific functions and performance. It is also about the overall capacity of a human society to monitor, assess, calibrate, adjust, and change, via institutional tools. This is an institutional function in itself" (2014: 36).

However tied the Ostroms may be to the public choice tradition, their understanding of institutional change, I argue, is *distinct*, though not separate, from the constitutional political economy of James Buchanan. In a letter dated 18 March 1977, Buchanan (1977) argues that the shared project between him and

Vincent Ostrom is grounded on two fundamental propositions: (1) institutions matter, and (2) institutions can be constructed. "We face opposition on both these counts," he adds. In that letter, Buchanan critiques Stigler and the modern Chicago School for explicitly denying the first, and also Hayek and other evolutionists for denying the second. However much both (1) and (2) may apply to the Ostroms and their understanding of political economy, *why* institutions matter and *how* institutions are constructed, according to the Ostroms, provides a distinct analytical framework that bridges James Buchanan's emphasis on institutional choice over the rules of the game (i.e. constitutional political economy) and F. A. Hayek's emphasis on institutional evolution.[1] Elinor Ostrom uses the term "rules" as a set of mutually-held relations that guide individual expectations about social interaction. "Rules are the result of implicit or explicit efforts by individuals to achieve order and predictability within defined situations" (E. Ostrom 1986: 5). She also refers to institutions as rules in order to distinguish them from physical laws and other constraints, which are not subject to human change. By doing so, she is able to illustrate the co-dependency between the evolutionary basis from which we inherit existing institutions, which nevertheless are the product of human action, though not of human design: "It is, of course, frequently difficult in practice to change the [existing] rules participants use to order their relationships. Theoretically, rules can be changed while physical and behavioral laws cannot. Rules are interesting variables precisely because they are potentially subject to change. That rules can be changed by humans is one of their key characteristics" (E. Ostrom 1986: 6).

To illustrate the point being raised regarding the distinctive nature of Ostromian institutional analysis, let us consider the following quotes by Hayek, on the one hand:

> At the moment our concern must be to make clear that while the rules on which a spontaneous order rests, may also be of spontaneous origin, this need not always be the case. Although undoubtedly an order originally formed itself spontaneously because the individuals followed rules which had not been deliberately made but had arisen spontaneously, *people gradually learned to improve those rules*; and it is at least conceivable that the formation of a spontaneous order *relies entirely on rules that were deliberately made*. (1973: 45, emphasis added)

---

1. Although not pertaining to the Ostroms directly, see Witt (1992) on endogenizing the public choice theorist as an agent of collective action, bridging the dichotomy between institutional construction and evolution.

And Buchanan (and Tullock) on the other:

> [O]ur analysis of the constitution-making process has little relevance for a society that is distinguished by a sharp cleavage of the population into distinguishable social classes or separate racial, religious, or ethnic groups sufficient to encourage the formation of predictable political coalitions and in which one of these coalitions has a clearly advantageous position at the constitutional stage.   (1962: 80)

Hayek's theory of institutional change is often interpreted as a theory based exclusively on evolution, with no basis for deliberate human action, the implications of which have done "great damage" because it presumes that "basic institutional change will somehow spontaneously evolve in the direction of structural efficiency" (Brennan & Buchanan [1985] 2000: 166*n*11), particularly if we are beginning our analysis in a world with deep social cleavages. This interpretation of Hayek by Buchanan and others is an oversimplification. The point here is not to adjudicate the perceived understanding, or misunderstanding, of the positions held between Buchanan and Hayek with regard to institutional change. Rather, it is to illustrate how the Ostroms are able to reconcile what otherwise might be perceived as mutually exclusive paradigms in institutional analysis, between institutional design on the one hand and institutional emergence on the other (see also Runst & Wagner 2011; Wagner 2014).

Raghuram Rajan has suggested that "a better starting point for analysis than a world with only minor blemishes may be a world where nothing is enforceable, property and individual rights are totally insecure, and the enforcement apparatus for every contract must be derived from first principles – as in the world that Hobbes so vividly depicted" (2004: 57). It is precisely this analytic starting point that illustrates two characteristics distinctive to Ostromian political economy. First, whereas Buchanan and Tullock regard social cleavages as a potential problem for the formation of institutions, the very same social cleavages, from an Ostromian perspective, may be regarded as a *source* of institutional formation. That is, the very reason *why* institutions emerge, and that individuals gradually *learn* to improve those rules is to exploit and utilize individual heterogeneity in knowledge, not only across time and place, but also across religious, ethnic, and other demographic groups.

The Ostroms also made contributions to understanding Buchanan's dual-analytic framework by stressing the entangled nature of constructivism and spontaneous order in "constitutional craftsmanship," as noted by Hayek in the quote above. The ability of individuals to craft rules that are effective within their own communities hinges upon the mutually agreed-upon rules of governance that then establish reliable expectations among the community. Elinor Ostrom emphasized the legitimacy of rules as essential to minimizing the enforcement and monitoring costs of rules (E. Ostrom 1990: 205). If rules are developed internally, by actors with local legitimacy and knowledge of the community's history, then monitoring can be a natural byproduct of the system of rules (E. Ostrom 1990: 96). Elinor Ostrom's interest in studying constitution-making from the bottom-up was partially inspired by Buchanan's constitutional political economy agenda; she described his work as "an important stimulus for our extensive studies of how many diverse peoples around the world have been able to organize their own rules" (E. Ostrom 2011b: 372). Precisely because of the empirical nature of institutional diversity, which cannot be derived *a priori*, the Ostroms developed the institutional analysis and development (IAD) framework as a conceptual tool, or "a metatheory of institutional mapping" (Aligica 2014: 95). The distinctive feature of the IAD framework for institutional mapping is that it nests different levels of institutional analysis, which interact with each other. At a higher level of analysis, the constitutional level of analysis refers to the rules governing future collective decision-making, while a lower level of institutional analysis, the collective-choice level, refers to the framework within which the interactions of individuals take place. Nested within the collective-choice level is the operational level of analysis, referring to the interactions of individuals within the overall set of rules governing decision-making (E. Ostrom 1990: 52).

Although these levels of institutional analysis are conceptually distinct, in reality, they are entangled in such a way that the distinction between selecting rules for a game and playing a game within those rules occur simultaneously and not sequentially. In such a way, distinguishing between different levels of analysis, analytically speaking, allows the Ostroms to incorporate both exogeniety and endogeneity to understanding institutional change that is *both* evolutionary and deliberative. As Elinor Ostrom states:

> The nesting of rules within rules is a source of considerable confusion and debate. Institutional theorists, who have attempted to make the choice of rules endogenous to an analysis, have been criticized because it is necessary to assume the presence of some rules that govern the choice of other rules. *Making the choice of operational-level rules endogenous does not imply the choice of collective-choice or constitutional-choice rules endogenous at the same time.* For the purposes of analysis, the theorist has to assume that some rules already exist and are exogenous for purposes of a particular analysis. The fact that they are held constant and unchanging during analysis, however, does not mean that they cannot be changed. *Those very same rules may themselves be the objects of choice in a separate analysis or in the context of a different area of choice.* (E. Ostrom 1990: 52, emphasis added)

Therefore, institutional change, in the Ostromian framework, occurs *on the margin*. Even if a given set of rules is not the result of deliberate construction at a particular moment in time, it does not necessarily follow that such rules were not the product of human action in the past. Neither does it follow that any given set of rules cannot be changed in the future as a result of reflection and choice. The link between these two features of institutional change – design and emergence – is the ability for human beings to learn and adapt to changing conditions *through time* within a given institutional framework. Vincent Ostrom best summarizes this relationship: "Perhaps the most distinctive characteristics of human beings is their capability for learning. Learning involves the development of an image about the order of events and relationships that occur. Where constraint exists, a learning organism can take advantage of that constraint by inducing variety in its own behavior so as to improve its adaptive potential" (1980: 310–11). Therefore, as Ostrom continues elsewhere on this point:

> Human beings thus face a paradoxical situation: they need order or constraint in their environment as a necessary condition for learning; but learning gives rise to new possibilities for increasing the potential variety of human behavior. Increasing potential variety in human behavior threatens the maintenance of a predictable order in which learning can occur. As the human adaptive potentials increase, we would anticipate that *mechanisms for ordering or constraining choice* must *simultaneously* occur if human development is to advance beyond very primitive levels. Features of human societies depend on *coevolutionary* patterns of development.   (1997: 135, emphasis original)

The best illustration of the relationship between institutional construction and institutional evolution via learning is best explored through the Ostroms' work on polycentricity and federalism, and the relationship between the two, as discussed in the next section.

Polycentricity and federalism: bridging the dichotomy between institutional construction and evolution

The concept of polycentricity had initially been developed by Michael Polanyi in *The Logic of Liberty* (1951). However, independent of Polanyi,[2] this theoretical concept was later developed by the Ostroms, initially by Elinor (1965) and

---

2. As Vincent Ostrom ([1991] 2014: 46) states, it was not until after he had published his seminal article (Ostrom, Tiebout & Warren 1961) that he had become aware of the prior use of the concept of polycentricity by Polanyi.

Vincent (1953a,b,c) in the context of water management in the western United states, but later in the context of public administration reform in metropolitan areas of the United States.[3] In the post-Second World War era, the presumption that emerged in the theory of public administration was one that stressed consolidation in the provision of public services by bureaucratic experts in the name of efficiency (V. Ostrom [1973] 2008: 5; see also Aligica 2019: 170). Just as Hayek ([1952] 1979) had railed against the uncritical and misplaced application of the methods of the natural sciences to the study of the social sciences (what he dubbed as "scientism") particularly in economics, Vincent Ostrom had been explicitly critical of a similar scientistic attitude that had come to prevail in the field of public administration.

> I have gradually come to conclude that the study of public administration should not be treated as strictly natural phenomena. The methods of the natural sciences are not fully appropriate to the study of public administration. Instead, we need first to look upon administrative tasks and administrative arrangements as works of art or as artifacts. Understanding works of art or artifacts may require somewhat different perspectives than understanding natural phenomena.
>
> (V. Ostrom 1980: 309).

The paradigm from which the Ostroms understood the problem of governance, particularly public administration, was not one of utilizing policy to generate a social outcome that is *ex ante* known and determined, as in a controlled scientific experiment, emanating from a single decision-making authority. This is what characterizes a monocentric paradigm of governance. The polycentric paradigm that the Ostroms developed was of crafting rules, and learning to gradually improve upon such rules, in order to harness the creative powers of heterogeneous individuals and facilitate the fulfillment of a diversity of human purposes, one in which the outcome is *ex ante* unknown.

A polycentric system of governance, broadly speaking, has three basic features. First, it consists of a multiplicity of autonomous decision centers formally independent of each other, yet act in ways that take account of the decisions of each other. Within such decision centers, individuals are the basic unit of analysis, whereby certain individuals will occupy positions acting on behalf of other individuals. Second, a polycentric system is structured by an institutional and cultural framework, providing an overarching system of rules governing

---

3. For further detail and deeper exposition of the intellectual context within which the Ostroms approached the study of polycentricity, see Aligica and Boettke (2009), Boettke, Coyne and Leeson (2011), McGinnis and Ostrom (2012), Boettke, Palagashivili and Lemke (2013) and Aligica (2014).

interjurisdictional competition and mutual adjustment between decision centers. Third, a polycentric system facilitates spontaneous order processes, generated by evolutionary competition between the different decision centers (Ostrom, Tiebout & Warren 1961; Aligica 2014: 58; V. Ostrom 1991 [2014]: 46).

A market economy illustrates the characteristics of a polycentric order quite well. For example, a market economy consists of a set of individuals, whereby production is mostly organized within firms. Such firms constitute a multiplicity of decision centers, within which the owner of the firm acts as the entrepreneurial decision-making agent, or residual claimant, acting on behalf of his or her employees. Although acting independently of one another, firms in a market economy are governed by a set of rules, namely private property and freedom of contract under the rule of law. Under such conditions, firms compete against each other in a peaceful and productive manner. The unintended consequence of such competitive behavior is the emergence of a particular spontaneous order, manifested in the price system, derived from the demands of consumers to which firms respond. It is the price mechanism that communicates both tacit and dispersed knowledge from among millions of consumers, coordinating the mutual adjustment of a multiplicity of firms responding to profits and losses that are revealed through the competitive market process.

Polycentricity, across time and place, describes the set of conditions by which various forms of competition emerge, applicable to both market as well as non-market settings. However, the manifestation of competition under any system of governance, either market or non-market, is institutionally contingent. "If polycentric arrangements were spontaneous systems of order," Vincent Ostrom writes, "we might expect peace to occur spontaneously throughout the world" (1991 [2014]: 56), independent of the institutional context within which those polycentric arrangements emerge. Moreover, spontaneity of outcomes is *not* mutually exclusive with *ex-ante* choice and reflection over the rules of the game. As Vincent Ostrom writes, if a polycentric order is to yield positive-sum outcomes, "the maintenance of such [polycentric] orders depends upon a sufficient level of intelligent deliberation to correct errors and reform themselves" (1991 [2014]: 58). The relationship between polycentricity and federalism illustrates this latter point.

Polycentricity and federalism are not synonymous with one another. While polycentricity is a *necessary condition* for federalism to yield positive-sum outcomes, it is *not a sufficient condition* for such a result. For example, Wagner and Yokoyama (2013; see also Wagner 2005) distinguish between two systems of federal governance: competitive federalism and cartel federalism. Competitive federalism consists of a polycentric structure of interjurisdictional competition, in which jurisdictions are autonomous and independent of each other, and therefore competition manifests itself in a positive-sum manner. Under competitive federalism, the types of services that jurisdictions offer will be governed by its ability to attract and satisfy the preferences of its citizenry, who exchange such services for tax revenue to provide such services. The presumption here is that jurisdictions face a hard budget constraint, and therefore cannot be bailed out by the central government. It is therefore incumbent on jurisdictions to structure institutional conditions in such a way that is conducive to productive specialization and wealth accumulation, such that they have a larger base from which to tax and offer public services against competing jurisdictions.

Cartel federalism consists of a monocentric structure, one in which a central government directs jurisdictions into a collusive manner. Although both competitive federalism and cartel federalism are nominally polycentric, cartel federalism is governed in reality under a monocentric structure, one in which competition between jurisdictions is redirected towards collusion. This is because, rather than competing to meet the preferences of its citizenry, jurisdictions under cartel federalism compete for grants and aid from a central government, contingent upon those jurisdictions conforming to requirements by the central government.

Moreover, federalism is not simply a decentralized form of public administration. For example, the US Federal Reserve System was designed as a decentralized form of central banking, with 12 regional Federal Reserve banks administering monetary policy within their assigned districts. Yet, monetary policy is centrally conducted from the top down by the Federal Open Markets Committee. Although the regional Federal Reserve banks are formally separate entities, interest rates do not emerge from the regional banks of the Federal Reserve System competing to supply loanable funds to customers.

Rather, federalism, as understood by the Ostroms, is a particular manifestation of a polycentric order that is institutionally contingent on adherence to predefined constitutional rules (V. Ostrom 1987). The concept of federalism more explicitly emphasizes the notion of design in crafting constitutional rules, yet the political outcome that emerges from such rules is not known *ex ante*. Federalism has two distinct connotations that are interrelated. The first connotation of federalism has an older meaning, derived from the Latin term *foedus*, meaning to covenant or enter into an agreement, which also shares a similar meaning with the Hebrew word, *b'rit*. The governing basis of such a relationship is adherence to a set of principles specifying the terms and conditions between two parties entering into agreement, such as a constitution, which may be written or unwritten. In this sense, *self-governance emerges by individuals subjecting themselves to rules, not to other individuals.* Such an understanding is in stark contrast to a hierarchical form of governance, where authority is derived from one party domineering and exercising discretion over the rest of society by setting the terms and conditions of governance.

A second, and more contemporary, meaning of federalism refers to "the creation of two or more units of government to exercise concurrent but limited authority to govern the same land and people" (Ostrom, Bish & Ostrom 1988: 14). According to such an understanding, the authority of states and national governments is derived from their citizenry entering into agreement, or covenant if you will, to uphold the terms and conditions of governance as outlined according to constitutional rules. The presumption is that no single government has the knowledge to govern across an entire geographic area. Therefore, a federalist structure of governance assigns jurisdiction over the administration, although not necessarily the production, of public services, including defense, fire protection, and building inspection. The boundaries of such jurisdiction coincide with the particular territory and individuals being served by a particular public service. For example, since defense is a public service that is regarded as national in scope, consumed simultaneously by all individuals of a particular country, provision of defense is more appropriately provided at the national level. However, since the scale of the spillover effects from administering the provision of fire protection or building inspection is far more limited than defense, to prevent free riding, it is more appropriate to internalize the costs and benefits of fire protection and building inspection by defining it a more localized level. By doing so, the threat of exit disciplines public administrators from deviating from citizens' preferences regarding public services and their provision (Ostrom, Tiebout & Warren 1961: 840).

When a federalist government is constitutionally constrained to predefined rules, positive-sum interjurisdictional competition can emerge by individuals sorting themselves according to their preferences (Tiebout 1956). As an unintended consequence of this competitive process, self-monitoring of political decision-making may emerge as sub-national units of government mutually adjust to one another. As a result, such a competitive process may yield constitutional change from the bottom-up that the designers of such a constitution may have never anticipated from the top down. This bi-directionality between institutional evolution and learning, on the one hand, and institutional choice and design on the other, is not only theoretically reconciled in the Ostroms' understanding of institutions, polycentricity, and federalism. It is empirically revealed by Lemke (2016) in the context of laws governing married women's property rights in the United States.

The design of the federalist structure of the United States, as outlined by the US Constitution, was without a doubt imperfect. For example, it initially denied political enfranchisement, not to mention legal personhood, to particular groups of individuals on the basis of their race and gender, specifically African Americans and women, in direct violation of the rule of law. However, what it means for American federalism to have been designed "imperfectly" can be understood in two different ways, yielding two different meanings of federalism. The first connotation would imply that American federalism was "flawed" or "sub-optimal" compared to an ideal form of federalism. Indeed the denial of economic property rights and political enfranchisement is a grave injustice built into any form of government. Moreover, the American federalist structure was unable to solve the question of slavery nationally without bloodshed, settling the issue by force of arms.

Having said this, comparing the American federalist structure, conceived at the Constitutional Convention of 1787, with an ideal form of federalism, shifts our analytical focus away from an Ostromian approach to understanding the imperfect nature of American federalism. A second connotation of the word "imperfect," when traced back to its Latin roots, suggests that imperfect means "incomplete," or to be more precise, "not thoroughly done." I raise this point to suggest that the exogenous design of the American federalist system, however much it fell short of the principles as outlined by the Declaration of Independence, nonetheless enabled the *possibility* of an endogenous realization of such principles through peaceful interjurisdictional competition.

Jayme Lemke (2016) has illustrated the process by which women in the United States become economically empowered throughout the nineteenth century, generating a more complete enforcement of women's property rights. At the beginning of the century, not only were women politically disenfranchised from state and national elections and from holding office; married women were not permitted to own property, enter into contracts without their husband's permission, or stand in court as independent persons. Moreover, "even if we assume the universal desirability of property rights reform, an unlikely proposition, legal reform is a public good. Identifying and implementing optimal laws is costly, and the non-rivalrous and non-excludable nature of reform is such that it is theoretically impossible for a private group to internalize benefits sufficient to motivate optimal provision of legal reform" (Lemke 2016: 292). How is it then that the interests of married women became aligned with political officials when they expressed no political voice through voting?

By the dawn of the twentieth century, legal reform in nearly every state had removed these restrictions by extending formal legal and economic rights to married women. Such legal reform was realized in part by women voting with their feet by moving westward across the United States. A process of interjurisdictional competition emerged as legislators, who held a vested interested in increasing the population of their territories in order to meet the requirements of statehood, took intentional efforts to attract female settlers. By strengthening women's rights, local political elites would gain job security and influence over political appointments made by the federal government (Lemke 2016: 307). Thus, an endogenous solution to imperfect institutional design had emerged.

Interjurisdictional competition, in effect, although not by design, incentivized legal reformers *to learn* and *discover* the preferences of women. Such legal reform occurred by political decision-makers gradually improving upon the existing constitutional rules, thus rendering the principles of life, liberty, and the pursuit of happiness more complete. Such a lesson from American federalism illustrates not only how public goods provision, but also constitutional craftsmanship, can emerge from the bottom-up, rather than top-down, through public entrepreneurship and interjurisdictional competition.

Polycentric governance unravelled: the case of Italian unification and its impact on Sicily

As discussed in the previous section, the degree to which polycentric processes are directed towards positive-sum outcomes or negative-sum outcomes is contingent upon constitutional rules that structure interjurisdictional competition. This point can be generalized across place and time to understand the de facto operation of governance structures in societies that are *de jure* monocentric. For example, Paul Craig Roberts (1969, 1971) utilized the concept of polycentricity to understand the de facto operation of the Soviet economy and its deviation from the dictates of *de jure* central planning. The primary purpose of this section is to suggest a theoretical framework that permits the political economy of Sicily to be understood, as neither monocentric nor anarchic, but as polycentric. Reframing pre-unification Sicily[4] from a polycentric perspective provides a preliminary analytic step to better understanding the negative impact that the hierarchical nature of Italian unification had on Sicilian governance institutions, which had incorporated both elements of design and evolution.

The prevailing view of Sicilian political economy, both prior to and after its political unification with the Italian peninsula throughout the nineteenth century, has been one of institutional inertia and conflict. Moreover, this prevailing view has been based upon two different theories regarding the institutional preconditions of feudal Sicily: one that hypothesizes a strongly centralized formal authority governed over Sicily, and one that hypothesizes a perpetual weakness of a formal centralized authority in Sicily.

The notion that the institutional conditions of feudal Sicily were hierarchical and authoritarian has been advanced by political scientist Robert Putnam (1993a). He emphasizes that the economic and political divergence between the

---

4. Although there are no exact dates defining this period, I use the term "pre-unification Sicily" interchangeably with "feudal Sicily" to refer to the period between the Norman conquest of Sicily in the eleventh century and the abolition of feudalism in 1812.

northern and southern parts of the Italian peninsula can be traced to their medieval institutional heritages. In northern Italy, the medieval city-states fostered an environment of "civic republicanism" and horizontal integration whereas the south, particularly Sicily, had inherited a heritage of autocracy and vertical integration of society. "The chief virtue in the South," as he states, "was the imposition of hierarchy and order on latent anarchy" (1993a: 130). That is, the political institutions in southern Italy undermined the horizontal integration of civil society and the formation of social capital.

More recently, Francis Fukuyama (2014) has argued that "the reality of Southern Italy was rather the opposite" of what Putnam had postulated, claiming instead that Sicily and southern Italy were characterized by "a persisting weakness of centralized authority that was unable to prevent exploitation of the peasantry by the aristocracy" (2014: 111). Similarly, Daniel Ziblatt (2006) has argued that the persisting weakness of centralized authority subsequent to the political unification of Italy was due to a lack of "infrastructural capacity" before unification, namely the ability to maintain civil order, the ability to tax resources effectively for the provision of public goods, and the ability to implement policy goals (2006: 80). Ziblatt compares the unification of Germany with that of Italy (2004, 2006), both of which were unified around a nucleus state, Prussia and Piedmont, respectively. In both cases, the political leaders of Prussia and Piedmont preferred to pursue unification in a federalist fashion (2004: 73). However, Ziblatt argues that the unitary, centralized path that characterized Italy's unification, compared to that of Germany, resulted from the fact that "*before* national unification, the states Piedmont inherited possessed limited institutional capacity to do the work of modern governance" (2006: 80, emphasis original). If the political "subunits of a potential federation are patrimonial states lacking constitutions, parliaments, and rationalized systems of administration, negotiation usually breaks down and the prospects of self-governance after state formation are limited, leading the way to unitary political institutions. When annexed, these states lack basic governance capacity vis-á-vis their own societies" (Ziblatt 2004: 78). Therefore, "it was *only* Piedmont that had the *state capacity* to carry out the unification of Italy" (2006: 72, emphasis original).

Neither rendition of the political economy of feudal Sicily fully captures the governance arrangements that prevailed during that period throughout its entire history. In fact, growing evidence from more recent empirical studies in history and social science has increasingly challenged the generalizability of the received wisdom about the South (Boettke & Candela 2020; Candela 2020; Sabetti 1984 [2002]). On this point, economic historian Stephan Epstein has argued that "as far as *territorial* dualism between northern and southern Italy is concerned, it appears that the view that the institutional weakness of southern towns was a cause of economic backwardness is misplaced" (1992: 158, emphasis original).

However controversial it may seem, at first blush, to analyze the political economy of feudal Sicily from a polycentric perspective, such an approach provides a useful analytical starting point to raise important questions that directly counter Putnam, on the one hand, and Fukuyama and Ziblatt, on the other. First, if Putnam is correct to characterize feudal Sicily as hierarchical, absolutist, and moncentric, why would the ruler of such a society ever cede power and subject itself to a parliament and constitutional arrangements limiting its power in the first place? Secondly, if Fukuyama and Ziblatt are correct that feudal Sicily lacked an effective overarching authority, why had there been a concerted effort after 1816[5] to abolish the parliamentary and constitutional framework that governed feudal Sicily?

The origins of Sicily's parliamentary institutions go back to Norman colonization, when Sicily's first parliament had been established in Palermo in 1130 by King Roger II (Mongitore 1749: 24). Like all medieval parliaments, its establishment was for the purpose of obtaining consent for taxation. In exchange for taxes granted to the Crown, Sicilian barons received political property rights to not only vote on taxation (*donativi*), but also to administer justice and governance (*mero e misto imperio*) over their respective fiefs (*latifundi*), the ownership from which they derived income in exchange for protecting the peasantry residing on their feudal land. As Congleton (2011) has written, this act of public entrepreneurship would unintendedly and gradually create a shift in authority from the Crown to Parliament throughout Europe, occurring over a period of centuries (see also Barzel 2000, 2002; Salter 2015a,b).

This constitutional exchange, which emerged with the original intention of benefiting Norman kings, evolved into a polycentric framework. At the constitutional level of analysis, Parliament provided overarching governance across feudal estates. At the collective-choice level of analysis, Sicilian barons held political and economic jurisdiction within feudal estates, or fiefs. At the operational level of analysis, the interaction between aristocracy and the peasantry residing within a fief was subject to an agreement, which became known as the Pacts of the Land (Sabetti [1984] 2002: 33). In theory, the abrogation of common property rights and other property rights within a respective fief, or *latifondo*, required unanimous consent of all inhabitants on a respective fief (Koenigsberger 1951: 78). In practice, "economic need served to check baronial excesses upon their local subjects, since egregious demands would only

---

5. In 1816, Sicily was reunited with the Kingdom of Naples as the Kingdom of the Two Sicilies, the first phase of Sicily's political absorption into the Italian peninsula. In 1861, the Kingdom of the Two Sicilies would be absorbed into the Kingdom of Italy.

aggravate rural flight" (Backman 1995: 159). A scarcity of agricultural labor relative to land, particularly after the Black Death, as well as individual mobility of inhabitants, was an important constraint that put checks on the discretionary rule of the Sicilian aristocracy (Epstein 1992: 319; see also North & Thomas 1971). The bundled nature of economic property rights and political jurisdiction would continue until 1806, after which time Sicily underwent British occupation during the Napoleonic Wars (see Roselli 1956).

However, the localized polycentric governance of feudal Sicily was by no means static, inevitable, or without contestation from the Crown. Two important constitutional-level changes occurred that redefined the allocation not only for political rights but also economic rights and also generated the conditions for the polycentric nature of governance in Sicily that characterized it up until the early nineteenth century, when thereafter this polycentric tendency was reversed by political centralization during the Italian unification process. As part of the political settlement following the Sicilian Vespers[6], King James I of Sicily and his successor, King Frederick III, implemented a set of constitutional limits on direct taxation, which were known as the *Capitulorum Regni Siciliae* or *Capitoli del Regno* (Epstein 1992: 375, 391). "The chapters that were enacted by Parliament in Palermo after the Coronation of Frederick were the *Magna Charta* of the island" (Spata 1865: 9, emphasis original). The acts, or chapters, outlined in the *Capitoli* stipulated that direct taxes (*donativi*) could only be collected through the consent of Parliament (Spata 1865: 11) and that declarations of war and peace could not occur without the assent of Parliament (Koenigsberger 1951: 149).

Second, with the coronation of King Frederick III, a new set of rules were created that changed those governing the ownership of property rights in Sicily. Prior to Frederick's reign, royal law prohibited the alienation of *latifondi* by Sicilian aristocrats. As stated in Title V, Chapter 57, in the Third Book of *Liber*

---

6. What is known as the Sicilian Vespers was an uprising in the Kingdom of Sicily against King Charles of the House of Anjou in 1282. Ascending to the throne in 1266, Charles took several measures that would lead to his deposition. He circumvented the custom whereby the King of Sicily was coronated by baronial election in Palermo. Visiting the island only once, he ruled from the city of Naples, rather than the traditional capital of Palermo. Perhaps most importantly, he circumvented parliamentary authority by resorting to forced loans and taxation, neither convening parliament nor acquiring parliamentary consent. Such affronts led to his expulsion from the island and Angevin French rule from Sicily, severing the Kingdom of Sicily into two kingdoms. Charles and his successors would be confined to the Italian peninsula south of the Papal States, henceforth known as the Kingdom of Naples. Only after the conclusion of the Napoleonic Wars in 1815 would these two kingdoms be reunited as the Kingdom of the Two Sicilies.

Augustalis, also known as the Constitutions of Melfi, "by this edictal law, which will be perpetually valid, we forbid all the *fideles* of our kingdom, counts, barons, knights, or any other person or cleric to dare to transfer property" ([1231] 1971: 108). However, a major institutional shift in the rules of the game occurred with establishment of the *Lex Volentes*, promulgated by Frederick III in 1296, which resulted in the de facto liberalization of the feudal land market, and legalized the sale of whole fiefs to individuals of "equal or greater dignity" than the seller (Epstein 1992: 165; see also Backman 1995: 167). The result of the *Lex Volentes* was that baronial title and the privileges that went with such title, including voting rights in Parliament, were owned not by virtue of heredity, but by virtue of purchase. In effect, such acts of public entrepreneurship, based on deliberate choice, unintendedly created a framework of rules that generated the conditions for polycentric governance, one in which the Sicilian aristocracy governed their feudal estates independently from each other.

However, both baronial political privileges as well as the *Lex Volentes* would become increasingly contested once the Crown in Sicily had shifted to the Neapolitan Bourbons, in which King Ferdinand IV of Naples also became King Ferdinand III of Sicily in 1759. In effect, although under different governments, the Kingdom of Naples and the Kingdom of Sicily underwent a regal union. Thereafter, a policy of centralization was initiated by the Viceroy of Sicily, Domenico Caracciolo, appointed by Naples in 1781. Caracciolo initiated a policy of attenuating the *Lex Volentes* as well as the baronial prerogative of *mero e misto imperio* to erode baronial power in Sicily. With their political rents in jeopardy, Sicily's barons seized the opportunity to abolish feudalism once the island had become shielded from Neopolitan rule by the British. This culminated with the installment of the Constitution of 1812, through which the Sicilian Parliament abolished feudalism and divested itself from Neopolitan rule. In effect, the Sicilian barons had exchanged away by constitutional reform the very baronial privileges they had obtained from the Crown for the ability to alienate their *latifundi*, unintendedly participating in the long evolution towards a system of private property, and the preconditions for democracy, that had begun with the establishment of parliament. The unintended effect of constitutional bargains in Sicily that had begun in Norman times was that the Sicilian Parliament institutionalized a set of constraints against the political privileges it had been designed to protect in the first place. However, with the end of the British occupation of Sicily, this evolution towards the rule of law, which had evolved in the previous seven centuries, would become eroded by the process of Italian political unification.

In 1815, the Congress of Vienna reconfigured the political borders of the Italian peninsula in the aftermath of the Napoleonic Wars. Sicily was united with Italy south of Rome as the Kingdom of the Two Sicilies, with its capital based in Naples. King Ferdinand I of the Bourbon dynasty was crowned its first monarch.[7] After 1815, severed from a decentralized feudal political tradition, Sicilian administration and bureaucracy would embrace a French-Napoleonic political tradition of centralization. By abolishing the Sicilian Parliament as well as the Constitution of 1812, which had stipulated the abolition of feudalism and the establishment of exchangeable private property rights over feudal lands, the Kingdom of the Two Sicilies had eliminated any credible commitment to uphold Sicilian institutions as a constraint against its political discretion.

Moreover, Sicily was to undergo a complete fusion into absolutist rule with the Neapolitan Bourbons and later political centralization under the Kingdom of Piedmont. After 1816, Sicily would be divided into 23 districts and seven provinces headed by non-elected intendants sent from Naples (Riall 1998: 32; Sabetti [1984] 2002: 57; Mack Smith 1968: 353). As Lucy Riall states, "Bourbon reformers had two related objectives: to undermine the economic and political power of the Sicilian barons, and to replace them with the rule of a single, centralized administrative authority based in Naples" (1998: 25). The means by which the Bourbons would achieve these objectives was through land reform:

> One of the original intentions of the Bourbon programme of land reform had been to improve the economy of the *latifondo* by ending the concentration of land in very few hands. The division of common land was meant to create a new class of small holders, thereby solving the problem of absenteeism, offering the rural poor a stake in improving land, and, it was hoped, providing a new source of support for the Bourbon government. (Riall 1998: 49)

The fundamental problem with land reform was that it required political discretion over the redistribution of property rights. Yet, by failing to credibly commit to institutional constraints that would constrain public predation, specifically by abolishing Sicilian parliamentary institutions, the resulting uncertainty over the assignment and enforcement of property rights by the state enabled private predation and the rise of the Sicilian mafia. Italy's lack of state capacity and inability to enforce private property rights was not due to the privatization of feudal estates. Rather, its incapacity to govern was a *byproduct* of the subsequent political unification process itself, which had failed to institutionalize a set of credible constraints that would prevent it from intervening in the exchange of private property rights. Therefore, by undermining any pre-existing conditions for federalism, which had been embryonic in feudal Sicily, the tendency toward

---

7. King Ferdinand I had previously been Ferdinand IV of Naples and Ferdinand III of Sicily (Mack Smith 1968: 352).

monocentric governance during the Italian unification process unintendedly created the conditions for social disorder and conflict.

Conclusion

At the end of her Nobel Prize address, Elinor Ostrom wrote that "to explain the world of interactions and outcomes occurring at multiple levels, we also have to be willing to deal with complexity instead of rejecting it" (2010a: 665). She asserted that institutional theorists across disciplines must go "beyond markets and states" to observe the multitude of alternative institutional arrangements that individuals craft to govern their interactions. In doing so, she also revealed another important lesson for institutional theorists: we must go beyond the dichotomy between institutional evolution and design. Both Elinor and Vincent Ostrom were pioneers in the theoretical formulation and the empirical application of institutional analysis, polycentricity, and federalism. Each of these concepts, although distinct from each other, are not mutually exclusive from one another. Analyzed together, they reveal that dynamic institutional change across time, not comparisons of institutions at points in time, incorporates reflection and choice in the emergence of institutions. Individuals may inherit a set of institutions by accident and force from the past, but from an Ostromian perspective, this is just the analytical starting point for what institutions *will become* through human reflection and choice, however marginal it may seem.

REFERENCES

Acemoglu, D. & J. Robinson 2012. *Why Nations Fail: The Origins of Power, Prosperity, and Poverty.* New York: Crown Books.

Ahn, T. & R. Wilson 2010. "Elinor Ostrom's contributions to the experimental study of social dilemmas". *Public Choice* 143(3): 327–33.

Aligica, P. 2003. "Rethinking institutional analysis: interviews with Vincent and Elinor Ostrom". Mercatus Center at George Mason University.

Aligica, P. 2014. *Institutional Diversity and Political Economy: The Ostroms and Beyond.* Oxford: Oxford University Press.

Aligica, P. 2015. "Public administration, public choice and the Ostroms: the achievements, the failure, the promise". *Public Choice* 163(1): 111–27.

Aligica, P. 2019. *Public Entrepreneurship, Citizenship, and Self-Governance.* Cambridge: Cambridge University Press.

Aligica, P. & P. Boettke 2009. *Challenging Institutional Analysis and Development: The Bloomington School.* London: Routledge.

Aligica, P. & P. Boettke 2011. "The two social philosophies of Ostroms' institutionalism". *Policy Studies Journal* 39(1): 29–49.

Aligica, P., P. Boettke & V. Tarko 2019. *Public Governance and the Classical-Liberal Perspective: Political Economy Foundations.* Oxford: Oxford University Press.

Aligica, P. & V. Tarko 2012. "Polycentricity: from Polanyi to Ostrom, and beyond". *Governance: An International Journal of Policy and Administration* 25(2): 237–62.

Aligica, P. & V. Tarko 2013. "Co-production, polycentricity, and value heterogeneity: the Ostroms' public choice institutionalism revisited". *American Political Science Review* 107(04): 726–41.

Alston, E., L. Alston, B. Mueller & T. Nonnenmacher 2018. *Institutional and Organizational Analysis: Concepts and Applications.* Cambridge: Cambridge University Press.

Alston, L., G. Libecap & B. Mueller 1999. *Titles, Conflict, and Land Use: The Development of Property Rights and Land Reform on the Brazilian Amazon Frontier.* Ann Arbor, MI: University of Michigan Press.

Anderson, T. & F. McChesney 2003. *Property Rights: Cooperation, Conflict, and Law.* Princeton, NJ: Princeton University Press.

Ariely, D. 2009. *Predictably Irrational: The Hidden Forces That Shape Our Decisions.* New York: Harper.

Aumann, R. 1976. "Agreeing to disagree". *Annals of Statistics* 4(6): 1236–9.

Austin, J. 1962. *How to Do Things with Words: The William James Lectures Delivered at Harvard University in 1955*. Oxford: Oxford University Press.

Backman, C. 1995. *The Decline and Fall of Medieval Sicily: Politics, Religion, and Economy in the Reign of Frederick III, 1296–1337*. Cambridge: Cambridge University Press.

Baier, A. 1997. "Doing things with others: the mental commons". In L. Alanen, S. Heinämaa & T. Walldren (eds), *Commonality and Particularity in Ethics*, 15–44. Basingstoke: Palgrave Macmillan.

Baron, J. 2014. "Rescuing the bundle-of-rights metaphor in property law". *University of Cincinnati Law Review* 82(1): 57–101.

Barwise, J. & J. Perry 1983. *Situations and Attitudes*. Cambridge, MA: MIT Press.

Barzel, Y. 1997. *Economic Analysis of Property Rights*. Second edition. New York: Cambridge University Press.

Barzel, Y. 2000. "Property rights and the evolution of the state". *Economics of Governance* 1(1): 25–51.

Barzel, Y. 2002. *A Theory of the State: Economic Rights, Legal Rights, and the Scope of the State*. New York: Cambridge University Press.

Bates, R. *et al.* 1998. *Analytic Narratives*. Princeton, NJ: Princeton University Press.

Becker, G. 2007. *Economic Theory*. Second edition. New Brunswick, NJ: Transaction.

Berggren, N. 2014. "The calculus of consent 'at Fifty': insights for liberalism". *The Independent Review* 18(3): 373–89.

Biggart, N. & M. Guillen 1999. "Developing difference: social organization and the rise of the auto industries of South Korea, Taiwan, Spain, and Argentina". *American Sociological Review* 64(5): 722–47.

Bish, R. 1971. *The Public Economy of Metropolitan Areas*. Chicago, IL: Markham Publishing.

Bish, R. 2014. "Vincent Ostrom's contributions to political economy". *Publius: The Journal of Federalism* 44(2): 227–48.

Bish, R. & V. Ostrom [1973] 1979. *Understanding Urban Government: Metropolitan Reform Reconsidered*. Washington, DC: American Enterprise Institute Press.

Blomquist, W., E. Schlager, S. Tang & E. Ostrom 1994. "Regularities from the field and possible explanations". In E. Ostrom, R. Gardner & J. Walker (eds), *Rules, Games, and Common-Pool Resources*, 301–18. Ann Arbor, MI: University of Michigan Press.

Blomquist, W., A. Thiel & D. Garrick (eds) 2019. *Governing Complexity*. New York: Cambridge University Press.

Boettke, P. 2012. *Living Economics: Yesterday, Today, and Tomorrow*. Oakland, CA: Independent Institute.

Boettke, P. & R. Candela 2020. "Productive specialization, peaceful cooperation and the problem of the predatory state: lessons from comparative historical political economy". *Public Choice* 182(3/4): 331–52.

Boettke, P., C. Coyne & P. Leeson 2011. "Quasimarket failure". *Public Choice* 149(1/2): 209–24.

Boettke, P., S. Haeffele-Balch & V. Storr 2016. *Mainline Economics: Six Nobel Lectures in the Tradition of Adam Smith*. Arlington, VA: Mercatus Center, George Mason University.

Boettke, P., L. Palagashvili & J. Lemke 2013. "Riding in cars with boys: Elinor Ostrom's adventures with the police". *Journal of Institutional Economics* 9(4): 407–25.

Boettke, P. & N. Snow 2014. "Political economy and the science of association: a suggested reconstruction of public choice through the alliance of the Vienna, Virginia, and Bloomington schools of political economy". *Review of Austrian Economics* 27(1): 97–110.

Bourdieu, P. 1986. "The forms of capital". In J. Richardson (ed.), *Handbook of Theory and Research for the Sociology of Education*, 241-58. New York: Greenwood Press.

Bowles, S. & H. Gintis 2011. *A Cooperative Species: Human Reciprocity and Its Evolution*. Princeton, NJ: Princeton University Press.

Bratman, M. 1992. "Shared cooperative activity". *Philosophical Review* 101(2): 327–41.

Bratman, M. 1993. "Shared intention". *Ethics* 104(1): 97–113.

Brennan, G. & J. Buchanan [1980] 2000. *The Power to Tax: Analytical Foundations of a Fiscal Constitution*. Indianapolis, IN: Liberty Fund.

Brennan, G. & J. Buchanan [1985] 2000. *The Reason of Rules: Constitutional Political Economy*. Indianapolis, IN: Liberty Fund.

Bromley, D. 1986. "Closing comments". In *Proceedings of the Conference on Common Property Resource Management*, 591–98.

Bruegge, C., T. Deryugina & E. Myers 2019. "The distributional effects of building energy codes". *Journal of the Association of Environmental and Resource Economists* 6(S1): S95–127.

Buchanan, J. 1950. "Federalism and fiscal equity". *American Economic Review* 40(4): 583–99.

Buchanan, J. 1959. "Positive economics, welfare economics, and political economy". *Journal of Law and Economics* 2: 124–38.

Buchanan, J. 1962. "Politics, policy, and the Pigovian margins". *Economica* 29(113): 17–28.

Buchanan, J. 1964. "What should economists do?" *Southern Economic Journal* 30(3): 213–22.

Buchanan, J. [1969] 1999. *Cost and Choice: An Inquiry in Economic Theory*. Indianapolis, IN: Liberty Fund.

Buchanan, J. [1975] 2000. *The Limits of Liberty: Between Anarchy and Leviathan*. Indianapolis, IN: Liberty Fund.

Buchanan, J. 1977. "Letter to Professor Vincent Ostrom". Blacksburg: Virginia Polytechnic Institute and State University.

Buchanan, J. [1979a] 1999. "Natural and artifactual man". In *The Logical Foundations of Constitutional Liberty*, 246-59. Indianapolis, IN: Liberty Fund.

Buchanan, J. [1979b] 1999. "Politics without romance". In *The Logical Foundations of Constitutional Liberty*, 45-59. Indianapolis, IN: Liberty Fund.

Buchanan, J. 1987. "Justification of the compound republic: the calculus in retrospect". *Cato Journal* 7(2): 305–12.

Buchanan, J. 1989. *Essays on Political Economy*. Honolulu, HI: University of Hawaii Press.

Buchanan, J. 1991. *The Economics and the Ethics of Constitutional Order*. Ann Arbor, MI: University of Michigan Press.

Buchanan, J. 1994. *Ethics and Economic Progress*. Norman, OK: University of Oklahoma Press.

Buchanan, J. 1995. "Federalism as an ideal political order and an objective for constitutional reform". *Publius: The Journal of Federalism* 25(2): 19–27.

Buchanan, J. 2005. "Afraid to be free: dependency as desideratum". *Public Choice* 124(1): 19–31.

Buchanan, J. & R. Congleton 1998. *Politics by Principle, Not Interest: Towards Nondiscriminatory Democracy*. Cambridge: Cambridge University Press.

Buchanan, J. & N. Devletoglou 1970. *Academia in Anarchy: An Economic Diagnosis*. New York: Basic Books.

Buchanan, J. & G. Tullock 1962. *The Calculus of Consent: Logical Foundations of Constitutional Democracy*. Ann Arbor, MI: University of Michigan Press.

Buchanan, J. & R. Wagner 1977. *Democracy in Deficit: The Political Legacy of Lord Keynes*. New York: Academic Press.

Burt, R. 2004. "Structural holes and good ideas". *American Journal of Sociology* 110(2): 349–99.

Buskens, V. & J. Weesie 2000. "An experiment on the effects of embeddedness in trust situations: buying a used car". *Rationality and Society* 12(2): 227–53.

Candela, R. 2020. "The political economy of insecure property rights: insights from the Kingdom of Sicily". *Journal of Institutional Economics* 16(2): 233–49.

Carlisle, K. & R. Gruby 2019. "Polycentric systems of governance: a theoretical model for the commons". *Policy Studies Journal* 47(4): 927–52.

Casey, K., C. Dewees, B. Turris & J. Wilen 1995. "The effects of individual vessel quotas in the British Columbia halibut fishery". *Marine Resource Economics* 10(3): 211–30.

Chambers, C. & F. Echenique 2016. *Revealed Preference Theory*. New York: Cambridge University Press.

Chamlee-Wright, E. 2005. "Entrepreneurial response to 'bottom-up' development strategies in Zimbabwe". *Review of Austrian Economics* 18(1): 5–28.

Chan, C. 2009. "Creating a market in the presence of cultural resistance: the case of life insurance in China". *Theory and Society* 38(3): 271–305.

Chivers, T. 2019. "What's next for psychology's embattled field of social priming". *Nature* 576(7786): 200–202.

Coase, R. 1937. "The nature of the firm". *Economica* 4(16): 386–405.

Coase, R. 1960. "The problem of social cost". *Journal of Law and Economics* 3: 1–44.

Coase, R. 1992. "The institutional structure of production". *American Economic Review* 82(4): 713–19.

Cole, D., G. Epstein & M. McGinnis 2019. "The utility of combining the IAD and SES frameworks". *International Journal of the Commons* 13(1): 244–75.

Cole, D. & M. McGinnis (eds) 2015a. *Elinor Ostrom and the Bloomington School of Political Economy, Volume 1: Polycentricity in Public Administration and Political Science*. Lanham, MD: Lexington Books.

Cole, D. & M. McGinnis (eds) 2015b. *Elinor Ostrom and the Bloomington School of Political Economy, Volume 2: Resource Governance*. Lanham, MD: Lexington Books.

Cole, D. & E. Ostrom 2012. "The variety of property systems and rights in natural resources". In D. Cole & E. Ostrom (eds), *Property in Land and Other Resources*, 37–64. Cambridge, MA: Lincoln Institute of Land Policy.

Coleman, J. 1988. "Social capital in the creation of human capital". *American Journal of Sociology* 94: S95–S120.

Committee for Economic Development 1970. *Reshaping Government in Metropolitan Areas: A Statement on National Policy*. New York: Committee for Economic Development.

Congleton, R. 2011. *Perfecting Parliament: Constitutional Reform, Liberalism, and the Rise of Western Democracy*. Cambridge: Cambridge University Press.

Cooper, M. 2018. "Governing the global climate commons: the political economy of state and local action, after the US flip-flop on the Paris Agreement". *Energy Policy* 118: 440–54.

Cosmides, L. & J. Tooby 1997. "Evolutionary psychology: a primer". https://www.cep.ucsb.edu/primer.html.

Cosmides, L. & J. Tooby 2006. "Evolutionary psychology, moral heuristics, and the law". In G. Gigerenzer & C. Engel (eds), *Heuristics and the Law*, 175–205. Cambridge, MA: MIT Press.

Cox, M., G. Arnold & S. Tomás 2010. "A review of design principles for community-based natural resource management". *Ecology and Society* 15(4): 38.

Coyne, C. & J. Lemke 2011. "Polycentricity in disaster relief". *Studies in Emergent Orders* 3: 45–57.

Craiutu, A. & S. Gellar 2009. *Conversations with Tocqueville: The Global Democratic Revolution in the Twenty-First Century*. Lanham, MD: Lexington Books.

Crawford, S. & E. Ostrom 1995. "A grammar of institutions". *American Political Science Review* 89(3): 582.

Denzau, A. & D. North 1994. "Shared mental models: ideologies and institutions". *Kyklos* 47(1): 3–31.

Durkheim, E. 1978. "Sociology and the social sciences". In M. Traugott (ed.), *On Institutional Analysis*, 71–99. Chicago, IL: University of Chicago Press.

Easterly, W. 2013. *The Tyranny of Experts: Economists, Dictators, and the Forgotten Rights of the Poor*. New York: Basic Books.

Eggertsson, T. 1990. *Economic Behavior and Institutions: Principles of Neoinstitutional Economics*. Cambridge: Cambridge University Press.

Epstein, S. 1992. *An Island for Itself: Economic Development and Social Change in Late Medieval Sicily*. New York: Cambridge University Press.

Feiock, R. 2009. "Metropolitan governance and institutional collective action". *Urban Affairs Review* 44(3): 356–77.

Feiock, R. 2013. "The institutional collective action framework". *Policy Studies Journal* 41(3): 397–425.

Feiock, R. & J. Scholz 2009. *Self-Organizing Federalism: Collaborative Mechanisms to Mitigate Institutional Collective Action Dilemmas*. New York: Cambridge University Press.

Fukuyama, F. 1995. *Trust: The Social Virtues and the Creation of Prosperity*. New York: Free Press.

Fukuyama, F. 2014. *Political Order and Political Decay: From the Industrial Revolution to the Globalization of Democracy*. New York: Farrar, Straus & Giroux.

Furubotn, E. & R. Richter 2005. *Institutions and Economic Theory: The Contribution of the New Institutional Economics*. Ann Arbor, MI: University of Michigan Press.

Galiani, S. & E. Schargrodsky 2014. "Land property rights". In S. Galiani & I. Sened (eds), *Institutions, Property Rights and Economic Growth: The Legacy of Douglass North*, 107–20. New York: Cambridge University Press.

Galiani, S. & I. Sened 2014. *Institutions, Property Rights, and Economic Growth: The Legacy of Douglass North*. New York: Cambridge University Press.

Gehlbach, S. & E. Malesky 2014. "The grand experiment that wasn't? New institutional economics and the postcommunist experience". In S. Galiani & I. Sened (eds), *Institutions, Property Rights, and Economic Growth*, 223–47. New York: Cambridge University Press.

Gibson, C., K. Andersson, E. Ostrom & S. Shivakumar 2005. *The Samaritan's Dilemma: The Political Economy of Development Aid*. Oxford: Oxford University Press.

Gibson, C., M. McKean & E. Ostrom (eds) 2000. *People and Forests: Communities, Institutions, and Governance*. Cambridge, MA: MIT Press.

Gigerenzer, G. 2008. *Rationality for Mortals: How People Cope with Uncertainty*. Oxford: New York: Oxford University Press.

Gigerenzer, G., P. Todd & ABC Research Group 1999. *Simple Heuristics That Make Us Smart*. New York: Oxford University Press.

Gigerenzer, G., R. Hertwig & T. Pachur (eds) 2011. *Heuristics: The Foundations of Adaptive Behavior*. Oxford: Oxford University Press.

Gilbert, M. 1989. *On Social Facts*. London: Routledge.

Gilbert, M. 2000. *Sociality and Responsibility: New Essays in Plural Subject Theory*. Lanham, MD: Rowman & Littlefield.

Gilbert, M. 2013. *Joint Commitment: How We Make the Social World*. Oxford: Oxford University Press.

Gintis, H. 2009. *The Bounds of Reason: Game Theory and the Unification of the Behavioral Sciences*. Princeton, NJ: Princeton University Press.

Granovetter, M. 1973. "The strength of weak ties". *American Journal of Sociology* 78(6): 1360–80.

Granovetter, M. 1985. "Economic action and social structure: the problem of embeddedness". *American Journal of Sociology* 91(3): 481–510.

Granovetter, M. 1992. "Economic institutions as social constructions: a framework for analysis". *Acta sociologica* 35(1): 3–11.

Granovetter, M. & R. Swedberg 2001. *The Sociology of Economic Life*. Boulder, CO: Westview Press.

Greif, A. 1998. "Self-enforcing political systems and economic growth: late medieval Genoa". In R. Bates *et al.* (eds), *Analytic Narratives*, 23-63. Princeton, NJ: Princeton University Press.

Greif, A. 2006. *Institutions and the Path to the Modern Economy: Lessons from Medieval Trade*. New York: Cambridge University Press.

Grüne-Yanoff, T., C. Marchionni & I. Moscati 2014. "Introduction: methodologies of bounded rationality". *Journal of Economic Methodology* 21(4): 325–42.

Hadfield, G. 2008. "The many legal institutions that support contractual commitments". In C. Ménard & M. Shirley (eds), *Handbook of New Institutional Economics*, 175–203. Berlin: Springer.

Haidt, J. 2005. *The Happiness Hypothesis: Finding Modern Truth in Ancient Wisdom*. New York: Basic Books.

Haidt, J. 2012. *The Righteous Mind: Why Good People Are Divided by Politics and Religion*. New York: Pantheon.

Haight, C., A. Marroquín & N. Wenzel 2011. "The calculus of consent: 50th anniversary". *Laissez-Faire* 35: 83–5.

Hampton, A. 2003. "Population control in China: sacrificing human rights for the greater good". *Tulsa Journal of Comparative and International Law* 11(1): 321–61.

Hardin, G. 1968. "The tragedy of the commons". *Science* 162(3859): 1243–48.

Hayek, F. 1948. *Individualism and Economic Order*. Chicago, IL: University of Chicago Press.

Hayek, F. [1952] 1979. *The Counter-Revolution of Science: Studies on the Abuse of Reason*. Indianapolis, IN: Liberty Fund.

Hayek, F. 1973. *Law, Legislation and Liberty, Volume 1: Rules and Order*. Chicago, IL: University of Chicago Press.

Hayek, F. 1988. *The Fatal Conceit*. Chicago, IL: University of Chicago Press.

Hayek, F. 1989. "The pretense of knowledge". *American Economic Review* 79(6): 3–7.

Heimer, R., Z. Iliewa, A. Imas & M. Weber 2020. "Dynamic inconsistency in risky choice: evidence from the lab and field". Social Science Research Network. SSRN Scholarly Paper. https://papers.ssrn.com/abstract=3600583.

Henderson, C. (ed.) 2015. *Tocqueville's Voyages: The Evolution of His Ideas and Their Journey beyond His Time*. Indianapolis, IN: Liberty Fund.

Henrich, J. et al. (eds) 2004. *Foundations of Human Sociality: Economic Experiments and Ethnographic Evidence from Fifteen Small-Scale Societies*. Oxford: Oxford University Press.

Herzberg, R. 2015. "Governing their commons: Elinor and Vincent Ostrom and the Bloomington School". *Public Choice* 163(1): 95–109.

Hess, C. & E. Ostrom 2007. "Introduction: an overview of the knowledge commons". In C. Hess & E. Ostrom (eds), *Understanding Knowledge as a Commons*, 3–26. Cambridge, MA: MIT Press.

Hobbes, T. [1651] 1965. *Leviathan or the Matter, Forme, and Power of a Commonwealth Ecclesiasticall and Civil*. Oxford: Clarendon Press.

Hume, D. [1739] 2000. *A Treatise of Human Nature*. Edited by D. Norton & M. Norton. Oxford: Oxford University Press.

Ingram, P., J. Robinson & M. Busch 2005. "The intergovernmental network of world trade: IGO connectedness, governance, and embeddedness". *American Journal of Sociology* 111(3): 824–58.

Isoni, A., G. Loomes & R. Sugden 2011. "The willingness to pay – willingness to accept gap, the 'endowment effect', subject misconceptions, and experimental procedures for eliciting valuations: comment". *American Economic Review* 101(2): 991–1011.

Jaynes, E. 2003. *Probability Theory: The Logic of Science*. Edited by G. Larry Bretthorst. Cambridge: Cambridge University Press.

Jehle, G. & P. Reny 2011. *Advanced Microeconomic Theory*. Third edition. Harlow: Pearson.

Jordan, A., D. Huitema, H. Van Asselt & J. Forster 2018. *Governing Climate Change: Polycentricity in Action?* New York: Cambridge University Press.

Kahneman, D. 2011. *Thinking, Fast and Slow*. New York: Farrar, Straus & Giroux.

Kirzner, I. 1997. "Entrepreneurial discovery and the competitive market process: an Austrian approach". *Journal of Economic Literature* 35(1): 60–85.

Kliemt, H. 1994. "The calculus of consent after thirty years". *Public Choice* 79(3/4): 341–53.

Knight, J. 1992. *Institutions and Social Conflict*. Cambridge: Cambridge University Press.

Knorr, K. & U. Bruegger 2002. "Global microstructures: the virtual societies of financial markets". *American journal of Sociology* 107(4): 905–50.

Koenigsberger, H. 1951. *The Government of Sicily under Philip II of Spain: A Study in the Practice of Empire*. London: Staples Press.

Kuhnert, S. 2001. "An evolutionary theory of collective action: Schumpeterian entrepreneurship for the common good". *Constitutional Political Economy* 12(1): 13–29.

Lange, O. 1936. "On the economic theory of socialism: part one". *Review of Economic Studies* 4(1): 53–71.

Lange, O. 1937. "On the economic theory of socialism: part two". *Review of Economic Studies* 4(2): 123–42.

Lasswell, H. & A. Kaplan [1950] 2014. *Power and Society: A Framework for Political Inquiry*. New Brunswick, NJ: Transaction.

Lavoie, D. [1985] 2015. *Rivalry and Central Planning: The Socialist Calculation Debate Reconsidered*. Fairfax, VA: Mercatus Center at George Mason University.

Lemke, J. 2016. "Interjurisdictional competition and the married women's property acts". *Public Choice* 166(3/4): 291–313.

Levi, M. 2010. An Interview with Elinor Ostrom. Annual Reviews Conversations. https://www.annualreviews.org/userimages/ContentEditor/1326999553977/Elinor OstromTranscript.pdf.

Lewis, D. 1969. *Convention: A Philosophical Study*. Cambridge, MA: Harvard University Press.

Lewison, R. *et al.* 2019. "Accounting for unintended consequences of resource policy: connecting research that addresses displacement of environmental impacts". *Conservation Letters* 12(3): e12628.

List, C. & P. Pettit 2011. *Group Agency: The Possibility, Design, and Status of Corporate Agents*. New York: Oxford University Press.

Locke, R. 1995. *Remaking the Italian Economy*. Ithaca, NY: Cornell University Press.

Lomborg, B. 2001. *The Skeptical Environmentalist: Measuring the Real State of the World*. Cambridge: Cambridge University Press.

Mack Smith, D. 1968. *A History of Sicily: Modern Sicily after 1713*. London: Chatto & Windus.

Maurer, A. 2012. "'Social embeddedness' viewed from an institutional perspective. Revision of a core principle of new economic sociology with special regard to Max Weber". *Polish Sociological Review* 180(4): 475–96.

McGinnis, M. (ed.) 1999a. *Polycentric Governance and Development: Readings from the Workshop in Political Theory and Policy Analysis*. Ann Arbor, MI: University of Michigan Press.

McGinnis, M. (ed.) 1999b. *Polycentricity and Local Public Economies: Readings from the Workshop in Political Theory and Policy Analysis*. Ann Arbor, MI: University of Michigan Press.

McGinnis, M. (ed.) 2000. *Polycentric Games and Institutions: Readings from the Workshop in Political Theory and Policy Analysis*. Ann Arbor, MI: University of Michigan Press.

McGinnis, M. 2005. "Beyond individualism and spontaneity: comments on Peter Boettke and Christopher Coyne". *Journal of Economic Behavior & Organization* 57(2): 167–72.

McGinnis, M. 2011a. "An introduction to IAD and the language of the Ostrom workshop: a simple guide to a complex framework". *Policy Studies Journal* 39(1): 169–83.

McGinnis, M. 2011b. "Networks of adjacent action situations in polycentric governance". *Policy Studies Journal* 39(1): 51–78.

McGinnis, M. 2015. "Polycentric governance in theory and practice: dimensions of aspirations and practical limitations". Mimeo, prepared for Polycentricity Workshop, Ostrom Workshop, IU Bloomington, 14–17 December 2015. Available at http://ssrn.com/abstract=3812455.

McGinnis, M. 2017. "The IAD framework in action: understanding the source of the design principles in Elinor Ostrom's governing the commons". In D. Cole & M. McGinnis (eds), *Elinor Ostrom and the Bloomington Schools of Political Economy*, 87–108. Lanham, MD: Lexington Books.

McGinnis, M. 2019. "Beyond a precarious balance: improving the scientific rigor and policy relevance of institutional analyses from the Bloomington School". In P. Aligica, P. Boettke & B. Herzberg (eds), *Ostrom's Tensions: Reexamining the Political Economy and Public Policy of Elinor C. Ostrom*, 19–72. Arlington, VA: Mercatus Center, George Mason University.

McGinnis, M. & E. Ostrom 1996. "Design principles for local and global commons". In O. Young (ed.), *The International Political Economy and International Institutions*, 465–93. Cheltenham: Elgar.

McGinnis, M. & E. Ostrom 2012. "Reflections on Vincent Ostrom, public administration, and polycentricity". *Public Administration Review* 72(1): 15–25.

McGinnis, M. & E. Ostrom 2014. "Social-ecological system framework: initial changes and continuing challenges". *Ecology and Society* 19(2): 30.

McGinnis, M. & V. Ostrom [1999] 2012. "Democratic transformations: from the struggle for democracy to self-governance?" In B. Allen (ed.), *The Quest to Understand Human Affairs: Essays on Collective, Constitutional, and Epistemic Choice*, vol. 2, 501–32. Lanham, MD: Lexington Books.

Ménard, C. & M. Shirley (eds) 2008. *Handbook of New Institutional Economics*. Berlin: Springer.

Ménard, C. & M. Shirley 2014. "The contribution of Douglass North to new institutional economics". In S. Galiani & I. Sened (eds), *Institutions, Property Rights and Economic Growth: The Legacy of Douglass North*, 11–29. New York: Cambridge University Press.

Mercier, H. & D. Sperber 2011. "Why do humans reason? Arguments for an argumentative theory". *Behavioral and Brain Sciences* 34(2): 57–74.

Metcalfe, J. 2007. "Policy for innovation". In H. Hanusch & A. Pyka (eds), *Elgar Companion to Neo-Schumpeterian Economics*, 943–66. Cheltenham: Elgar.

Miettinen, J., C. Shi & S. Liew 2011. "Deforestation rates in insular Southeast Asia between 2000 and 2010". *Global Change Biology* 17(7): 2261–70.

Milgrom, P., D. North & B. Weingast 1990. "The role of institutions in the revival of trade: the law merchant, private judges, and the Champagne fairs". *Economics & Politics* 2(1): 1–23.

Miller, G. 1992. *Managerial Dilemmas: The Political Economy of Hierarchy*. Cambridge: Cambridge University Press.

Mises, L. von [1920] 1975. "Economic calculation in the socialist commonwealth". In F. Hayek (ed.), *Collectivist Economic Planning: Critical Studies on the Possibilities of Socialism*. London: Routledge & Kegan Paul.

Mises, L. von [1949] 1966. *Human Action: A Treatise on Economics*. Chicago, IL: Henry Regnery.

Mitchell, M. & P. Boettke 2017. *Applied Mainline Economics: Bridging the Gap between Theory and Public Policy*. Arlington, VA: Mercatus Center, George Mason University.

Mitchell, W. 1988. "Virginia, Rochester, and Bloomington: twenty-five years of public choice and political science". *Public Choice* 56(2): 101–19.

Mitchell, W. 1999. "Political science and public choice: 1950–70". *Public Choice* 98: 237–49.

Moe, T. 1990. "Political institutions: the neglected side of the story". *Journal of Law, Economics, & Organization* 6: 213–53.

Mokyr, J. 2014. "Culture, institutions, and modern growth". In S. Galiani & I. Sened (eds), *Institutions, Property Rights and Economic Growth: The Legacy of Douglass North*, 151–91. New York: Cambridge University Press.

Mongitore, A. 1749. *Parlamenti Generali Del Regno Di Sicilia Dall'anno 1446 Sino al 1748: Con Le Memorie Istoriche Dell'antico, e Moderno Uso Del Parlamento Appresso Varie Nazioni, Ed in Particolare Della Sua Origine in Sicilia, e Del Modo Di Celebrarsi*. Palermo: Presso P. Bentivenga.

Murtazashvili, J. 2016. *Informal Order and the State in Afghanistan*. Cambridge: Cambridge University Press.

National Research Council, Division of Behavioral and Social Sciences and Education, and Committee on the Human Dimensions of Global Change 2002. *The Drama of the Commons*. Washington, DC: National Academies Press.

Nee, V. & P. Ingram 1998. "Embeddedness and beyond: institutions, exchange, and social structure". In M. Brinton & V. Nee (eds), *The New Institutionalism in Sociology*, 19–45. New York: Russell Sage Foundation.

North, D. 1982. *Structure and Change in Economic History*. New York: Norton.

North, D. 1990a. *Institutions, Institutional Change and Economic Performance*. Cambridge: Cambridge University Press.

North, D. 1990b. "A transaction cost theory of politics". *Journal of Theoretical Politics* 2: 355–67.

North, D. 1994. "Economic performance through time". *American Economic Review* 84(3): 359–68.

North, D. 2005. *Understanding the Process of Economic Change*. Revised edition. Princeton, NJ: Princeton University Press.

North, D. 2008. "Institutions and the performance of economies over time". In C. Ménard & M. Shirley (eds), *Handbook of New Institutional Economics*, 21–33. Berlin: Springer.

North, D. & R. Thomas 1971. "The rise and fall of the manorial system: a theoretical model". *Journal of Economic History* 31(4): 777–803.

North, D. & R. Thomas 1973. *The Rise of the Western World: A New Economic History*. Cambridge: Cambridge University Press.

North, D., J. Wallis & B. Weingast 2009. *Violence and Social Orders: A Conceptual Framework for Interpreting Recorded Human History*. New York: Cambridge University Press.

North, D. & B. Weingast 1989. "Constitutions and commitment: the evolution of institutions governing public choice in seventeenth-century England". *Journal of Economic History* 49(4): 803–32.

Oakerson, R. 1999. *Governing Local Public Economies: Creating the Civic Metropolis*. Oakland, CA: ICS Press.

Oakerson, R. & R. Parks 1988. "Citizen voice and public entrepreneurship: the organizational dynamic of a complex metropolitan county". *Publius* 18(4): 91–112.

Oakerson, R. & R. Parks 2011. "The study of local public economies: multi-organizational, multi-level institutional analysis and development". *Policy Studies Journal* 39(1): 147–67.

Olson, M. 1965. *Logic of Collective Action: Public Goods and the Theory of Groups*. Cambridge, MA: Harvard University Press.

Ostrom, E. 1965. "Public entrepreneurship: a case study in ground water basin management". University of California, Los Angeles.

Ostrom, E. 1972. "Metropolitan reform: propositions derived from two traditions". *Social Science Quarterly* 53(3): 474–93.

Ostrom, E. (ed.) 1976. *The Delivery of Urban Services: Outcomes of Change*. London: Sage Publications.

Ostrom, E. 1983. "A public choice approach to metropolitan institutions: structure, incentives, and performance". *Social Science Journal* 20(3): 79–96.

Ostrom, E. 1986. "An agenda for the study of institutions". *Public Choice* 48(1): 3–25.

Ostrom, E. 1989. "Microconstitutional change in multiconstitutional political systems". *Rationality and Society* 1(1): 11–50.

Ostrom, E. 1990. *Governing the Commons: The Evolution of Institutions for Collective Action*. Cambridge: Cambridge University Press.

Ostrom, E. 1991. "Rational choice theory and institutional analysis: toward complementarity". *American Political Science Review* 85(1): 237–43.

Ostrom, E. 1994. "Constituting social capital and collective action". *Journal of Theoretical Politics* 6(4): 527–62.

Ostrom, E. 1996. "Crossing the great divide: coproduction, synergy, and development". *World Development* 24(6): 1073–87.

Ostrom, E. 1998a. "A behavioral approach to the rational choice theory of collective action: presidential address, American Political Science Association, 1997". *American Political Science Review* 92(1): 1–22.

Ostrom, E. 1998b. "The comparative study of public economies". Speech on acceptance of the Frank E. Seidman Distinguished Award in Political Economy. Memphis, TN: Seidman Foundation.

Ostrom, E. 2000a. "Collective action and the evolution of social norms". *Journal of Economic Perspectives* 14(3): 137–58.

Ostrom, E. 2000b. "Crowding out citizenship". *Scandinavian Political Studies* 23(1): 3–16.

Ostrom, E. 2005a. *Understanding Institutional Diversity*. Princeton, NJ: Princeton University Press.

Ostrom, E. 2005b. "Unlocking public entrepreneurship and public economies". UNU-WIDER, Discussion Paper No. 2005/01. https://www.wider.unu.edu/publication/unlocking-public-entrepreneurship-and-public-economies.

Ostrom, E. 2006. "Converting threats into opportunities". *PS: Political Science & Politics* 39(1): 3–12.

Ostrom, E. [2006] 2015. "A frequently overlooked precondition of democracy: citizens knowledgeable about and engaged in collective action". In D. Cole & M. McGinnis (eds), *Elinor Ostrom and the Bloomington School of Political Economy: Polycentricity in Public Administration and Political Science*, 337–52. Lanham, MD: Lexington Books.

Ostrom, E. 2007a. "Challenges and growth: the development of the interdisciplinary field of institutional analysis". *Journal of Institutional Economics* 3(3): 239–64.

Ostrom, E. 2007b. "A diagnostic approach for going beyond panaceas". *Proceedings of the National Academy of Sciences* 104(39): 15181–7.

Ostrom, E. 2010a. "Beyond markets and states: polycentric governance of complex economic systems". *American Economic Review* 100(3): 641–72.

Ostrom, E. 2010b. "Polycentric systems for coping with collective action and global environmental change". *Global Environmental Change* 20(4): 550–57.

Ostrom, E. [2010] 2016. "Beyond markets and states: polycentric governance of complex economic systems". In *Mainline Economics: Six Nobel Lectures in the Tradition of Adam Smith*, 191–250. Arlington, VA: Mercatus Center, George Mason University.

Ostrom, E. 2011a. "Background on the institutional analysis and development framework". *Policy Studies Journal* 39(1): 7–27.

Ostrom, E. 2011b. "Honoring James Buchanan". *Journal of Economic Behavior & Organization* 80(2): 370–73.

Ostrom, E. 2012. "Green from the grassroots". *Project Syndicate*. 12 June; https://www.project-syndicate.org/commentary/green-from-the-grassroots.

Ostrom, E. 2014a. "Institutions and sustainability of ecological systems". In. S. Galiani & I. Sened (eds), *Institutions, Property Rights and Economic Growth*, 84–106. New York: Cambridge University Press.

Ostrom, E. 2014b. "A polycentric approach for coping with climate change". *Annals of Economics and Finance* 15(1): 97–134.

Ostrom, E. 2016. "The comparative study of public economies". *American Economist* 61(1): 91–107.

Ostrom, E., W. Baugh, R. Gaurasci, R. Parks & G. Whitaker 1973a. *Community Organization and the Provision of Police Services*. Beverly Hills, CA: Sage Publications.

Ostrom, E. & M. Cox 2010. "Moving beyond panaceas: a multi-tiered diagnostic approach for social-ecological analysis". *Environmental Conservation* 37(4): 451–63.

Ostrom, E., M. Janssen & J. Anderies 2007. "Going beyond panaceas". *Proceedings of the National Academy of Sciences* 104(39): 15176–8.

Ostrom, E., R. Parks & G. Whitaker 1973b. "Do we really want to consolidate urban police forces? A reappraisal of some old assertions". *Public Administration Review* 33(5): 423–32.

Ostrom, E., R. Parks & G. Whitaker 1978. *Patterns of Metropolitan Policing*. Cambridge, MA: Ballinger Publishing.

Ostrom, E. & V. Ostrom 1977. "Public goods and public choices". In E. Savas (ed.), *Alternatives for Delivering Public Services: Toward Improved Performance*, 7–49. Boulder, CO: Westview Press.

Ostrom, E. & V. Ostrom 2004. "The quest for meaning in public choice". *American Journal of Economics and Sociology* 63(1): 105–47.

Ostrom, E. & V. Ostrom [2004] 2014. "The quest for meaning in public choice". In P. Aligica & F. Sabetti (eds), *Choice, Rules, and Collective Action: The Ostroms on the Study of Institutions and Governance*, 61–93. Colchester: ECPR Press.

Ostrom, E. & J. Walker 1991. "Communication in a commons: cooperation without external enforcement". In T. Palfrey (ed.), *Laboratory Research in Political Economy*: 287–322. Ann Arbor, MI: University of Michigan Press.

Ostrom, V. 1953a. *Metropolitan Los Angeles: A Study in Integration. VIII. Water Supply*. Los Angeles: Haynes Foundation.

Ostrom, V. 1953b. "State administration of natural resources in the West". *American Political Science Review* 47(2): 478–93.

Ostrom, V. 1953c. *Water and Politics: A Study of Water Politics and Administration in the Development of Los Angeles*. Los Angeles, CA: Haynes Foundation.

Ostrom, V. 1972. "Polycentricity". Workshop in Political Theory and Policy Analysis Working Paper W72-2. Available via the Digital Library of the Commons, Workshop in Political Theory and Policy Analysis, Indiana University Bloomington; http://hdl.handle.net/10535/3763.

Ostrom, V. [1973] 2008. *The Intellectual Crisis in American Public Administration*. Third edition. Tuscaloosa, AL: University of Alabama Press.

Ostrom, V. 1980. "Artisanship and artifact". *Public Administration Review* 40(4): 309–17.

Ostrom, V. 1987. *The Political Theory of a Compound Republic*. Second edition. Lincoln, NE: University of Nebraska Press.

Ostrom, V. 1988. "The foundations of institutional analysis and development". Workshop in Political Theory and Policy Analysis. Working Paper W88-3. Available via the Digital Library of the Commons, Workshop in Political Theory and Policy Analysis; Indiana University Bloomington, http://hdl.handle.net/10535/7455.

Ostrom, V. 1989. *The Intellectual Crisis in American Public Administration*. Second edition. Tuscaloosa, AL: University of Alabama Press.

Ostrom, V. 1991a. *The Meaning of American Federalism: Constituting a Self-Governing Society*. San Francisco, CA: Institute for Contemporary Studies Press.

Ostrom, V. 1991b. "Polycentricity: the structural basis of self-governing systems". In *The Meaning of American Federalism*, 223–48. San Francisco, CA: ICS Press.

Ostrom, V. [1991] 2014. "Polycentricity: the structural basis of self-governing systems". In P. Aligica & F. Sabetti (eds), *Choice, Rules and Collective Action: The Ostrom's on the Study of Institutions and Governance*, 45–60. Colchester: ECPR Press.

Ostrom, V. 1993. "Epistemic choice and public choice". *Public Choice* 77(1): 163–76.

Ostrom, V. 1997. *The Meaning of Democracy and the Vulnerability of Democracies: A Response to Tocqueville's Challenge*. Ann Arbor, MI: University of Michigan Press.

Ostrom, V. 2006. "Citizen-sovereigns: the source of contestability, the rule of law, and the conduct of public entrepreneurship". *PS: Political Science & Politics* 39(1): 13–17.

Ostrom, V., R. Bish & E. Ostrom 1988. *Local Government in the United States*. San Francisco, CA: ICS Press.

Ostrom, V. & E. Ostrom 1965. "A behavioral approach to the study of intergovernmental relations". *Annals of the American Academy of Political and Social Science* 359(1): 137–46.

Ostrom, V. & E. Ostrom 1971. "Public choice: a different approach to the study of public administration". *Public Administration Review* 31(2): 203–16.

Ostrom, V., C. Tiebout & R. Warren 1961. "The organization of government in metro-politan areas: a theoretical inquiry". *American Political Science Review* 55(4): 831–42.

Parks, R. 1985. "Metropolitan structure and systemic performance: the case of police service delivery". In K. Hanf & T. Toonen (eds), *Policy Implementation in Federal and Unitary Systems*, 161–91. Dordrecht: Springer.

Pettit, P. 2008. *Made with Words: Hobbes on Language, Mind, and Politics*. Princeton, NJ: Princeton University Press.

Pincus, S. & J. Robinson 2014. "What really happened during the Glorious Revolution?" In S. Galiani & I. Sened (eds), *Institutions, Property Rights, and Economic Growth*, 192–222. Cambridge: Cambridge University Press.

Plott, C. & K. Zeiler 2005. "The willingness to pay-willingness to accept gap, the 'endow-ment effect', subject misconceptions, and experimental procedures for eliciting valuations". *American Economic Review* 95(3): 530–45.

Pohl, R. (ed.) 2016. *Cognitive Illusions: Intriguing Phenomena in Judgement, Thinking and Memory*. Second edition. London: Psychology Press.

Polanyi, K. 1957. *The Great Transformation: The Political and Economic Origins of Our Time*. Second edition. Boston, MA: Beacon Press.

Polanyi, M. 1951. *The Logic of Liberty: Reflections and Rejoinders*. London: Routledge & Kegan Paul.

Portes, A. 1998. "Social capital: its origins and applications in modern sociology". *Annual Review of Sociology* 24(1): 1–24.

Portes, A. 2000. "The two meanings of social capital". *Sociological Forum* 15(1): 1–12.

Portes, A. & J. Sensenbrenner 1993. "Embeddedness and immigration: notes on the social determinants of economic action". *American Journal of Sociology* 98(6): 1320–50.

Posner, R. 1993. "The new institutional economics meets law and economics". *Journal of Institutional and Theoretical Economics (JITE)/Zeitschrift für die gesamte Staatswissenschaft* 149(1): 73–87.

Poteete, A., M. Janssen & E. Ostrom 2010. *Working Together: Collective Action, the Commons, and Multiple Methods in Practice.* Princeton, NJ: Princeton University Press.

Powell, J. (trans.) [1231] 1971. *The Liber Augustalis or Constitutions of Melfi promulgated by the Emperor Frederick II for the Kingdom of Sicily in 1231.* Syracuse, NY: Syracuse University Press.

Putnam, R. 1993a. *Making Democracy Work: Civic Traditions in Modern Italy.* Princeton, NJ: Princeton University Press.

Putnam, R. 1993b. "The prosperous community: social capital and public life". *The American Prospect* 13 (Spring), vol. 4.

Putnam, R. 1995. "Bowling Alone: America's Declining Social Capital". *Journal of Democracy* 6(1): 65–78.

Putnam, R. 2000. *Bowling Alone: The Collapse and Revival of American Community.* New York: Simon & Schuster.

Rajan, R. 2004. "Assume anarchy". *Finance and Development* 41(3): 56–7.

Ravindra, K. *et al.* 2016. "Air pollution in India: bridging the gap between science and policy". *Journal of Hazardous, Toxic, and Radioactive Waste* 20(4): A4015003.

Riall, L. 1998. *Sicily and the Unification of Italy: Liberal Policy and Local Power, 1859–1866.* Oxford: Clarendon Press.

Richman, B. 2017. *Stateless Commerce: The Diamond Network and the Persistence of Relational Exchange.* Cambridge, MA: Harvard University Press.

Ridley, Matt 1996. *The Origins of Virtue: Human Instincts and the Evolution of Cooperation.* New York: Viking.

Rizzo, M. & G. Whitman 2019. *Escaping Paternalism: Rationality, Behavioral Economics, and Public Policy.* Cambridge: Cambridge University Press.

Robbins, L. [1952] 1965. *The Theory of Economic Policy in English Classical Political Economy.* London: Macmillan.

Roberts, P. 1969. "The polycentric Soviet economy". *Journal of Law and Economics* 12(1): 163–79.

Roberts, P. 1971. *Alienation and the Soviet Economy: The Collapse of the Socialist Era.* Albuquerque, NM: University of New Mexico Press.

Roselli, J. 1956. *Lord William Bentinck and the British Occupation of Sicily: 1811–14.* New York: Cambridge University Press.

Runst, P. & R. Wagner 2011. "Choice, emergence, and constitutional process: a framework for positive analysis". *Journal of Institutional Economics* 7(1): 131–45.

Sabetti, F. [1984] 2002. *Village Politics and the Mafia in Sicily.* Montreal: McGill-Queen's University Press.

Sabetti, F. 2004. "Local roots of constitutionalism". *Perspectives on Political Science* 33(2): 70–78.

Sabetti, F. & D. Castiglione (eds) 2017. *Institutional Diversity in Self-Governing Societies: The Bloomington School and Beyond.* Lanham, MD: Lexington Books.

Salter, A. 2015a. "Sovereignty as exchange of political property rights". *Public Choice* 165(1): 79–96.

Salter, A. 2015b. "Rights to the realm: reconsidering Western political development". *American Political Science Review* 109(4): 725–34.

Schelling, T. 1960. *The Strategy of Conflict*. Cambridge, MA: Harvard University Press.

Schelling, T. 1984. "Self-command in practice, in policy, and in a theory of rational choice". *American Economic Review* 74(2): 1–11.

Schlager, E. & M. Cox 2017. "The IAD framework and the SES framework: an introduction and assessment of the Ostrom workshop frameworks". In C. Weible & P. Sabatier (eds), *Theories of the Policy Process*, 225–62. Boulder, CO: Westview Press.

Schlager, E. & E. Ostrom 1992. "Property-rights regimes and natural resources: a conceptual analysis". *Land Economics* 68(3): 249–62.

Schleifer, J. 2018. *Tocqueville*. Cambridge: Polity.

Schumpeter, J. [1926] 1934. *The Theory of Economic Development*. Trans. Redvers Opie. Cambridge, MA: Harvard University Press.

Schumpeter, J. 1942. *Capitalism, Socialism and Democracy*. New York: Harper.

Searle, J. 1965. "What is a speech act?" In M. Black (ed.), *Philosophy in America*, 221–39. London: Allen & Unwin.

Searle, J. 1969. *Speech Acts: An Essay in the Philosophy of Language*. New York: Cambridge University Press.

Searle, J. 1995. *The Construction of Social Reality*. New York: Free Press.

Searle, J. 2002. *Consciousness and Language*. Cambridge: Cambridge University Press.

Searle, J. 2006. "Social ontology: some basic principles". *Papers: Revista de Sociología* 80: 51–71.

Searle, J. 2010. *Making the Social World: The Structure of Human Civilization*. Oxford: Oxford University Press.

Shah, T., D. Molden, R. Sakthivadivel & D. Seckler 2001. "Global groundwater situation: opportunities and challenges". *Economic and Political Weekly* 36(43): 4142–50.

Shear, M. 2017. "Trump will withdraw US from Paris Climate Agreement". *New York Times*. 1 June; https://www.nytimes.com/2017/06/01/climate/trump-paris-climate-agreement.html.

Shepsle, K. 2010. *Analyzing Politics: Rationality, Behavior and Institutions*. Second edition. New York: Norton.

Shermer, M. 2007. *The Mind of the Market: Compassionate Apes, Competitive Humans, and Other Tales from Evolutionary Economics*. New York: Times Books.

Simon, H. 1955. "A behavioral model of rational choice". *Quarterly Journal of Economics* 69(1): 99–118.

Simon, H. 1969. *The Sciences of the Artificial*. Cambridge, MA: MIT Press.

Simon, H. 1979. "Rational decision making in business organizations". *American Economic Review* 69(4): 493–513.

Simon, H. 1991. "Organizations and markets". *Journal of Economic Perspectives* 5(2): 25–44.

Simon, H. 1997. *Administrative Behavior: A Study of Decision-Making Processes in Administrative Organization*. Fourth edition. New York: Free Press.

Smelser, N. & R. Swedberg 1994. "Introducing economic sociology". In N. Smelser & R. Swedberg (eds), *The Handbook of Economic Sociology*, 3–25. Princeton, NJ: Princeton University Press.

Smith, A. [1759] 1793. *The Theory of Moral Sentiments; or, an essay towards an analysis of the principles by which men naturally judge concerning the conduct and character, first of their neighbours, and afterwards of themselves*. Vol. 2. Basil: Tourneisen.

Smith, A. [1759] 2002. *Adam Smith: The Theory of Moral Sentiments*. Cambridge: Cambridge University Press.

Smith, A. [1776] 1976. *An Inquiry into the Nature and Causes of the Wealth of Nations*. Edited by Edwin Cannan. Chicago, IL: University of Chicago Press.

Smith, V. 2007. *Rationality in Economics: Constructivist and Ecological Forms*. Cambridge: Cambridge University Press.

Sozou, P. 1998. "On hyperbolic discounting and uncertain hazard rates". *Proceedings of the Royal Society of London. Series B: Biological Sciences* 265(1409): 2015–20.

Spata, G. 1865. *Capitula Regni Siciliae Recensioni Francisci Testa*. Panormi: ex Tipis Diarii Siciliae.

Stigler, G. 1962. "The tenable range of functions of local government in federal expenditure policy for economic growth and stability". In E. Phelps (ed.), *Private Wants and Public Needs*, 167–76. New York: Norton.

Stigler, G. & G. Becker 1977. "De gustibus non est disputandum". *American Economic Review* 67(2): 76–90.

Stinchcombe, A. 1983. *Economic Sociology*. New York: Academic Press.

Storr, N., E. Chamlee-Wright & V. Storr 2015. *How We Came Back: Voices from Post-Katrina New Orleans*. Arlington, VA: Mercatus Center, George Mason University.

Swann, W. & S. Kim 2018. "Practical prescriptions for governing fragmented governments". *Policy & Politics* 46(2): 273–92.

Swedberg, R. 1991. "Major traditions of economic sociology". *Annual Review of Sociology* 17(1): 251–76.

Swedberg, R. 2003. *Principles of Economic Sociology*. Princeton, NJ: Princeton University Press.

Swedberg, R. 2004. "What has been accomplished in new economic sociology and where is it heading?" *European Journal of Sociology/Archives Européennes de Sociologie* 45(3): 317–30.

Swedberg, R. 2008. "Theoretical versus practical explanation in political economy and economic sociology: the case of Tocqueville". *Socio-Economic Review* 6(3): 427–47.

Swedberg, R. 2009. *Tocqueville's Political Economy*. Princeton, NJ: Princeton University Press.

Tarko, V. 2017. *Elinor Ostrom: An Intellectual Biography*. London: Rowman & Littlefield.

Thaler, R. 1991. *Winner's Curse: Paradoxes and Anomalies of Economic Life*. New York: Free Press.

Thaler, R. & C. Sunstein 2008. *Nudge: Improving Decisions About Health, Wealth, and Happiness*. New Haven, CT: Yale University Press.

Thomas, M. 2018. "Reapplying behavioral symmetry: public choice and choice architecture". *Public Choice* 180(1/2): 11–25.

Tiebout, C. 1956. "A pure theory of local expenditures". *Journal of Political Economy* 64(5): 416–24.

Tocqueville, A. de [1805–59] 1998. *The Old Regime and the Revolution.* Two volumes. Chicago, IL: University of Chicago Press.

Tocqueville, A. de [1835] 2012. *Democracy in America.* Two volumes. Indianapolis, IN: Liberty Fund.

Tullock, G. [1965] 2005. *Bureaucracy.* Indianapolis, IN: Liberty Fund.

Tullock, G. 1972. *Explorations in the Theory of Anarchy.* Blacksburg, VA: Center for the Study of Public Choice, Virginia Polytechnic Institute and State University.

Tullock, G. 2004. "Part 1, Genesis". In C. Rowley (ed.), *Selected Works of Gordon Tullock, Volume 1: Virginia Political Economy*, 1–47. Indianapolis, IN: Liberty Fund.

Tullock, G. 2005. *The Social Dilemma: Of Autocracy, Revolution, Coup D'Etat, and War.* Indianapolis, IN: Liberty Fund.

Tuomela, R. 2007. *The Philosophy of Sociality: The Shared Point of View.* New York: Oxford University Press.

Tuomela, R. 2013. *Social Ontology: Collective Intentionality and Group Agents.* New York: Oxford University Press.

United Nations 2015. "Paris Agreement". Paris: United Nations.

Uzzi, B. 1996. "The sources and consequences of embeddedness for the economic performance of organizations: the network effect". *American Sociological Review* 61(4): 674–98.

Uzzi, B. 1997. "Social structure and competition in interfirm networks: the paradox of embeddedness". *Administrative Science Quarterly* 42(1): 35–67.

Uzzi, B. 1999. "Embeddedness in the making of financial capital: how social relations and networks benefit firms seeking financing". *American Sociological Review* 64(4): 481–505.

Wagner, R. 2005. "Self-governance, polycentrism, and federalism: recurring themes in Vincent Ostrom's scholarly oeuvre". *Journal of Economic Behavior & Organization* 57(2): 173–88.

Wagner, R. 2014. "Design vs. emergence in a theory of federalism: toward institutional reconciliation". *Journal of Public Finance and Public Choice* 32(1/2): 197–213.

Wagner, R. 2016. *Politics as a Peculiar Business: Insights from a Theory of Entangled Political Economy.* Cheltenham: Elgar.

Wagner, R. & A. Yokoyama 2013. "Polycentrism, federalism, and liberty: a comparative systems perspective". *Journal of Public Finance and Public Choice* 31(1/3): 179–97.

Weber, M. [1905] 1998. *The Protestant Work Ethic and the Spirit of Capitalism.* Los Angeles, CA: Roxbury.

Weber, M. 1949. *Max Weber on the Methodology of the Social Sciences.* New York: Free Press.

Weingast, B. 1995. "The economic role of political institutions: market-preserving federalism and economic development". *Journal of Law, Economics, & Organization* 11(1): 1–31.

Wendt, A. 2004. "The state as person in international theory". *Review of International Studies* 30(2): 289–316.

Wicksell, K. [1896] 1958. "A new principle of just taxation". In R. Musgrave & A. Peacock (eds), *Classics in the Theory of Public Finance*, 72–118. London: Palgrave Macmillan.

Williamson, O. 1975. *Markets and Hierarchies: Analysis and Antitrust Implications*. New York: Free Press.

Williamson, O. 1985. *The Economic Institutions of Capitalism*. New York: Free Press.

Williamson, O. 1996. *The Mechanisms of Governance*. Oxford: Oxford University Press.

Williamson, O. 2010. "Transaction cost economics: the natural progression". *American Economic Review* 100(3): 673–90.

Williamson, O. & S. Winter (eds) 1993. *The Nature of the Firm: Origins, Evolution, and Development*. New York: Oxford University Press.

Wilson, D., E. Ostrom & M. Cox 2013. "Generalizing the core design principles for the efficacy of groups". *Journal of Economic Behavior & Organization* 90 (supplement): S21–32.

Witt, U. 1992. "The endogenous public choice theorist". *Public Choice* 73(1): 117–29.

Wood, A., M. Graham, V. Lehdonvirta & I. Hjorth 2019. "Networked but commodified: the (dis)embeddedness of digital labour in the gig economy". *Sociology* 53(5): 931–50.

Woolcock, M. 1998. "Social capital and economic development: toward a theoretical synthesis and policy framework". *Theory and Society* 27(2): 151–208.

Woolcock, M. & D. Narayan 2000. "Social capital: implications for development theory, research, and policy". *World Bank Research Observer* 15(2): 225–49.

Worm, B. *et al*. 2006. "Impacts of biodiversity loss on ocean ecosystem services". *Science* 314 (5800): 787–90.

Zagorski, N. 2006. "Profile of Elinor Ostrom". *Proceedings of the National Academy of Sciences of the United States of America* 103(51): 19221–23.

Zeiler, K. 2011. "The willingness to pay-willingness to accept gap, the 'endowment effect', subject misconceptions, and experimental procedures for eliciting valuations: reply". *American Economic Review* 101: 1012.

Zelizer, V. 1978. "Human values and the market: the case of life insurance and death in 19th-century America". *American Journal of Sociology* 84(3): 591–610.

Zelizer, V. 2011. *Economic Lives: How Culture Shapes the Economy*. Princeton, NJ: Princeton University Press.

Ziblatt, D. 2004. "Rethinking the origins of federalism: puzzle, theory, and evidence from nineteenth-century Europe". *World Politics* 57(1): 70–98.

Ziblatt, D. 2006. *Structuring the State: The Formation of Italy and Germany and the Puzzle of Federalism*. Princeton, NJ: Princeton University Press.

INDEX